Political Consultants and Campaigns

TRANSFORMING AMERICAN POLITICS

Lawrence C. Dodd, Series Editor

Dramatic changes in political institutions and behavior over the past three decades have underscored the dynamic nature of American politics, confronting political scientists with a new and pressing intellectual agenda. The pioneering work of early postwar scholars, while laying a firm empirical foundation for contemporary scholarship, failed to consider how American politics might change or recognize the forces that would make fundamental change inevitable. In reassessing the static interpretations fostered by these classic studies, political scientists are now examining the underlying dynamics that generate transformational change.

Transforming American Politics brings together texts that address four closely related aspects of change. A first concern is documenting and explaining recent changes in American politics—in institutions, processes, behavior, and policymaking. A second is reinterpreting classic studies and theories to provide a more accurate perspective on postwar politics. The series will look at historical change to identify recurring patterns of political transformation with in and across the distinctive eras of American politics. Last and perhaps most important, the series presents new theories and interpretations that explain the dynamic processes at work and thus clarify the direction of contemporary politics. All of the books focus on the central theme of transformation—transformation in both the conduct of American politics and in the way we study and understand its many aspects.

BOOKS IN THIS SERIES

Political Consultants and Campaigns

ONE DAY TO SELL

Jason Johnson

WESTVIEW
PRESS
A Member of the Perseus Books Group

Westview Press was founded in 1975 in Boulder, Colorado, by notable publisher and intellectual Fred Praeger. Westview Press continues to publish scholarly titles and high-quality undergraduate- and graduate-level textbooks in core social science disciplines. With books developed, written, and edited with the needs of serious nonfiction readers, professors, and students in mind, Westview Press honors its long history of publishing books that matter.

Find us on the World Wide Web at www.westviewpress.com.

Every effort has been made to secure required permissions for all text, images, maps, and other art reprinted in this volume.

Westview Press books are available at special discounts for bulk purchases in the United States by corporations, institutions, and other organizations. For more information, please contact the Special Markets Department at the Perseus Books Group, 2300 Chestnut Street, Suite 200, Philadelphia, PA 19103, or call (800) 810-4145, ext. 5000, or e-mail special.markets@perseusbooks.com.

Library of Congress Cataloging-in-Publication Data

Johnson, Jason.
    Political consultants and campaigns : one day to sell / Jason Johnson.
        p.   cm. — (Transforming American politics)
    Includes bibliographical references and index.
    ISBN 978-0-8133-4488-1 (pbk. : alk. paper) — ISBN 978-0-8133-4556-7 (e-book)
    1. Political consultants—United States.   2. Political campaigns—United States.   3. Campaign management—United States.   I. Title.
    JK2281.J627 2011
    324.70973—dc22

                                                                                2011004728

10 9 8 7 6 5 4 3 2 1

Contents

Introduction

American elections are one of the most studied and analyzed areas in political science. Arguably, everything from the behavior of mayors, congressmen, and presidents to the implementation of policy at all levels of government is influenced by political campaigns (Mayhew 1974; Randon Hershey 1984; Johnson-Cartee and Copeland 1997; Thurber, Nelson, and Dulio 2000; Nelson, Dulio, and Medvic 2002; Sabato 2006). However, all too often, election research proposes theories, reaches conclusions, and leaves campaign managers, consultants, and organizers—*actual* political professionals—out of the equation. This is akin to seeing a group of well-dressed, high-minded art critics crowded around a painting and discussing its implications, all the while ignoring the artist who is standing right next to the work. At the same time, many political professionals believe that academic theory comes from men and women locked away in ivory towers and that it has no place in the real world of political campaigns (Johnson-Cartee and Copeland 1997; Thurber 1998a; Jamieson and Waldman 2001; Craig 2006).

The goal of this book is to bridge the gap between these two groups, to find out where political science theory and political professionals agree and where they disagree. The hope is that this research will not only teach us more about campaign managers and political professionals but also give us more insight into how exactly political science theory can be helped or improved by consistently including the men and women pulling the strings in American politics. In order to show where this book will take political science research on campaign managers, it is first necessary to explain where the research has been.

The Personal Era, 1950–1970

Although there have always been men and women involved in running political campaigns, there was very little political science research on political managers until fairly recently. The first era of work on campaign professionals is best described as sporadic and personal. The advent of modern polling technology in the 1950s, and dynamic innovations in campaign strategy (demonstrated in John F. Kennedy's presidential campaign in 1960), brought about more sophisticated discussions of American elections in political science, but work on actual campaign managers was still fairly sparse.[1] Much of the knowledge about political professionals in the 1950s and 1960s came from the professionals themselves (Perry 1968; Pritchell 1958) in the form of memoirs[2] or oral histories collected for archives and journalists (Shadegg 1964; Kirwan and Redding 1964; Scott 1968). The principals of Baus and Ross, one of the first fully functioning political consulting firms in America, put together a "how-to book" for budding political campaigners that hinted at overarching campaign theories without explicitly stating any. Baus and Ross wrote, "Forcing the issue transcends merely debating acknowledged issues. The winning offensive strategy is to convince the voters that the issue is what the winner says it is, not what his opponents say it is. The winner forces the loser to fight on terrain of the winner's choosing" (1968, 120). While Baus and Ross hinted at issue positioning strategy, they did not go so far as to suggest how this might apply across various types of elections. The majority of the work in this era either by consultants or by academics spoke little to campaign strategy beyond the particular races individuals ran, and there was little or no work done on the profession in general. Campaign managers were an afterthought in political science research on campaigns, and campaign managers themselves seldom referenced political science in their musings.

The Professionalization Era, 1970–1980

Changes by national parties in the presidential primaries, the passage of the Federal Election Campaign Act of 1974, and the creation of the American Association of Political Consultants (AAPC) all led to slightly more study of campaign strategy and managers in the 1970s.[3] The average voter was introduced to political professionals when Mike Wallace, host of the news program *60 Minutes*, interviewed Joe Napolitan, founder and first president of the newly created American Association of Political Consultants. With a full-fledged association for political professionals in existence, a few brave political scientists with an interest in campaign politics began to take a look at the professionals who worked behind the scenes in campaigns. At the time, most researchers were not sure if this new group should be what Nimmo (1970) called "campaign managers" or what others dubbed "implementers of campaign strategy" (Parkinson 1970; Shadegg 1964; Napolitan 1972 cited in Perlmutter 1999). Barkan and Bruno suggested calling them "business marketers who've gone political or just a new generation of political organizers." Clearly, an increased "professionalization" in politics began and was here to stay. Research on campaign operatives began to veer from purely anecdotal discussions, and for the first time some political scientists began to bring social science studies and technology into analyzing campaigns and even suggesting improvements to campaign managers. For example, Barkan and Bruno first suggested the use of political science theories to improve targeting partisans during a campaign. "To activate an electoral majority, campaign strategists must first identify and geographically locate those segments of the electorate which are most likely to constitute a base of partisan support. . . . Though campaign managers usually make intuitive judgments in this regard detailed maps of the geographical distribution of party identification across a constituency are rarely made because of the difficulties involved" (1974, 710). Voter targeting existed long before political scientists took notice and was not always guided by the guts and instincts of campaign managers, but their interest made it clear that a change was coming. Blydenburgh (1976) used game theory to explain the behavior of campaign managers. Hershey (1973), on the other hand, assessed whether consultants were influenced by "minimum winning coalition theory." Finally, Price and Lupfer's concerns dealt not with what theories a given campaign used but with how the political science theories could be applied (1973, 412). A very small but consistent group of political scientists began to realize that campaign managers were here to stay—even if the methods with which to identify and research campaign managers had not been established (Wilson 1966; Nimmo 1970; Hiebert et al. 1971; Rosenbloom 1973). It would not be until the next era that the *impact* of this new profession started to receive serious analysis in political science.

The Party Downfall Era, 1980–1990

Campaigns and Elections, the first and still most influential trade magazine for political consultants, launched in 1980, established that enough self-described campaign managers existed across the nation to support a magazine that shared tactics and strategies. With a trade magazine, some intrepid political scientists began the first systematic analysis of campaign managers and their impact on the American electoral system. In the 1980s political scientists Larry Sabato (1983, 1989a, 1989b, 1989c; Sabato and Larson 1987) and Paul Herrnson (1986, 1988, 1989) led the way theoretically and methodologically for the analysis of campaign professionals as a distinct group. The rise of political consultants (also the title of Larry Sabato's seminal book [1983]) as a topic of research in political science coincided with new research showing that the power of the Republican and Democratic parties over candidates and campaigns locally as well as nationally was starting to fade (Blumenthal 1980; Sabato 1989a, 1989b; Salmore and Salmore 1989; Petracca 1989; Everson 1992). At the time, researcher Walter DeVries explained the relationship between the weakening parties and the rise of consultants: "A major reason—if not the only reason—for having campaign consultants is that political parties basically failed to do their job in a changing technological and social environment" (1989, 21). Celinda Lake's study showed that "political consultants were bringing new and innovative technology into the campaign world, playing a huge role in the recruiting of candidates." Her study also pointed out that "managers were playing an increasingly important role in image creation and policy stances for candidates, all areas that were once mostly in the control of state or national party leaders" (1989, 26).

The impact of political consultants had grown so fast that their influence led to debates in political science and journalism about whether this influence on American democracy represented a positive or a negative development. Some people had concerns that American politics was being taken over by hired guns who slipped in and out of politics and cared more about money and wins than good government (DeVries 1989; Petracca 1989; Rosenberg and McCafferty 1987). However, Lake viewed the consultants and managers as "breaking the hold of party bosses, opening up the electoral process and giving candidates a chance to speak to the people unfiltered" (1989, 26).

This meteoric rise also led to the first academics decrying the lack of reliable systematic analysis about who political consultants were, what they were doing, and how their actions should be studied (Petracca 1989, 12). Consequently, campaign management schools and institutes popped up across the country at various colleges, giving academics and practitioners a chance to work together.[4] However, the newfound togetherness between the academic world and the practitioner world did not change the minds of many skeptics in either domain. Although former AAPC president Joe Napolitan noticed the increasing interest in campaign professionals among a small cadre of academics in the 1980s, he was not impressed: "I see little relationship, if any, between political science and politics. Political Science, in my opinion, is an academic pursuit of what happened; politics is the pursuit of making things happen" (Binford 1985, 89).

Despite skepticism on the part of most practitioners and academics, political science programs and a very small but dedicated group of researchers began to focus on campaign managers as a topic of analysis. The increasing focus resulted in (by the end of the 1980s) political scientists outlining the methods to actually study campaign managers on a large scale. The methods ranged from simply observing campaign managers in the process of their jobs to the old standby of consultant interviews (Howell 1980; Bositis 1985; Goldenberg, Traugott, and Baumgartner 1985). For the first time, large-scale empirical surveys were conducted that looked at campaign managers across the nation as well as how the public viewed the actions of campaign managers (Herrnson 1988; Petracca 1989; Binford 1985).

The Celebrity Manager Era, 1990–2000

The 1990s brought political consultants out of the back rooms of politics and into the limelight in a way that surprised the public, including academics and journalists. Successful consultants emerged as pundits, writing books and appearing on television shows, and they became part of American popular culture. Steven K. Medvic and Silvo Lenart, two of the few political scientists studying consultants at the time, commented on these newfound political celebrities: "The role of political consultants in the U.S. electoral process has increased exponentially in the last few decades such that, in the current political landscape, they are often as prominent as the politicians for whom they work" (1997, 61). In particular, Bill Clinton's cadre of political consultants, George Stephanopoulos, James Carville, and Dick Morris, became the topics of gossip magazines and pop culture icons in addition to staying on in his administration past the election to create policy and messages. However, not everyone was thrilled with these political viziers coming out from behind the curtain. At one point, disgusted with attention-hogging consultants, then-candidate Bill Clinton said to two of his top aides, "I don't want to read about you in the press. I'm sick and tired of consultants getting famous at my expense. Any story that comes out during the campaign undermines my candidacy" (Johnson 2000, 3).[5] Of course, candidates were not the only ones getting tired of the celebrity campaign game: "I cringe when I see consultants write 'kiss and tell' books that reveal embarrassing information about their candidates. . . . Most important, a consultant owes a certain amount of loyalty to his candidates—even after the election" (Perlmutter 1999, 6). Some consultants actually began to see the trend as harmful not only to the candidates but also to the public perception of the profession. Perlmutter quoted another prominent consultant of the era: "Each public utterance by the consultant in this context [media] becomes a reminder to the television viewer or newspaper reader that the candidate in question is a creature of his handlers. . . . It actually insults and devalues the candidate and breeds further cynicism towards the political process" (ibid., 296).

Despite grumblings from some inside the profession and in politics, the tidal wave of celebrity campaigners could not be stopped, and the very nature of political science research on consultants and campaigns, when it occurred, was caught up in the wave. Popular films like *The War Room* (1992), *Wag the Dog* (1997), and *Primary Colors* (1998) actually provided information about campaign consultants and strategy but were dramatized by Hollywood for public consumption. Big-name consultants wrote a spate of personal campaign memoirs that further mixed up the waters (Morris 1997, 1998; Carville and Matalin 1995). When James Carville, Clinton's top campaign manager, and Mary Matalin, Bush's top campaign manager, wrote *All's Fair: Love, War, and Running for President* in 1995, detailing how they met and fell in love while running opposing presidential campaigns, the fusion of campaign managers and celebrity life finally came full circle.[6] At the same time, many political scientists were writing books for and about political consulting with political consultants that mixed anecdotes and social science that were great for the emerging culture of "political junkies" and "pundits" but did not necessarily move the political science or theoretical discussion forward (Carville and Matalin 1995; Carville 1996; Morris 1997, 1998; Perlmutter 1999; Strother 2003; Moore and Slater 2003; Bailey and Faucheux 2000; Watson and Campbell 2003). Ironically, with the rise of consultants in almost every sector of American popular culture, scholarship on consultants still remained the work of a few outliers, scholars who dabbled in the subject but usually as a backdrop to larger discussions about political campaigns. The work that did emerge provided some initial examples of fusing theory and scholarship on political consultants: Scholars now viewed them as partners instead of usurpers of the two major parties, investigated consultant views on negative advertising, and examined the role of campaign managers in enhancing voter turnout and fund-raising; all these subjects were bolstered by scholarship in this era despite the cacophony of celebrity books, movies, and television programs (Nelson 1998; Kolodny and Logan 1998; Theilmann and Wilhite 1998; Medvic 1998). The methods of analyzing political consultants also advanced during this period due to greater visibility of consultants as well as better communications technology. The majority of the political science work still relied on consultant interviews (Magleby and Patterson 1998; Nelson 1998; Kahn and Kenney 1997). Researchers such as Glaser (1996) used observation, but several new methods for studying political consultants were introduced. Some political scientists began to use data from the magazine *Campaigns and Elections* to determine which campaigns used consultants as well as how extensive consultant activities were to start their analyses. In some cases academics used either *Campaigns and Elections* or the membership roster of the American Association of Political Consultants to survey or record the actions of political consultants (Medvic and Lenart 1997; Herrnson 1992; Kolodny and Logan 1998; Medvic 1998). Nevertheless, this represents a minuscule amount of research in the ocean of political science work on campaigns. There were still "too many theories and too many campaign managers running around that weren't being connected in any meaningful way, and the calls for change within the profession became louder" (Medvic and Lenart 1997, 61–77).

In 1998, James Thurber of the Center of Congressional and Presidential Studies at American University led the clarion call for aggressive and empirical work on political consulting. In his aptly titled article "The Study of Campaign Consultants: A Subfield in Search of a Theory," Thurber threw down the proverbial gauntlet to political science to investigate further this key part of the discipline: "Though professional political consulting outside of political party organizations has been around since the 1930's, it has only recently sparked interest among some political scientists. Why have consultants been ignored by political scientists? Why have consultants ignored political scientists? Why is there little or no theory related to political consultants? Why do we know so little about the profession of political consultants? What subfield houses the study of political consulting? Elections and voting behavior, political parties, political communications, political advertising, campaign management?" (1998b, 145). Thurber's words were heard across political science, especially in a new generation of graduate students who came of age in the celebrity culture of the 1990s. A new generation of researchers saw campaign managers to be as viable and worthy a topic of study as members of Congress, voters, and members of the media. What happened next was a full-fledged research revolution.

The Modern Era, 2000–2010

More than ten years after Thurber's call, political science arguably knows a little more about political consultants as a whole. A cottage industry of sorts has arisen based on the work of a few key researchers, many of whom spring from Thurber's research center (Thurber and Nelson 2000; Thurber 2001; Thurber, Nelson, and Dulio 2000; Nelson, Dulio, and Medvic 2002; Rampton and Stauber 2004). The *Journal of Political Marketing*, launched in 2002, was the first peer-reviewed academic journal to focus specifically on political campaigns, managers, strategy, and theory. The *JOPM* became the academic and theoretical yin to the practical and functional yang of *Campaigns and Elections*. The fusion of work between consultants and academics on the ethics and professional norms of political consulting also defined this period. After the celebrity campaign era, many consultants and academics became concerned not just with the negative impact that some rogue campaigners may have on democracy but also on the profession of campaign management in general. Increased media attention, "spin doctors" manipulating public perception of debates, and a few high-profile scandals involving consultants that rocked the political world got many academics and consultants talking.[7] In addition, the concern about the long-term impact of the "permanent campaign" wherein consultants moved from the campaign field to essentially run operations from within the statehouse or White House got academics and consultants working together on a plan to clean up the profession before things spun out of control (Panagopoulos 2006; Norton and Goethals 2004; Auer 2003; Edsall and Rosin 1999; Holmes 1996).

With a large grant from the Pew Charitable Trust, researchers at American University began a semiannual survey of consultants' views on ethics and professional norms in an attempt to rein in some of the more unruly managers out in the field and lay the groundwork for professional standards and rule enforcement. Acknowledging perhaps for the first time how consultants and academics really needed and could help each other, the Campaign Management Institute announced in its *Improving Campaign Conduct* packet a program to improve consulting as a profession and campaign research at the same time. It read in part, "CMI (Campaign Management Institute) will work with the American Association of Political Consultants (AAPC) to share its research and begin a series of discussions to form consensus around useful industry codes and standards. At the same time, CMI will launch an effort to bring campaign training schools together into an informal association to share the consultant research and involve schools in conversations about campaign standards and practices" (Thurber 1999, 1). At the end of the decade, political science studies of political consultants as a distinct group worthy of critical analysis are in pretty good shape. Heading into the next era, the question is: Where do we go from here?

The Research

Although there has been a tremendous amount of work over the past decade in political science on campaign managers and consultants, there still is no comprehensive work that examines various theories of political campaigns against what consultants are actually doing in the field. Yes, we now know consultants will attack under some circumstances and what they think is ethical professionally, but in so many areas crucial to campaign studies, such as message theory, candidate theory, and even Internet technology, we still have little or no idea if existing theory really approximates or explains what political operatives are doing in the field. This book proposes to take the best of the various eras of research and analyze political consultant attitudes, practices, and beliefs across the entire spectrum of campaign activities. Although this is clearly an ambitious task, this book will provide a better picture of not only where consultants are in today's dynamic campaign environment but also how effective current political science theories are in explaining the actions and behaviors of political managers.

Methods and Definitions

This book is based on an extensive online survey of political operatives' beliefs and attitudes on issue strategy, message strategy, candidate traits, negative advertising, and Internet campaigning. You will notice that throughout this book I interchangeably use the terms *consultant, campaign manager,* and *political operative*; this is intentional, given that we operate under a very broad definition of *campaign operative*. Medvic defined the term *political consultant* as "anyone who worked in two or more congressional and or statewide campaigns during the most recent campaign cycle, was among the highest grossing consultants in his/her field, or was a member of the American Association of Political Consultants" (1998, 150). Sabato similarly defined the term as "a professional who is engaged primarily in the provision of advice and services (such as polling, media creation and production and direct mail fundraising) to candidates, their campaigns, and other political committees" (1983, 8). These definitions possess much insight, but adherence to them would fall short of the purposes of this book. My goal is to capture campaign managers, consultants, and operatives at all levels of political campaigns, and my interest is more in surveying those who are involved in the strategy and organization of a campaign than with what services campaign operatives provide and for how long they do so. For the purposes of this work, my definition of *political consultant* is "anyone who worked on a political campaign from beginning to end, such that that person was involved in developing campaign strategy. This can include but is not limited to campaign managers, consultants, political organizers, or candidates who ran their own campaigns." With the thousands of campaigns across America every year, the best way to comprehend who managers are, and how they think, would be to include a sample that ranges from highly paid consultants to the local manager who no one will ever see on MSNBC, CNN, or FOX. This belief serves as the main driving force behind defining a political operative so broadly. The survey captures the consultant who has been running statewide races on behalf of presidential candidates for the past twenty years as well as the public schoolteacher who has taken a semester off every two years for the past twenty to manage his wife's state senate campaign.

In addition to calling campaigns all across the United States, I sent surveys to professional campaign schools, including the Women's Campaign School at Yale, George Washington University's School of Campaign Management, Regent University, and the Bliss Institute at the University of Akron.[8] More than 350 consultants responded to the survey, and I analyzed their beliefs, attitudes, and practices against existing political science theory.

Chapter Outline

This book will proceed in the following order. Chapter 1 focuses on political candidates and the theories surrounding them. I first take a look at existing theory on candidate traits in political science and then examine whether consultants have similar views to voters on the weights and import of candidate traits from current national election surveys. Then I examine the governing-versus-campaigning conundrum and analyze if consultants see a difference in what it takes to be a good campaigner compared to an effective elected official. Finally, I discuss what it takes for a candidate to be "electable" in the minds of campaigners, the press, and academics.

Chapter 2 examines the role that political messages play in the strategies of political consultants. I distill the five key defining messages in political campaigns and discover exactly what factors drive message strategy for consultants. I also look at the influence of message discipline and consistency on campaign success according to consultants.

Chapter 3 is dedicated to issue-position strategy for political consultants. I examine which theories of candidate positioning from political science best describe and explain how political consultants set position strategy during campaigns. I also take a look at "issue ownership" and "deliberative priming" theories and how these concepts may or may not explain consultant strategy.

Chapter 4 delves into negative-advertising strategy and how campaign managers and consultants organize attacks. First, I try to find a functional definition of negative advertising that actually includes input from campaigners out in the field. Then I examine how on-the-ground factors like the district demographics and candidate party identification compare to situational factors like position in the polls in explaining consultant strategies.

Chapter 5 brings us to a discussion of the use of the Internet in modern political campaigns. I look at the role of Internet optimists and pessimists in driving campaign theory and consultant strategy and then examine how consultants use various tools, from campaign Web sites to Facebook and Twitter, to help their candidates.

Finally, in Chapter 6 I wrap up all that we have learned from consultants and discuss the implications for the profession and existing political science theory and, most importantly, I discuss what it really takes to win according to the respondents in my survey. Each chapter will have case-study examples from campaigns across the country over the years to demonstrate the principles being discussed in that section, in addition to interviews with various consultants.

The Appendix serves multiple purposes in support of this text as well. First, it provides in-depth ouputs from SPSS that formed the backbone of the numerous tables in the book. Further, it gives more detailed explanations of the variables, definitions, and procedures that were used to make the book accessible for academics, students, and political practitioners alike.

This Book Is for You

Right after college I took a job as a campaign manager in South Carolina. I was responsible for running two statehouse races after redistricting forced a special election, and I felt prepared for what was ahead. I had read just about every book on campaigns that was available at the time and had taken a Campaigns and Elections class under Larry Sabato while a student at the University of Virginia. Yet just about everything I was trying to do as a manager in my first race was not working. I would knock on doors for my candidate, and people would laugh at my canvassing questions or want to set me up with their daughters. My campaign staff thought posters were silly and did not believe in polling. Nobody on the ground had ever heard of a "strategy box" and did not want to, either.

In frustration, I talked with one of the higher-ups in the state campaign and asked for advice about the "profession." "This isn't a profession," he said.

"It's a bare-knuckles trade. . . . You're selling something to people, and it has to be good." And that is when it dawned on me: All of the work I had done in college about campaigns was not enough; there had to be some real-world applications as well. A political campaign is a marketing campaign, with academic research and theory thrown in for good measure. You have about a year to find a product (the candidate), test-market that product (the primary), create a slogan for the product (message and advertising), and then get it to the public as creatively as possible (the Internet). But unlike a new pair of shoes, a new gaming system, or a car, a political candidate has only *one day to sell*, and that is election day. Either the voters buy your product, or they do not; there is no second chance. I went on to win both of my races with more than 60 percent of the vote.

If you are reading this book, you already have some interest in how political campaigns in America are run. Perhaps you are a campaign manager yourself, looking to learn something else about the trade, or perhaps you are a young volunteer needing a refresher, a political science student reading for class, or just a political junkie looking for an interesting read. Regardless of what has brought you to this work, there is something for everyone to learn, question, and analyze in our journey into the world of campaign theory and campaign managers. It is my hope that after reading this book you will understand some of the theories, beliefs, and attitudes behind all the men and women (from the ivory tower to the feet on the ground) involved in the campaign process.

1

The Candidate

There was an old story about President Bill Clinton that used to circulate in Washington during the 1990s. It was said that Bill Clinton could enter a room of 300 people knowing full well that 299 of them adored him and supported everything he did and stood for. But Clinton would spend the entire evening working on changing the mind of that one person out of 300 who had not already come under his sway of charm. His ability to work a room, let alone be singularly focused on changing hearts and minds, represents a significant reason Bill Clinton was one of the most successful political candidates in American history over the past forty years.

The focus of this book is on political operatives from low-level campaign managers to highly paid political consultants and all the men and women in between. Although the experience level and campaign sophistication of the men and women in the sample of operatives may vary, they all have one thing in common: They are trying to get a candidate elected. Therefore, our journey into the world of political consultants begins with candidates, without whom political operatives would have nothing to do and no one to work for.

When you talk to campaigners in the field, you are always drawn back to that most basic of questions: What makes someone a good candidate? Or to delve deeper into the political jargon of the press, what makes a candidate "electable"? This chapter analyzes what makes someone an electable candidate in the minds of academics, pundits, and political consultants and what factors, such as race, class, or even the "post-9/11" world, impact whether someone has a good chance of moving from candidate to elected official. We will also look at the transition from being a candidate to an elected official. Are the traits needed for one role suitable to the other? Or are consultants promoting one product during the election that turns out to be something else once someone is sworn into office? Finally we will look at the extent to which consultants are making lemonade out of sour lemons. Very few campaign managers are influential enough and sought-after enough that they get a choice of for whom they work. Therefore, when we view these political operatives' answers, we see what they view as the best traits in a candidate that, for better or worse, they are stuck with. That might give us a better reflection of what the elusive concept of the "electable candidate" is all about.

The Traits That Rate

Political candidates are a unique mixture of product and the "real thing." They are men and women, black, white, Asian, and Latino, from all creeds and belief systems. Yet they have to make themselves fit in with an image of the "candidate" and "elected official" that voters want to pay attention to, donate money to, and vote for on election day. That is where their campaign managers, consultants, and other staffers come in, to help them in this process of becoming a candidate that the public wants to support in the general election. Despite what the television and radio pundits might want you to think, Americans *want* to like their politicians; there is a reason that people watched *The West Wing* and were heartbroken when President Palmer died on *24*.[1] Candidates and elected officials hold both Americans' dreams for the future and their concerns about power in one tight bundle.

Political science literature has focused on researching the four main traits on which voters evaluate candidates based on the American National Election Survey that is conducted during major election years in the United States (Iyengar and Kinder 1985; Funk 1996). These four traits are competence, integrity, empathy, and leadership. These traits carry a great deal of importance in understanding America's political system, since voters weigh these traits differently depending on a host of factors yet still use them to make judgments about a candidate's policies and fitness to serve. If you are a conservative Republican, what appeals to you in a candidate differs from what appeals to a liberal Democrat. But what happens if you are a liberal Democratic woman living in New York City who lived through 9/11? Or what if you are a conservative Republican man living in New Orleans who lived through Hurricane Katrina? Perhaps what appeals to you in a candidate has changed, and you might put more emphasis on one trait over another. Political scientists and academics have argued for decades about how different traits and characteristics influence how or why citizens perceive and evaluate candidates the way they do (Rapoport, Metcalf, and Hartman 1989; Pierce 1993; Hardy and Jamieson 2005). The majority of debates and discussions revolve around what value can be found in these candidate traits and how voters evaluate them under different circumstances (Keeter 1987; Alexander and Andersen 1993; Funk 1996, 1997, 1999; Fox and Smith 1998; Hayes 2005). No one, however, has examined how any of these factors, time, space, or place might influence how a campaign manager or consultant looks at the traits of their candidate. In this next section we will be taking a look at some of the existing theories on what factors influence how voters evaluate candidates, and we will use those theories to get a better idea as to how a consultant might be influenced by the same variables.

Party

As I mentioned in the Introduction, party identification, or "partisanship," influences how one looks at a political candidate (Stoker 1993; Goren 2002; Klein and Ahluwalia 2005). Of course, how that partisanship interacts with demographic traits about the voter and their environment is something subject to a great deal of discussion in political science. Some political scientists have focused on how party voters look at candidate traits in particular campaign years. Analyzing the 1996 presidential election, Alvarez and Glasgow found that Democrats evaluated Bill Clinton highest on his leadership skills and also found leadership to be the most important trait for someone running for office (1998, 148). Since Republican voters valued integrity as the most important trait in a candidate, conservatives rejected Bill Clinton because of his various extramarital affairs. In another analysis of the 1996 presidential election, other researchers found that Clinton received equally high marks from Republican and Democratic voters on empathy, but the two partisan groups parted ways regarding his intelligence. Democrats thought of him as a genius, whereas Republicans thought of him as well short of that mark (Klein and Ahluwalia 2005, 132).

Researchers Hansen and Otero found that not only is partisanship the best predictor of how people will vote, but it is also a stronger predictor of the weight placed on candidate traits (2007, 36). Leadership and compassion seemed to be the most important traits to both parties from 1988 to 2004, with the candidate rated highest in one or both of those categories by Democratic and Republican partisans usually winning the day. This suggests not only that partisanship might matter as an individual predictor for the candidates but that the partisan leanings of a district might come into play as well. Most researchers have found that campaign context—such as whether the district was leaning Republican or Democratic or if it was a "good" year for either party—influences how candidate traits are viewed (Funk 1999; see also Goren 2002; Doherty and Gimpel 1997; Kinder et al. 1980). In fact, one of the few researchers who posit that partisanship is not the most important factor in determining how a candidate is evaluated says this is the case because the voter's race trumps partisanship in those evaluations (Colleau et al. 1990, 386).

What is most interesting about the partisan effect on candidate evaluation discussions is that it plays out in a very real way in most elections. Former president George W. Bush was a classic example of this partisan evaluation. Democrats, progressives, and left-leaning analysts and columnists remarked on the infamous "Bush smirk." *Huffington Post.com* columnist Bob Cesca dedicated an entire article to this "smirk" and pulled no punches: "His uncomfortably ridiculous smirks and smiles illustrate his inadequacies as a leader: his fugacious attitude; his vacant stature; and, most strikingly, his apparent inability to grasp the reality of his decisions. It's all right there on the screen—underlined by those tiny baby teeth" (2007). Yet at the Republican convention in 2004, when former Tennessee senator Fred Thompson narrated President Bush's photo-essay introduction, some of those same pictures deemed as "smirks" by liberals and Democrats were said to demonstrate "his lack of pretension, a sincerity both of action and purpose. . . . There's a sense of humor that's natural. He's even been known to kid around with folks."[2]

Which was the real reflection of Bush's infamous "smirk"? No academic or analyst can truly say; the truth was in the eye of the beholder, and the beholder saw a different truth whether they were Republican or Democrat.

Type of Race: Challenger, Open Seat, or Incumbent

There are three ways in which a candidate starts a race: He or she is either seeking an open seat, challenging the current seat holder, or the incumbent defending his or her seat. Depending on what position one is in, political science research shows that how traits are evaluated can change significantly. Carolyn L. Funk, one of the originators of modern candidate trait research in political science, argues against this theory, suggesting that evaluations are all about the specific candidates involved, and what type of race they are running really does not make a difference (1999, 2). Other researchers, however, have shown that incumbents and challengers are evaluated differently by voters and observers. Kinder et al. (1980) found that voters tended to judge incumbents on integrity and leadership first and then take a look at the challenger. Alvarez and Glasgow (1998) and Goren (2002) found that challengers are evaluated more harshly than incumbents on their competence, since voters do not know if they can truly get the job done. Trait evaluations in open-seat races tend to be more of a mixed bag, with most researchers not finding significant differences in voter evaluations of candidates when both parties are trying out for a new position (Kinder et al. 1980; Alvarez and Glasgow 1998; Goren 2002; Arnold and Hawkins 2002).

Finally, in addition to what kind of position a candidate is in at the beginning of the race, the position they seek, be it legislative or executive, can influence how their competence is viewed as well as their leadership ability (Nadeau et al. 1995; Burden 2002; Atkinson and Partin 2001; Arnold and Hawkins 2002). Atkinson and Partin find that voters view the responsibilities and competencies of gubernatorial and senatorial candidates differently (2001, 796). Whereas governors are seen as being more caring about and responsible for the poor, senators are seen as more likely to take strong leadership stands on international issues. Burden's work discusses the difficulties Senate candidates face in their pursuit of the White House, in part because they are evaluated differently on traits and issues from those running for executive positions (2002, 82). There is evidence to suggest that because those seeking and serving in executive positions are viewed and evaluated differently from those serving in and seeking legislative positions, the traits upon which they are evaluated will differ as well.

Gender

Most political science research on gender and candidate traits looks at how the candidate's gender and the gender of the voters influence how voters evaluate the candidate. Initially, many researchers suggested that there was not any real difference in how voters evaluated women compared to male candidates (Darcy and Schramm 1977; Eckstrand and Eckert 1981). However, since the late 1980s and the increase in women candidates running for higher office, especially executive positions, researchers have found that there was a fascinating mix of how gender and policy issues played off each other in female candidate evaluations. For example, Rosenwasser et al. found that women were deemed as highly "competent" on "feminine" issues such as education and civil rights, while they were evaluated as less competent on issues such as foreign affairs and the military by the average voter (1987, 193). Sanbonmatsu found similar results, in that female candidates were found to be generally more empathetic than men, and that empathy also played a larger role in how voters evaluated them (2002, 22). Further, while women were found to be just as competent as men, this evaluation varied according to what issues were placed before the public. In explaining 1992, "The Year of the Woman," when an unprecedented number of women candidates were successful in gaining office, especially on the federal level, Jennifer L. Lawless, director of the Women and Politics Institute at American University, reiterated this relationship between gender issues and women candidates' success. The year "1992 was an election cycle where women's issues and women's ability to lead was at the forefront of these campaigns. The Clarence Thomas and Anita Hill hearings and the Family Medical Leave Act are just two of the issues that were prioritized by a lot of the women running" (Horn 2010). Women candidates who focus on a few issues that are seen as their inherent strengths or political environments where "women's issues" are at the forefront may lead to women candidates being as or more successful than male candidates (Clayton and Stallings 2000; Hansen and Otero 2007). Continuing on this theme, women candidates' traits are also more positively evaluated for certain positions than men's. Some analysts find that voters think women are much better suited for legislative positions like city council or school board member than "leadership" positions like mayor or governor (Hedlund et al. 1979; Huddy and Terkildson 1993a and 1993b; Ballew and Todorov 2007; Dolan 2004b).

This belief can put women candidates and the consultants that are working for them in a real bind when it comes to running for higher office positions, especially in the post-9/11 world of federal politics. Most voters see women as being more capable as legislators and on domestic issues, but a woman seeking higher office or an executive position faces a "glass ceiling" of stereotypes and expectations. This is one of the reasons Hillary Clinton worked so hard to create a hawkish image of herself during her time in the Senate, because she knew as a woman it would be critical for her to appear tough on foreign policy issues. Clinton's increasingly aggressive foreign policy positions as she moved from candidate to senator to presidential candidate were well chronicled in the press. Even the slightly right-leaning *Real Clear Politics* site noticed this transformation. Cofounder and executive editor of the Web site Tom Bevan said, "Never known as an ardent supporter of the U.S. military, Clinton secured a coveted seat on the Armed Services Committee upon entering the Senate and has worked diligently on military issues. In the wake of Sept. 11, she became devoted to homeland security and supported military action in Afghanistan and Iraq. It's no secret critics suggest Clinton's transformation to foreign policy hawk is a calculated move designed to help achieve her ultimate goal of becoming the first woman president" (Bevan 2006). Now, one might argue that making hawkish moves in a post-9/11 world is something that any ambitious candidate would do regardless of gender, especially one coming from New York. However, given the existing research demonstrating that many voters do not see women candidates as being as competent or capable in handling foreign affairs as men, these moves became even more important for someone like Hillary Clinton. In a survey of one hundred Republican and Democratic political "insiders" by the *Atlantic Monthly* in late 2005 about Clinton's chances as a presidential candidate in 2008, one of the specific hurdles she was seen as facing was her gender in relation to foreign policy and leadership issues. One Republican insider stated, "While it's difficult to pick just one, Hillary's gender will more than likely be the biggest obstacle to her becoming President. The bottom line—with such uncertainty in foreign and world affairs, the United States will not elect a woman to be the leader of the free world" (Barnes and Bell 2005).

In fact, under the strong advice of her campaign staff, Clinton went out of her way to brandish her toughness on foreign policy issues, and then went a little too far. In one of the more critical events in the 2008 Democratic primary, Clinton claimed to have been under sniper fire when coming off an airplane for a state visit to Bosnia as first lady in 1996. When reporters and even a stand-up comedian who attended the trip with her disputed this account, and video of her state visit was discovered showing clear skies and no snipers, she was caught in a serious political lie that dogged her campaign for weeks. Analyzing the Hillary Clinton presidential campaign as symptomatic of the challenges that female candidates face on certain issues, Lawrence and Rose assert, "Clinton's 'Bosnia Fairy Tale' highlights, among other things, the imperative for the female presidential candidate to burnish her national security credentials. Clinton may have felt pressure to exaggerate her foreign policy experience to establish her 'toughness' in the foreign policy area, especially in a time of war" (2010, 74).[3]

When evaluating how a candidate's gender influences trait evaluation, one of the challenges in political science has been the relative paucity of subjects to examine. While the number of female candidates for higher office, especially executive positions, continues to grow, there has been a relatively small sample of prominent women presidential candidates to analyze.[4] Consequently, the role of gender in campaign studies has often been viewed from the side of the voter in terms of how men and women evaluate candidate traits. Since the vast majority of political candidates running for high office are men, sometimes gender plays a role in trait evaluation from the demographics of the voter, not the candidate. Doherty and Gimpel found that women tended to trust Bill Clinton more than George Bush across the board, especially on economic issues, in spite of the fact that Clinton had been caught in various extramarital affairs (1997, 178). At the same time, men often found Bill Clinton lacking in leadership compared to both Bush and Dole.

Political science literature does not have a definitive answer about how gender influences candidate evaluations, but there are a few things we can surmise. First, women are viewed differently from men, and whether that is a positive or negative has to do with what the issues in the campaign are and what position is being sought. Second, the way that women are evaluated when running for office is really driven by the context of the campaign environment, which in many respects does not differ that much for men.

Race

Both the race of the candidate and the race of the voters have an impact on how candidates and candidate traits are evaluated. Most academics agree that white voters tend to have harsher evaluations of black candidates than white ones, especially when it comes to leadership and competence (Colleau et al. 1990; Wright 1995; Hajnal 1998; Jeffries 2002; Burden 2002; Liu 2003; Abrajano 2005). Black candidates can counter this lingering prejudice if they focus on certain issues that white voters do not find as threatening or establish their competence by having held previous office or having a stellar record of success (Colleau et al. 1990; Gimpel and Doherty 1997; Hajnal 1998; Clayton and Stallings 2000). This can usually be done with a focus on "valence issues," that is, issues where there is near-universal support or disapproval from the voters.[5]

Many political commentators believe that the existing research on the effect of a candidate's race on how they are evaluated has been turned on its head over the past three years because of the election of Barack Obama (Hollinger 2008; Collins 2008; Taranto 2009; Steele 2008). Or has it? Some researchers have shown that were he a white male, candidate Obama's election margin would have been much larger (Lewis-Beck and Tien 2009). Other political pundits and leaders claimed that if he was not black, he would not have even won the nomination, such as Geraldine Ferraro, who in 1984 was selected by Walter Mondale to be the first female vice presidential nominee for a major party. She infamously said in an interview with California's *Daily Breeze* newspaper, "If Obama was a white man, he would not be in this position. . . . And if he was a woman (of any color) he would not be in this position. He happens to be very lucky to be who he is. And the country is caught up in the concept" (Maddaus 2008). Ferraro's suggestion that being African American was actually an *advantage* in running for president of the United States was met with both scorn and support in public discourse. Ultimately, her comments and the discussions that followed just further muddled the role race could play in such a high-profile election.

For their part the Obama campaign staff was consistently coy about any racial issue throughout the primary and into the general election. In late 2007, long before the actual presidential primary, Barack Obama trailed Hillary Clinton by double digits among African American Democrats, yet "his strategists nonetheless, resisted any temptation to run a more race conscious campaign. Most of Obama's top staffers viewed his ambiguity on matters of race as an asset; they decided therefore to soldier on with the racial balancing act that Obama had been engaged in since the 2004 Democratic Convention" (Sears and Tesler 2010, 5). Like Hillary Clinton's role in political science research on female candidates, Barack Obama's role in influencing research on candidates' race has been significant as well.[6] If an African American man can get elected to the highest office of the land, does that mean that race is no longer a detriment to minorities running for higher office? Not likely, but it does suggest that perhaps conventional wisdom and observation on race in American elections needs to be reevaluated and that political operatives working with minority candidates might have some insights into race and the electorate that are missing in existing political science work. Much of the existing political science and cultural writing on African Americans in politics deals with those men and women who have already been elected, as opposed to suggestions or proposals for how minorities can be elected (Howell and McLean 2001). The amount of work on Latino elected officials is similar, focused more on those who have already achieved office rather than those who are running (Kam 2007; Kaufmann 2003). The prevailing wisdom about the impact of race on political candidates prior to the election of Barack Obama fell to three main ideas. Sigelman et al. noted that the majority of white voters were still reluctant to support African American candidates over white candidates for higher office (regardless of what they might have said to preelection pollsters) because whites did not believe blacks had the proper traits (intelligence, discipline) to serve (1995, 244). This diminishing support from whites for black candidates by election day is colloquially referred to as the "Bradley Effect." Although this phenomenon does not always result in the minority candidate losing, the belief is that white support cannot be fully trusted when cameras are not watching and people are safe in the voting booth. The phrase originated when Tom Bradley, a long-term African American mayor of Los Angeles, ran for governor of California as a Democrat in 1982. Polls prior to the race showed him with a substantial lead over rival Republican candidate George Deukmejian. In October, just about a month before the election in an interview with the *Los Angeles Times*, Bill Roberts, campaign manager for Deukmejian, stated, "If we are down only 5 points or less in the polls by election time, we're going to win (because of) the hidden anti-black vote. . . . It's (the hidden anti-black vote) just a fact of life. If people are going to vote that way, they certainly are not going to announce it for a survey (poll) taker. You will not get the truth from people regarding the race issue." Not only did Bradley lose the race, but subsequent high-profile races across America have reinforced this theory.[7] The second piece of conventional wisdom about African American candidates is that white political candidates will exploit lingering racism in order to improve their chances of success against a black candidate.[8] Finally, the way that African American candidates have to counter this exploitation is by running "deracialized" campaigns defined as "conducting a campaign in a stylistic fashion that defuses the polarizing effects of race by avoiding specific reference to race specific issues, while at the same time emphasizing those issues that are perceived as racially transcendent thus mobilizing a broad segment of the electorate for the purposes of capturing or maintaining public office" (Orey and Ricks 2007, 325; see also Austin and Middleton 2004). This concept is challenging, since it is almost impossible for an African American, Latino, or other minority candidate to not in some way remind white voters that they exist. Nonetheless, the prevailing suggestion to minority candidates to at least remain "ambiguous" on those issues likely to cause racial anxiety in white voters when they are needed to win an election has persisted. One could argue that theories one and two were in play during the Obama campaign, but his campaign staff helped him to successfully adhere to theory three so well that he still won the election.

The race of the candidate is not the only racial factor that influences trait evaluation; the racial composition of the election district has an impact as well. Although it is known that African American voters form a pretty consistent voting bloc for Democrats, the number of minorities in a district also has an impact on trait evaluation (Miller and Miller 1975; Tate 1991; Lublin 1999; Austin and Middleton 2004). African American voters may view some traits as more important than Latino or Asian American voters. Moreover, the size of a minority population in a campaign area has a significant impact on what policies are promoted or discussed by candidates. Immigration reform is a make-or-break issue for candidates running in Texas, Arizona, and Nevada, because each of these areas has large Latino voting populations. But a candidate is going to get a lot of blank stares if they base their 2011 campaign on closing the borders when they are running for mayor of

Dayton, Ohio (Alvarez and Glasgow 1998; Doherty and Gimpel 1997; Alvarez and Bedolla 2003; Leal 2004; Alexander 2006; Arnold and Hawkins 2002; Burden 2002).

What is important to remember is that race has a dual role in how political candidates are evaluated, which is reflected in most political science work. As with gender, the race of the candidate and the race and number of the voters play off each other to paint the campaign environment in different ways. It is the job of the campaign manager to determine the best way to use these various elements to the advantage of the candidate.

Education

The more educated you are, the more likely you are to pay attention to politics and the more complex your evaluation of candidates will become. This is not to say that less educated voters do not care about politics, but it is simply a fact that the more educated you are, the more likely you are to care about the issues in a campaign (Kinder et al. 1980; Alvarez and Glasgow 1998; Pierce 1993; Goldthwaite 2002). The same logic applies to candidate evaluations: More educated voters look at things differently than less educated voters. Peterson shows that the more sophisticated a voter is, the more certain they are about the candidate's policy stands and thus use them to make assessments of the candidate's character traits (2005, 3). Lavine and Gschwend show that the less sophisticated the voter, the more time they spend judging candidates by personality traits as opposed to their actual words or stands on policy issues (2007, 142). In many political science studies there appears to be a consensus that the more sophisticated the voter, the more heavily they weighed a candidate's competence, and the less sophisticated the voter, the more they focused on the candidate's empathy or integrity. The importance of leadership seemed to vacillate with particular candidates and campaign years (Kinder et al. 1980; Pierce 1993; Doherty and Gimpel 1997; Alvarez and Glasgow 1998; Goldthwaite 2002; Bartels 2002).

What this amounts to for our research is that the level of education among the voting population should influence how a campaign manager sees the importance of candidate traits as well. If you are running a campaign in the college town of Chapel Hill, you want to focus a campaign on different traits than if you are running a campaign in rural Tupelo, Mississippi.

9/11 Terrorist Attacks

The terrorist attacks on New York City and Washington, D.C., on September 11, 2001, have irrevocably changed American politics, from the issues that are raised to the manner in which voters respond to candidates, especially for federal office (Lawless 2004; Murphy 2003; Norpoth and Sidman 2007). Understandably, it has also changed how political consultants and analysts interact with political candidates and how they package their traits to the voters. Jordan Lieberman, former publisher of the trade magazine *Campaigns and Elections*, put it succinctly: "9/11 changed everything. Real is in. Candidates have to be authentic now, especially on national security issues" (Johnson 2010a). No one candidate exemplified this change more than former New York mayor and 2008 Republican presidential nomination candidate Rudy Giuliani. Lawrence Haas, a Democrat who worked in the Clinton White House, spoke to Giuliani's strengths as a candidate in this post-9/11 era: "Something changed on 9/11. . . . Many Americans came to realize that they are seriously threatened by dangerous enemies, and Giuliani personifies the determination to confront those enemies. So Republicans are holding their collective noses on social issues and flocking to his side" (Cannon n.d.). Haas pointed out two things that are critical to political consultants and trait theory for candidates. First, Giuliani was not just a candidate; he had come to personify traits and a determination that Americans desperately needed after the 9/11 attacks. A candidate who can represent several traits at once, based on one particular event, is usually in good shape politically. Moreover, the strength of those traits associated with Giuliani were such that many Republican elites were willing to overlook his somewhat more liberal positions on issues like gay marriage and gun control. Of course, one seemingly powerful candidate was not enough to quell the arguments on how best to use the events of 9/11 in a campaign environment.

For years Republicans and Democrats have traded barbs suggesting which party did or did not fully recognize how national security priorities had changed since the terrorist attacks. This became a common theme in many political campaigns on the national level. On the one hand, parties used the event to ridicule the opposition: "Democrats have a post-9/11 worldview and many Republicans have a pre-9/11 worldview. Democrats think it is wrong to trust a state that recognized the Taliban as the legitimate government of Afghanistan, Republicans think it's right. That doesn't make them unpatriotic but it does make them wrong—deeply and profoundly and consistently wrong."[9] And in other instances, political campaigns used 9/11 to criticize other campaigns for using 9/11 too often. In one of the most memorable quotes from the 2008 presidential primary season, Senator Joe Biden chastised Rudy Giuliani for focusing too much on the terrorist attacks to bolster his résumé for running for president: "There's only three things he mentions in a sentence: a noun, and a verb and 9/11!"[10]

Ultimately, among other factors perhaps influencing how a candidate's traits are evaluated, we must take into consideration whether the campaign was run before or after the 9/11 attacks. One would predict that not only would there be significant relationships between how campaign managers evaluate traits and 9/11, but certain traits like leadership and integrity would likely prove to be more important in their estimation.

The aforementioned analyses of candidate evaluations are mostly from academic research over the past several decades. However, most of what the average voter knows about candidate traits and evaluation comes from the twenty-four-hour news channels, blogs, and their friends. If you ask a thirty-seven-year-old African American female with a college degree living in Utah how she views a candidate's competence, she will likely give you whatever answer comes off the top of her head. Like most voters, her evaluation is based on environment and who is asking the question at the time. So this leads to our research: Although it is nice to know what influences how voters look at candidate traits, do these same factors influence how campaign managers and consultants look at traits? Voters have the luxury of deciding about candidate evaluation at their leisure, but a political consultant's very livelihood depends on their ability to figure out who is a good candidate and who is not or, moreover, how to turn what may be a bad candidate into an "electable" one. We will now begin to take a look at what actual consultants think about candidate traits and what influences that thinking.

What Makes a Great Candidate?

The best way to learn about candidates is to simply ask the men and women who work for them. The campaign managers in my study were asked the open-ended question, "What is your candidate's best attribute?" This simple question opens the door to our overall discussion of candidates, traits, and electability that we will explore in this chapter. First, we want to see what consultants think of the men and women they work for and find out if the traits they find important in the candidates match up with the four main traits that most political science literature has been using to evaluate candidates over the years. There is an inherent strength and weakness to this type of analysis, however. On the one hand, we are asking political operatives in the sample to give the best trait of the candidate that they happen to be working with in the race that is the focus of the survey they completed. There is a difference between asking "What is *your* candidate's best trait?" and "What are the best traits a candidate *can have*?" However, this is also a strong point of this line of questioning. In this initial question we are simply trying to discover if the traits that consultants look at are in any way consistent with the traits that voters appear to care about based on the ANES survey and existing political science research. Given the freedom to choose any trait from a range of election levels, even if the results are time bound, they still give us a worthwhile sample of what consultants in a particular election cycle thought were the most valuable candidate traits.

There were a wide range of traits mentioned by political consultants as the "best traits" of the candidates, but by and large they fell into a few basic categories. The responses were combined according to theme (great speaker and great communicator were merged, for example) to get a better handle on the main traits.[11] There did not appear to be any strong differences in responses based on the gender of the candidates, or the type of race being run, but there were differences according to the party of the consultants. Below I lay out some of the main differences among Republicans and Democrats who described their candidates' best traits.

Democrats on Best Traits

Out of the 117 Democrats who responded to this section of the survey, "ambition" was seen as the most important trait. In this survey "ambition" was a collection of various statements or traits that all denoted candidates were willing to work hard, so responses such as "hard worker," "dedicated," and "willing to do what was needed to win" were included in the "ambition" category. We take ambition to have a fairly broad meaning, but I am confident that it encapsulated the feelings being expressed by the consultants in the

TABLE 1.1 Most-cited "best trait of candidate": Democratic consultants

Trait	Number	Percentage
Good communicator	17	14.5
Integrity/honesty	17	14.5
Résumé	9	7.7
Intelligence	12	10.3
Personality	15	12.8
Hard worker	22	18.8
Experience	21	17.9
Miscellaneous	4	3.4
Total	117	100

sample. When your job is on the line, what good is it to have a charismatic speaker who will not put in the time to make fund-raising phone calls? The next most cited trait in the Democratic sample was "experience," which many consultants cited, even when they were working with challengers. In the case of experience, this exact term was used by the consultants in all but a few instances, and experience can apply not just to having served in office but also to background with the issues that will be faced once in office. Conspicuously absent were many of the terms that are used to assess candidates in the ANES survey given to voters by academics over the years. Only one manager cited leadership as their candidate's best attribute, and only one consultant cited competence.

Republican "Best Traits"

Republican campaign managers saw different "best traits" in their candidates than their Democratic competitors. What jumps out first is the importance of integrity in the minds of the Republican consultants; almost twice as many stated this as the most important trait of their candidate, followed closely by résumé, and the rest of the traits were mentioned infrequently. In this regard Republican managers at least seemed to identify one of the traits most often used by academics in assessing their candidates in the real world. One important trait that came up several times among Republicans that did not appear on any Democratic responses was issue position. Although still a relatively small number, only Republican consultants cited their candidates' positions on tough issues or ability to stand firm on tough issues as their best trait.

TABLE 1.2 Most-cited "best trait of candidate": Republican consultants

Trait	Number	Percentage
Personality	7	14
Integrity	18	36
Résumé	11	22
Intelligence	0	0
Communicator	1	2
Hard worker	5	10
Experience	5	10
Positions	3	6
Total	50	100

Overall, we see a pretty good cross-section of what Democratic and Republican campaign managers and political consultants consider to be the best traits of their candidates in this sample, and just about none of their responses match up with how most researchers have been looking at how voters evaluate political candidates. Although this is only a sample of the thousands of consultants who work campaigns across the country, the absolute lack of congruence between their identification of best traits and that of most voters is worthy of note. Might this suggest a fundamental problem in how well our modern electoral system is working? If what voters say they look for in a candidate and what campaign managers look for in a candidate are so different, can we still achieve effective representation through the election process? No one is suggesting that political operatives do not care what voters think, but don't we have a problem in American democracy if the consumers of campaigns and the producers of campaigns do not see eye to eye on what is being sold?

Governing Versus Campaigning

In his seminal work *Congress: The Electoral Connection*, David Mayhew argued that a legislator's primary motivation in all activities was to be reelected. In claiming that all legislators are "single minded seekers of re-election" (1974, 5), he detailed how this primary focus affected everything from the policies initiated to the structure of Congress itself and suggested the major conflict between voters and elected officials (and by extension political consultants) was the tension between governing and campaigning. Consultants want candidates who exhibit the traits needed to get elected, whereas voters seek candidates with traits needed to be good elected officials, and, as Mayhew suggested years ago, these traits and motivations may not overlap. Are consultants just trying to get a win and then riding off into the sunset without a care about how the official performs once in office?

In one of the earliest surveys taken of political professionals by James Thurber, he discovered that consultants often did regret helping to get candidates elected if they later found out that those candidates did not serve well. Thurber noted:

> Almost 51% of all consultants said that they have helped a candidate get elected only to regret it later. . . . Overall this indicates that many consultants who helped elect a candidate they were later sorry to see serve felt that way because their candidate seemingly pandered to voters, and told the public what they wanted to hear, instead of what the candidate intended to do. . . . Our analysis demonstrates that consultants are not pleased to see a client elected at any cost. Indeed consultants hope their candidates truly mean what consultants help them to say. (1998b, 2)

Some works by consultants have further suggested that this difference in skill sets may actually have electoral consequences. Jim Jordan, John Kerry's campaign manager during the 2004 presidential campaign, commented, "John's not an instinctive politician. He doesn't understand the rhythms of a campaign. He's a very gifted man in ways that are more analogous to being a good president than a good campaigner" (Thomas 2005, 14).

Even if we were to accept the notion that consultants do care one way or another about how a candidate eventually serves, it does not change the fact that the attributes needed to run a successful campaign may or may not automatically mesh with what it takes to serve in office. Obviously, with presidential campaigns starting earlier and earlier, we have entered the era of the permanent campaign where the lines between serving in office and running are blurred (Jones 2000; Tenpas 1998). Moreover, political operatives are in the unique position of often being able to see both sides of this equation. While some move on after their campaigns, many go on to serve in some capacity in the new official's office, or at least somewhere in government. With that in mind, we want to know what if any difference, according to campaign

TABLE 1.3 **Frequency of consultants' opinion about the relationship of candidate traits: Running and serving**

Survey option	Frequency	Percentage
They have a very strong correlation. The way they run and behave in a campaign says a lot about how they will govern.	110	63.6
They have no correlation. Being a great campaigner says little about how they will actually govern.	59	34.1
I don't know. I don't keep up with candidates after the race is over.	4	2.3
Total	173	100

managers, is there in the traits you need to run for office and the traits you need to actually govern?

To tackle this question we use a two-pronged approach. First, we have to find out if consultants in the sample actually see a difference in what it takes to campaign versus govern, and then we have to look at how these traits may differ for those who are campaigning versus governing. When asked if they see a difference between how someone runs a campaign and how they govern, the majority of consultants do see a relationship.

With more than 60 percent of consultants responding that they believe the behavior of a candidate in a campaign correlates to how someone will do their job as an elected official, we can rest assured that many of these consultants are not hired guns just running from one election to another. Ultimately, how is your business model helped if you get a reputation for electing folks who do a bad job? More important, if you want repeat clients, it is in your best interest to work with clients who can do their job effectively. Of course, now that we see that consultants view campaigning as a window into governing, let us try to get more specific. There are literally dozens of variables in the campaign environment that impact how voters see candidates, as we have discussed before, so shouldn't those same variables potentially impact how consultants think? To get a deeper examination of the question of governing versus campaigning, I looked at various environmental factors, such as what region of the country a consultant is in, along with demographic factors, such as the race of the candidate, and performed a logistic regression. The goal was to see, once I controlled for other variables, what is truly driving why consultants feel the way they

TABLE 1.4 **Significant predictors by feelings on governing versus campaigning by environmental and demographic variables**

Model	Significant predictor	Interpretation
Campaigning versus governing	Elections after 9/11	You are less likely to see a connection between campaigning and governing if you worked on a campaign that took place after 9/11
Campaigning versus governing	Working for a challenger	You are less likely to see a connection between campaigning and governing if you are working for a challenger

do about the connection between campaigning and governing. The results are shown in Table 1.4.

Not many factors influenced how consultants felt about the connection between campaigning and governing, and the two that did, 9/11 and being a challenger, make sense given the research. The September 11 terrorist attacks have been a key political football for years, but if there is one thing that they have shown campaign strategists and managers, it is that you cannot predict even half of what your candidate will face once they are in office. George W. Bush ran a campaign with a message of "Compassionate Conservatism" and said repeatedly in debates with Vice President Al Gore that the United States did not need to be in the business of nation building. Yet less than a year into office the world changed in such a way that many of the principles and themes that he campaigned on were put aside in favor of the events directly in front of the nation. It is not so much about lying or selling the public on a candidate, as much as campaign managers realize perhaps better than most that although how you campaign does tell something about your governing style, there are some events that might occur that will completely change the dynamic of being an elected official versus being a candidate. The second result also makes sense: If you are working for a challenger, your single-minded focus on beating the incumbent may not necessarily reflect how you will operate once in office. When you have two candidates running for an open seat who have never held that position, the campaign is an extended commercial about their ability to do the job, but when you are running a challenger's campaign you simply want to beat the incumbent and then make promises about what you will do once that person is no longer at the wheel of government.

Adding More Traits While Running or Campaigning

How do political operatives' views of candidate traits and their beliefs about governing versus campaigning match up with the traits used by most academics? We decided to take a look at how managers and consultants viewed the four traits from the ANES (competence, integrity, intelligence, and empathy) for a candidate who is running for office and serving in office, with the additional trait of ambition. Ambition was added to the mix due to the strong response levels gained from the open-ended questions about "best traits" from consultants. Political commentators and academics have often looked at the role political ambition can play in a candidate's success (Schlesinger 1996; Terrelonge-Stone 1980; Mezey 1970; Fox and Lawless 2005, 644).

Candidates who do not show a significant amount of ambition or passion for the campaign seldom make it out of the primary, as was the case with Fred Thompson and Rudy Giuliani, two highly touted but ultimately less than motivated campaigners during the 2008 Republican presidential primary. In a particularly telling piece on *Slate.com*, political writer John Dickerson pointed out how Thompson's country charm and easygoing manner may have worked for his roles in *The Hunt for Red October* and on *Law and Order*, but they did not fit well in the 2008 campaign: "Thompson's outsider strategy also gives his opponents an opportunity. One of the biggest (and longstanding) knocks against the former senator is that he doesn't have the heart for the race or the job. In short: He's lazy. . . . It looks like he's trying to elevate laziness into a virtue. Several of Thompson's rivals, who know him from his time in Washington, elaborate on that theme. He wasn't known for his hard work in the Senate" (2007).

Occasionally, ambition becomes a subject during the general election, and this trait, or lack thereof, can be deadly for a candidate. When Democrat Martha Coakley was running during a special election in January 2010 to replace Ted Kennedy in Massachusetts, she was asked about how far she was going out of her way to connect with voters. Her answer did not inspire a great deal of confidence that she was intensely seeking the job, as seen in this story from the *Boston Globe*: "There is a subdued, almost dispassionate quality to her public appearances, which are surprisingly few. Her voice is not hoarse from late-night rallies. Even yesterday, the day after a hard-hitting debate, she had no public campaign appearances in the state." Coakley bristled at the suggestion that, with so little time left, in an election with such high stakes, she was being too passive. "'As opposed to standing outside Fenway Park? In the cold? Shaking hands?' she fires back, in an apparent reference to a Brown online video of him doing just that. 'This is a special election. And I know that I have the support of Kim Driscoll. And I now know the members of the [Salem] School Committee, who know far more people than I could ever meet'" (Filipov 2010). After reading this quote on the air, Jon Stewart of the *Daily Show* lambasted Coakley for her lack of campaign ambition, detachment from Boston culture, and the campaign in general, stating: "Coakley was asked her favorite cream pie and she said banana. . . . Coakley believes that Larry Bird is a *Sesame Street* character, and she went into the bar at Cheers and didn't know anybody's name!"[12] Coakley never fully recovered from the impression that she just "wasn't that into" the job of campaigning and lost in a major upset to Republican Scott Brown. This is not to take away from Brown, who ran a good campaign, but Coakley did not do herself any favors by appearing uninterested in the grunt work of the race.

Candidate George W. Bush's passion for campaigning was questioned as well in the 2000 general election, but he and his campaign staff managed to stave off such questions by suggesting that Bush really was working even if the public did not see him as often as they wanted to. And campaign officials worked to head off a second *Wizard of Oz*–style problem: that he did not have the heart for a tough campaign. Voters "like fighters," said Stuart Rothenberg, editor of a nonpartisan political newsletter based in Washington. "They liked Bush better when he was fighting. [Bush] wants to avoid the appearance that he is more interested in jogging than overseeing education policy." Bush's staff eventually resorted to counting up the hours Bush spent campaigning and giving the figure to reporters to quash the story. While the doubt about Bush's passion for the job continued to linger, even into his presidency he did show enough passion through the campaign to get 49 percent of the popular vote.

The Results

Consultants were asked "How important are the following traits when running for office?" and "How important are the following traits when govern-

TABLE 1.5 How important are the following traits while running? Republicans

Trait	Very important N (%)	Somewhat important N (%)	Neither to very unimportant N (%)
Integrity	40 (75.5)	10 (18.9)	3 (5.7)
Leadership	40 (75.5)	10 (18.9)	3 (5.7)
Empathy	20 (37.7)	21 (39.6)	12 (22.7)
Competence	37 (69.8)	13 (24.5)	3 (5.7)
Ambition	19 (35.8)	25 (47.2)	9 (17.0)

Note: N = actual number of responses. (%) = percentage of total.

TABLE 1.6 How important are the following traits while running? Democrats

Trait	Very important N (%)	Somewhat important N (%)	Neither to very unimportant N (%)
Integrity	83 (79.8)	16 (15.4)	5 (4.8)
Leadership	78 (75.0)	24 (23.1)	2 (1.9)
Empathy	48 (46.2)	35 (33.7)	21 (20.2)
Competence	80 (76.9)	20 (19.2)	4 (3.9)
Ambition	23 (22.1)	43 (41.3)	38 (36.5)

Note: N = actual number of responses. (%) = percentage of total.

ing or serving as an elected official?" When looking at the five criteria upon which candidates are evaluated, under the lens of running or campaigning one result jumps out among all of the rest. Most of the consultants responded that just about every trait—competence, leadership, and so on—was "very important." The only seeming outliers were empathy and ambition, which consultants viewed as "somewhat important." However, no consultants responded in the majority that any trait was unimportant. Because most consultants found all of the traits important, the real distinction between parties, winners, losers, and other types of campaigns is between who saw traits as "very important" and who saw them as "somewhat important." Tables 1.5 and 1.6 show how Democratic and Republican consultants viewed these traits while their candidates were running for office.

There were slight differences between Democratic and Republican campaigners in the survey sample on the importance of candidate traits while their candidate was running for office. For Republicans, integrity and leadership were tied in importance at 75.5 percent each, with competence coming in third at 69.8 percent. Although the top three most important traits among Democratic campaigners in the sample were the same, their rankings differed. Democrats ranked integrity as the most important trait for a candidate while running, with competence and leadership closely ranked as second and third in importance, respectively. The rankings of empathy and ambition were the same for campaign operatives for both parties. The one major difference worthy of note in this initial question was which trait the campaign managers thought was "unimportant." The most unimportant trait among 20 percent of Republican respondents was empathy, whereas for Democrats it was ambition. At first blush these are both surprising and expected reactions. Republican candidates are not generally known for their empathy, which is why George W. Bush had to cast himself as a "compassionate conservative" in the 2000 presidential election, and clearly this survey seems to suggest that empathy (compassion) is not a priority to consultants in this sample during the campaign. On the other hand, the Democratic response is surprising. In the open-ended question about candidate traits Democrats were consistent in their responses that being a hardworking or ambitious candidate was the best trait, yet when compared to other traits from the ANES, they found ambition to be the least important. The fact that both Republican and Democratic consultants ranked the candidate traits similarly, though, implies that there may be a consistent idea among political professionals about what makes a good candidate. As mentioned before, there is a substantive difference between asking what is "your candidate's" best trait and what is the "best trait in general." It would seem that, in general, leadership and integrity are deemed most important, at least when a candidate is running for office. We now look at campaign manager responses to the importance of traits when someone is actually serving as an elected official.

The results for how consultants viewed candidate traits when serving as an elected official are actually similar to the value they placed on traits when someone was running for office. With some slight variation in order, the respondents ranked the traits integrity, leadership, and competence as the top

TABLE 1.7 How important are the following traits while governing? Democrats

Trait	Very important N (%)	Somewhat important N (%)	Neither to very unimportant N (%)
Integrity	63 (60.6)	26 (25.0)	15 (14.4)
Leadership	62 (59.6)	27 (26.0)	15 (14.4)
Empathy	50 (48.1)	38 (36.5)	16 (15.4)
Competence	52 (50.0)	37 (35.6)	15 (14.4)
Ambition	38 (36.5)	45 (43.3)	21 (20.2)

Note: N = actual number of responses. (%) = percentage of total.

TABLE 1.8 How important are the following traits while governing? Republicans

Trait	Very important N (%)	Somewhat important N (%)	Neither to very unimportant N (%)
Integrity	48 (90.6)	4 (7.5)	1 (1.9)
Leadership	46 (86.8)	5 (9.4)	2 (3.8)
Empathy	23 (43.4)	21 (39.6)	9 (17.0)
Competence	41 (77.4)	10 (18.9)	2 (3.8)
Ambition	11 (20.8)	13 (24.5)	29 (54.7)

Note: N = actual number of responses. (%) = percentage of total.

three, with empathy and ambition bringing up the rear in the category of "very important" traits. One marked difference between the governing and campaigning trait evaluations by political operatives was the degree to which they felt some traits were unimportant. Both Democrats (20.2 percent) and Republicans (54.7 percent) agreed that ambition is not very important when someone is actually serving in office. In most of the responses all traits were rated as "very important," and our analysis simply has to do with the degree to which the campaigners said that the trait is important. In this case, ambition was actually deemed more unimportant than any other trait in the survey. What might this mean as far as our survey? First, it suggests that our interpretation of ambition as being synonymous with "hardworking" might be a bit too broad. It is hard to imagine that campaign managers would actually argue that being hardworking is not an important trait to have while serving in public office. In addition, we are probably seeing a difference in interpretation of what ambition really amounts to. The overly ambitious politician in the minds of campaigners and those in Washington is not always a good thing. An "ambitious" politician could be someone who is not necessarily driven to do a good job in the current position but sees it only as a stepping-stone to get to the next office. The ambitious public official is the one who voters soon realize does not care about being their mayor or senator because they have their eyes on Congress, the governor's mansion, or some other higher office. There are various examples of this in recent electoral politics.

In referring to Ed Case, a former congressman from Hawaii, the local *Hawaiian Free Press* made the case against the "ambitious" politician: "Ed Case's inflated ego and unabashed ambition to climb the political ladder is once again rearing its ugly head. The former Member of Congress from Hawaii's Second Congressional District has announced that he will seek the First Congressional District seat in 2010. Case, who has run for state House, Governor, U.S. Congress in the Second District as well as the U.S. Senate, now has his eye on the First as his next stepping stone to higher office" (*Hawaii Free Press* 2009). In fact, stating that one has ambitions beyond their current office is a political no-no for most elected officials because it suggests that they are not truly dedicated to the office that they have earned. Ben Quayle, son of former vice president Dan Quayle who won a congressional seat in Arizona during the Republican sweep in the 2010 midterm elections, is a perfect example. Quayle's famous father (or infamous, depending on how you remember Vice President Dan Quayle), his youth, and his election to a safe Republican seat in Arizona have already raised talk that he might have ambitions for higher office. In an article in *Politico* about the new GOP star, the stage was already set for Quayle's ambitions to be a point of contention before he was even sworn into office: "The idea that Ben Quayle might find the House seat to be a useful steppingstone has become so prevalent that his Democratic opponent, businessman Jon Hulburd, has argued that voters who are uncomfortable with Quayle are better off supporting a Democrat to avoid the possibility of a long-term Quayle political career and to give another Republican a shot at the seat in 2012" (Hunt 2010). Quayle quickly dismissed any interest in serving in any capacity beyond Congress, which is totally unbelievable to any keen political observer, but it is part of the dance that elected officials must play with their peers and the public. And while Congress, the governors' mansions, and presidential primaries are filled with men and women who have adamantly stated "I have no interest in running for [fill in the blank]," the fact remains that to say otherwise risks political alienation and criticism. Our consultants see that while working hard on the campaign trail and elected office is key, you cannot have your eyes too focused on the future, at least publicly.

Now that we have looked at how political operatives view the candidate traits of their own candidates and the value of these traits in general, we move from the abstract to the specific. Clearly, current political science literature and political thought note that the political environment has an influence on how one evaluates candidate traits, but what about campaign managers? Do they change the weight they place on traits based on the demographics of their district or the campaign environment? We approach that question in our next section.

Who You Are Is What You Think

Over the years I have worked for both Democratic and Republican candidates on various levels. This was as much about learning the political process as any ideological leaning, and one of the most universal lessons about how political candidates and their traits can be interpreted depending on political context occurred while working as a campaign researcher for the Maryland Democratic state senate slate in 1998. During this time, a series of corruption scandals ranging from bribery to theft levied by a local historically black college weighed down the powerful Democratic nominee, Larry Young. The campaign staff struggled to figure out how to properly navigate the scandals. On the one hand, many white and suburban voters perceived Young to be corrupt, but on the other hand, many of his poor and working-class black constituents from Baltimore considered Young a man of the people. Democratic senator Michael Collins, charged by the ethics committee to investigate Young's misdeeds, faced a tough Republican challenger who ran on cleaning up the statehouse. To make matters worse, rumors swirled around both campaigns that Collins, Young, or both might be homosexual. The campaign team met to figure out how to mitigate suburban voters' concerns about a corrupt Baltimore senator and play up a Democrat being investigated by another Democrat without creating a rift in the party before the fall election. Needless to say, the meeting burned red with intensity.

Eventually, the chief strategist quieted the room with the following statement: "We just have to see what middle-class white voters hate more, an uppity black man or a closeted [expletive]." The room got quiet, nobody questioned the strategist's statement, and everyone got to work on figuring out the best way to exploit prejudice and bigotry to win the election. Collins won with room to spare as he rode the wave of heroism pushed ashore by suburban white voters who thought of him as a hero for standing up to the black political machine. Eventually, the ethics committee removed Young from the state senate because of ethics violations. He was a pariah in statewide politics but remained a hero in the eyes of many local constituents. Years later he served as the inspiration for the corrupt "Senator Clay Davis" character on the popular HBO series *The Wire*.[13] The moral of this story is simple: Hero or villain, there are a lot of factors that influence how a candidate's traits are viewed during the campaign season (Waldron and Daemmrich 1998).

Rich, poor, college educated, white, Latino, black, suburban, or urban: All are descriptions that can influence how a voter sees a political candidate's traits. By extension these are all variables and circumstances that influence how a consultant might weigh a candidate's traits as well. The skills or traits needed to be a great candidate in suburban Maryland in 1998 might not have worked as well in inner-city Detroit that same year. Rumors about sexual orientation might have weighed more heavily in a mid-Atlantic state senate campaign in the late 1990s than in a race for governor in rural Washington State a few years later. What makes a candidate "electable" one year may be a death knell for them in another year. The real challenge for the political consultant is to find out what factors determine which of these traits will work best for your candidate and where, and then focus the voters on that trait.

So much of what political consultants do is driven by their political and campaign environment, so why should their views of candidate traits be any different? I performed a logistic regression analysis on each of the five candidate traits both while running and while governing. I put various factors found in the campaign environment in the model and tried to determine

TABLE 1.9 **Significant predictors by candidate trait model from logistic regression analyses**

Model	Significant predictor	Interpretation: Trait very important if
Integrity while running	Position sought	seeking executive position
	Region of the country	running in the South
	Post-9/11	running before 9/11
	Federal or state race	seeking a federal office
Integrity while governing	None	
Leadership while running	Party identification	you are a Republican
	Federal or state race	seeking a federal office
Leadership while governing	None	
Empathy while running	Federal or state race	seeking a federal office
Empathy while governing	Education	district is more educated
Competence while running	Party identification	you are a Republican
	Minority percentage in district	higher minority percentage in district
Competence while governing	None	
Ambition while running	None	
Ambition while governing	None	

which if any of these factors influenced how consultants in the sample felt about the importance of these traits. Table 1.9 shows the results for which factors influenced how consultants felt about candidate traits while someone was running for office and when someone was actually serving in office.[14] The first column is the trait and the situation of the candidate (running or governing), the second column is the variable or factor that has a significant relationship with the trait evaluation, and the third column is how the absence or abundance of that variable influences how the trait is viewed by political operatives.

I used the following independent variables: Election pre- or post-9/11; Region; State or federal office sought; Incumbent, challenger, or open seat; Campaign war chest; Win or lose; Executive or legislative position sought; Minority percentage in district; Education level in district; District party preference; Your candidate's race; Your candidate's gender.

Integrity

None of the contextual or demographic variables from the survey had an impact on how campaign managers felt about a candidate's integrity while they served in office, but we do see that several variables influenced how important integrity was while running. Campaign managers working for a candidate seeking executive office or running for federal office were much more likely to say that integrity was important, which makes sense. The higher the public office, the greater the scrutiny by the press and the public; if you are working for or with someone who is corrupt, you do not want them running for president while you are attached to the campaign. We also see that running a campaign in the South makes consultants more likely to weigh integrity heavily. The most surprising result had to do with the influence of September 11. Campaign managers expressed that showing integrity while running for office was *less* important post-9/11 than before the terrorist attacks. Does this mean they think we lived in a simpler time before 9/11, where good and evil were easier to distinguish? Was this a statistical anomaly? Running the analysis with several other factors to control for variance and comparing past data showed that, in fact, integrity has become less important to consultants for candidates running after 9/11 (Johnson 2009). The most charitable interpretation of these results is that campaign managers think that integrity is important but not as much as they used to, and this is just a reflection of the increasing cynicism in American politics. A more disturbing interpretation is that the 9/11 attacks have opened the door to easier and crasser political marketing; under the guise of fighting terror, a candidate can say or do anything they want. Throughout this book we will look at how campaign managers viewed 9/11 as a factor in campaigns, and we can comfortably say right from the start that despite the public rhetoric, the terrorist attacks may not be changing campaign politics for the better.

Empathy

Campaign managers responded that showing empathy while running is very important when seeking a federal office and very important while governing if the constituency is educated. When a candidate is running for federal office, the constituency is likely much wider and more diverse, so it behooves a good manager to tell their candidate that showing a little love for the needs of all citizens in the state, not just your hometown or district, is very important. The results showing the importance of empathy while a governing official were interesting, given that much of current political science work suggests that less educated voters are more moved by emotional and sympathetic candidates (Hayes 2005; see also Pierce 1993). Research has shown that the more educated people are, the more concerned they are about people besides their immediate family, and consultants see that an educated constituency is going to want a candidate to show that they care about everyone, regardless of who voted for them.[15]

Leadership

Showing leadership while running for office is more important to Republican consultants and candidates than to Democratic consultants and candidates. This is consistent with much of existing research, where the leadership trait was weighed much more heavily by Republican voters than Democratic ones. It stands to reason that Republican campaign managers would feel the same way. When seeking a federal office, demonstrating leadership, even if the candidate is going to Congress, where they will be one of hundreds of other men and women, is understandably more important than when seeking a lower-level position. Again, it is important to note that most traits are deemed "very important" by consultants; the question is simply how much more important is that trait with these factors in play. There were no variables that influenced how consultants viewed the importance of leadership traits while governing. Again, what is worth noting is that 9/11 did not have an impact on leadership, despite the direct association between leadership and fighting terror that is so often drawn in federal and national campaigns. Given that 9/11 also did not have a statistically significant relationship with integrity, we might be seeing the beginning of a trend that 9/11 may show up in rhetoric but not necessarily manifest as statistically significant in our analysis.

Ambition

Clearly, the ambitious candidate was not particularly popular with political operatives in the sample, and the trend continues when we look at factors influencing the evaluation of candidate ambition. None of the variables in the model had an impact on how campaign managers viewed the importance of ambition as a candidate trait. We can fairly assume from now on that the hardworking but perhaps not the ambitious candidate is more valuable to campaign managers.

Competence

The last candidate trait proved to be important for consultants who were dealing with two demographic variables: candidate party identification and minorities in the district. A Republican consultant is more likely to value competence in their candidate while running than a Democratic consultant. If we look back at our initial tables showing how respondents weighed traits from "very important to unimportant," it is clear that Republicans weighed traits with more intensity than Democrats. Along those same lines, even though competence was only the third most important trait in most of the direct surveys when controlling for other factors, it was clearly more important to Republicans when running. The second significant variable is a surprise: The higher the minority percentage in the district, the more campaign managers thought it was important for the elected official to demonstrate competence. Are minorities more demanding? Do districts with large minority populations have more complex concerns that managers have to consider? These results might capture an urban district, given the large minority populations in most urban areas, and cities, where daily service problems such as trash removal and water are key, and thus competence might prove to be even more essential. Previous research did show that minorities evaluated candidates in different ways than whites, and this result may be a reflection of one of those differences in candidate evaluation.

So far we have learned that consultants see a connection between governing and campaigning, and that it is influenced by several variables. We have also learned that how campaign managers weigh the importance of traits while a candidate is running or governing is influenced by both environmental and demographic factors. So where does all of this information about consultants and candidates take us? Back to the question that drives every single political operative during election season: "Is this guy (or gal) really electable?"

With the information learned above, we will take a look at this electability concept again through a case study about a recent election that was completely driven by the electability theme.

The 2004 Presidential Election and the Fallacy of Electability

> *"You've only got one problem. The media says you're unelectable."*
> *"But I am electable . . . if you vote for me."*
> 　　　　　　—Exchange between a reporter and Democratic
> 　　　　　　presidential candidate Dennis Kucinich
> 　　　　　　before the Iowa caucuses in 2004

In 2004 electability was defined as the ability to beat George W. Bush head-to-head in the fall election. The environment of post-9/11 America had a major impact on the candidates running in the Democratic field, and thus their electability was viewed in terms of their ability to combat a sitting commander in chief as well. Of the major candidates competing for the Democratic nomination, they overlapped in the areas that political pundits and many consultants thought were key for electability that year. Many of the major contenders had either held executive office or served in some federal capacity (Governor Howard Dean [D-VT], Senator John Kerry [D-MA], Senator Joe Lieberman [D-CT]), a number of them had prestigious military backgrounds (Senator John Kerry [D-MA], Gen. Wesley Clark), and many of them were from critical electoral regions of the country (Senator John Edwards [D-NC], Congressman Dick Gephardt [D-MO]).

The candidates were in a battle to show which traits they exemplified best, but all had to consider the campaign environment, which was a nation at war that was also experiencing an economic slowdown. The Democratic campaign teams were in a tough battle to help their candidate stand out. In writing about the campaign, one of John Kerry's consultants stated, "Every candidate faces a problem of 'product differentiation'—that is, distinguishing himself from others in the field yet remaining credible enough to compete. Because there were three Southern candidates, none of them could claim being from that region as an advantage" (Nelson 2005, 24). Although most voters felt more passionately about Howard Dean, or were more impressed with Edwards or Clark, the various traits that John Kerry appeared to have cobbled together were what voters wanted, according to political scientist Michael Nelson, who wrote, "Although a small state governor grabbed the lead for a while, Democratic voters eventually turned to a more 'electable' candidate who had served with honor in Vietnam" (23).

The influence that electability questions have on the primary season is subject to intense debate (Abramowitz 1989). Some argue that primary voters are driven by their ideology and issues and that these weigh more than electability (Marlantes 2004). Others, such as Geer (1988) and Norrander (1989), find that primary voters are just as concerned about electability as general election voters. Wattier states that when you are an "out party" voter, practical considerations outweigh ideology. He goes on to say, "The contextual imperative for the out party is to find a 'sure winner,' a candidate widely perceived as possessing the mythical quality of electability. Primary voters in the out-party nomination contest may support the candidate they perceive as having the best chance of winning the November general election" (2003, 2).

The results of the 2004 primary seem to lean toward proving researchers like Wattier and Geer correct. In exit poll after exit poll Democratic primary voters voted for John Kerry (the eventual nominee) not based on his inherent popularity but on whether he would be seen as "electable" in the minds of non-Democratic voters. Consultants actually organized their strategies around convincing voters that despite misgivings, "their" candidate was more electable (i.e., could beat Bush) than the others. William Saleton, a national correspondent for the magazine *Slate*, captured this complicated phenomenon when discussing the surprising ascendancy of John Kerry to win the Democratic presidential nomination in 2004. Among voters who voted for a candidate who matched their beliefs or whom they were excited about, Kerry fared poorly against Howard Dean and John Edwards. However, among voters who thought he could convince red-state voters to vote for him he blew away the competition. Saleton reported, "Let me say again: Among voters who picked the candidate they wanted based on issues, not the candidate they thought somebody else wanted, Kerry did not win the New Hampshire Primary" (2004).

Political science research suggests that Kerry fared reasonably well among Democratic voters on the most important traits, scoring highest on competence but lowest on leadership among strong Democratic partisans. Goren stated, "Even the highest evaluations of John Kerry didn't match those of Bush; strong partisans for Bush believe he was almost 20 points more of a leader, even if they viewed his competence about the same as Kerry" (2002, 628). Eventually, this electability logic collapsed upon itself. Democrats picked a candidate who did not inspire them, hoping he would inspire their neighbors. These neighbors, in turn, taking a cue from uninspired Democrats, did not have much of a bandwagon to jump onto. Kerry lost a tight election, and conventional wisdom says he should have beaten Bush handily.

So what is the lesson here? John Kerry scored high on all of the most important candidate traits, but not as high as his opponent. He was the most "electable" of the candidates that Democrats had available, but he still failed to win the election, despite having money, a unified party behind him, and going up against a sitting president with approval ratings below 50 percent. Perhaps in order to be electable it is not just the campaign environment, the intensity with which people evaluate your traits, or how you directly match up against your opponent but also how much you inspire your own voters vis-à-vis the opposition. And that may or may not be something that a campaign manager can actually teach.

Conclusion

As humbling as it may be for political consultants and managers to admit, electable political candidates are more often born than made. *Political Image Makers*, one of the first books written for and about the emerging professional campaign manager culture in the 1970s, put it bluntly: "A far more important truth, however, has always been that good candidates make political advertising experts [consultants]. It simply is not the other way around" (Hiebert et al. 1971, 96).

This is not to suggest that a candidate's actions do not have an impact, but there is only so much that a campaign manager can do to enhance a dud candidate, and that is perhaps less than they have to do to win with a great candidate. Overall, the most successful political candidates in the minds of consultants seem to be those who are hardworking, demonstrate leadership, and stick to their beliefs. Campaign managers do not evaluate candidates based on the same criteria as voters in most national surveys when asked to freely give their opinions. However, when given the same choices as voters, Republican and Democratic campaign operatives tend to weigh the traits with a surprising level of consistency. To this end, at least, some areas of political science studies on candidate traits hold up well without consultant input. However, the divergence between consultant views and voter views in general suggests that political scientists cannot simply assume that the way voters weigh traits is automatically accepted and translated by the managers responsible for displaying those candidate traits right back at the voter.

More generally, from our last case study it seems that voters and by extension consultants like candidates who are also good communicators and have that "it" factor of charisma that can enhance or overcome any trait benefits or deficiencies the candidate might have. Candidates who jog or lose weight, like candidate Bill Clinton or Mike Huckabee, are viewed with enthusiasm by voters. Minority candidates who are nonthreatening to whites or have a lighter skin tone are perhaps more successful in certain statewide contests than others, according to some analysts. But ultimately the best candidate is the one who can capture the hearts and minds of voters, who can use their natural personality to overcome or combat any perceived negative traits they have and win over an environment no matter what obstacle they are facing. The following anecdote captures this concept perfectly.

In 1996 Republican senator Strom Thurmond was ninety-three years old and seeking to return to Washington as the oldest member of Congress. His challenger in the general election was political novice Elliot Close, a forty-three-year-old real estate developer. Close had begun his campaign by repeatedly vowing not to make age an issue, which coincidentally raised age as a campaign issue. Although Thurmond continued to make public appearances, many were tightly scripted, and Thurmond pointedly refuse to debate his opponent.

Late in the campaign, after not making much headway in the polls against Thurmond, Close reluctantly aired a commercial highlighting Thurmond's age and whether South Carolina needed to "turn the page" on Thurmond. Essentially, Thurmond was "too old" to serve in office and was no longer competent enough or ambitious enough to serve the needs of South Carolinians in the new century. Shortly after the commercial aired in late October, Close and Thurmond were campaigning at a University of South Carolina football game. With thousands of voters tailgating outside the stadium, Close planned to approach Thurmond and issue a personal challenge to debate. He never got the chance. The throngs of voters surrounding Thurmond, seeking to shake his hand, provided a literal and electoral barrier too tall to overcome. Close, on the other hand, was confronted with catcalls from an inebriated football fan, claiming, "You shouldn't have run that commercial." Thurmond's victory was never in doubt after that. You can have all of the traits and money in the world, but if your candidate has the right personality, in the right place, at the right time, they will always find a way to win.[16]

Campaigns are built on the idea of making the best out of whatever materials are available. The purpose of the political campaign is not so much to create a great candidate as it is to focus the voter on whatever trait your candidate already has that will most likely meet their campaign needs, if not their electoral needs (Funk 1999, 716). Of course, this will not stop political consultants from claiming someone can become the next Obama or Ronald Reagan on the campaign trial if only they did X, Y, and Z. In the next chapter we will address the question of just how the effective campaign manager creates their candidate's sales pitch: It's all in the messaging.

2

The Message

Once a campaign manager has been either assigned to or hired by a candidate, the campaign manager must explain why anyone would want to vote for his or her candidate. In my early years as an assistant slate director in the Maryland Senate, my coworkers and I would often perform extensive interviews with candidates at the beginning of the campaign. No matter if the candidates approached the election as either long-term incumbents or as new challengers chomping at the bit to campaign, we would ask them the same question every time: "How would you convince your spouse to vote for you?" It sounds like a simple question, but you would be amazed by how many candidates cannot articulate why anybody should vote for them, let alone why anybody should not vote for the other candidate. The point of the exercise was simple: If a candidate cannot explain to the people who know him best why they should bother to vote for him, then he certainly will not be able to convince thousands of voters who may not have ever heard of his campaign. Thus, raising consciousness and persuading the electorate represents the power of the *campaign message*. The campaign message articulates why the candidate desires to run for office and implicitly articulates why the voter should not vote for the other person running. In this chapter we will analyze how political scientists and campaign professionals look at the creation, distribution, and selection of messages. We will also look at some of the main message definitions used in campaign politics and explore the best strategies to implement them, according to political scientists and managers. Finally, we will take a look at existing political science and journalists' theories on message consistency

and see if they actually reflect how consultants and political operatives behave in the field.

Many elements to a candidate's message exist, such as the theme of a campaign, the image, the slogans, and how campaign operatives develop each of
these highly interconnected variables of the modern political campaign. To
begin this discussion, we must first address what a campaign message is and
then examine how consultants and candidates create and use such messages
before delving into our specific research questions.

What Is a Message?

The message of a campaign is absolutely essential for the success of a candidate because it answers the most fundamental question driving any political
campaign. According to Thurber and Nelson, "There may be many examples of the message and many different specifics used to illustrate it, but all
those examples must add up to one point: a campaign message that is the rationale for the candidate's election and the opponent's defeat" (2004, 52). If
the campaign's message provides the rationale for running and electing one
candidate over another, how do we disentangle that concept from images,
themes, and slogans, which are often used interchangeably with messages in
political science literature? This is where the existing literature from political
science and even practitioners can be somewhat muddled.

More often than not, researchers do not consistently distinguish between
verbal and image messages, themes, and slogans across the discipline. For
example, when Covington et al. discuss the use of images by Ronald Reagan's managers during the 1980 campaign, they also include theme and messages: "The homogeneity of a candidate's messages is defined as the degree
to which the messages delivered to the press over some period in time are
unified in content creating a single easily identified theme. A single repeated
message is most likely to influence the public's image of a candidate" (1993,
785). Hall also employs the terms *message* and *theme* interchangeably when
discussing the inability of the Bush campaign team to settle on a communication strategy, saying, "To the chagrin of speechwriters such as Curt Smith
no efforts were made by the campaign manager to work with them in creating lines that would resonate with voters. . . . Finally Teeter's inability and in-
decision in selecting a central campaign theme or 'message' proved costly"

(2002, 532). Finally, when Wattenberg and Brians discuss how negative advertising may affect voter turnout, they suggest that the message and theme of political communication might be extensions of each other, but they do not clarify, as in the following: "The substantive message certainly permeated the electorate. The fact that respondents showed an awareness of the ad's theme had higher turnout rates appears inconsistent with the demobilization hypothesis" (1999, 891). Political consultants often combine the concepts as well. S. Daley, writing for *Onlinecandidate.com*, a Web site promoting online campaigning, considers messages and themes to be the same, but he does not speak to image. Daley states: "A campaign theme is the message used by a political campaign to communicate why a candidate is running for office. It is also shaped by an overall campaign identity. The goal of this campaign theme is to influence voters and gain the support needed to win an election. At its essence, a campaign theme is simply a message that states why voters should elect a candidate" (2010). He goes on to say that slogans are simply shortened versions of one's campaign message and that slogans are most effective when they relate back to the theme of the campaign. When a campaign manager considers both the verbal and the visual interpretations of a message in political science along with the fact that most political operatives do not care about these distinctions, no uncertainty exists as to why some elements of message research in political campaigns remain neglected.

Regarding messaging, verbal and written messages primarily concern us. Even though the question of how a candidate dresses and styles himself or herself serves as part of the message-making process, a detailed discussion of that element of messaging lands beyond the scope of this chapter. Furthermore, distinguishing between messages, slogans, and themes will be very important to understand the rest of this section. Even if political scientists may disagree, consultants do not care, and voters may not notice, we must understand the differences between messages, slogans, and themes in order to move the discussion forward. What the campaign managers want you to *feel* operates as the *theme* of the campaign; it is the idea or emotion that ties the entire enterprise together. This may or may not be explicitly stated during the campaign. The *slogan*, however, embodies a simple phrase or series of words that encapsulates the campaign's theme. Finally, the *message* is the reason that voters should vote for a candidate and not their opponent. Many campaign managers and political scientists do not truly make these distinctions, and the reasons are pretty obvious. It is hard to distinguish one from the other and, depending on the level, expense, and range of the campaign slogans and other rhetorical creations, may not even be a part of the electoral strategy.

For example, when interviewing Reese Edwards, a government affairs consultant in New Mexico, I asked him to tell me the most memorable slogan he had heard in the past few years. He said, "I can only remember one slogan from the last few years, which was from someone who ran for Agriculture commissioner in South Carolina. The slogan was 'Keep Your State on Your Plate'" (Johnson 2010b). The slogan was created by Emile DeFelice, a hog farmer who ran against dairy farmer and incumbent Hugh Weathers for the office of commissioner of South Carolina's Department of Agriculture in 2006. DeFelice, not a typical hog farmer most Americans would expect, earned his bachelor's degree at Emory University and his master's degree in international relations at the University of South Carolina. At forty-one years of age, DeFelice had already started the first year-round all-local farmers' market in Columbia, South Carolina, and his organic hog farms, known for their humane treatment of the stock, had been written up in *Bon Appétit* and *Forbes*. DeFelice ran for office because he felt the state's incumbent agriculture commissioner did not adequately promote residents' buying locally grown and harvested food. Since DeFelice worked as an organic farmer in South Carolina, promoting organic farming meant a lot to him. As part of his campaign, DeFelice handed out green plates at rallies with his slogan emblazoned on them. Local bloggers loved his slogan, and DeFelice's message and theme were hitting home as well. A local food blog, *The Gurgling Cod*, wrote about DeFelice's dynamic campaigning and his communications strategy, stating:

> Cool news out of South Carolina: Emile DeFelice has taken the Eat Local Challenge and made it the focus of his campaign for Commissioner of Agriculture. They seem to take "Put Your state on Your plate" seriously—in an unprecedented move, the heart of the DeFelice campaign appears to be a food blog, including such entries as "put My pork on Your fork" and "put Your soul in Your bowl." Puns aside, DeFelice seems to be the real deal—he raises heirloom breeds of pork on an organic farm, and understands the office he is running for is one that involves promoting and supporting local

agriculture. In a state where fealty to corporate interests is too often synonymous with good citizenship, this DeFelice will be fighting an uphill battle,
but I wish him well. (2006)

The blogger's quote demonstrates perfectly how the slogan made various
themes clear to the voting public, and it hammered home the campaign's
primary message. DeFelice did not win his campaign against Weathers, but
his motto became so popular that the reelected commissioner grudgingly
adopted the slogan and the theme when he returned to office. Writing about
the campaign for the University of South Carolina's Moore School of Business, Jan Collins wrote: "The electorate liked the motto and the idea behind
it. (Weathers says the slogan may have been DeFelice's, but the idea of local
products being the foundation of South Carolina agriculture was hatched 'at
a strategic planning retreat in 2005 with state agricultural leaders.') The local
foods campaign in the Palmetto State, now championed by Weathers, is
called 'Certified S.C. Grown'" (2009). We can gather the theme, slogan, and
message of this campaign, even if Emile DeFelice did not delineate each one.
The theme of the campaign or the feeling that the candidate and his team
wanted voters to feel was *pride* in their local products. The slogan of the
campaign was "Put Your State on Your Plate," which captured the theme of
agricultural pride in a snappy rhyming slogan. The message of the campaign
was simple: "The current agriculture commissioner is not doing enough to
promote small farmers and local farmers in the state." But DeFelice's challenger message did not just come across in words. His life story as an educated young man who migrated to the state to work what many would
consider a difficult job, who also started up a farmers market to help out local agriculture business, expressed his message as well.

Depending on how themes, slogans, and messages are defined, the reactions of the public and campaign operatives differ. In some cases, campaigns
and political observers do not know or cannot make a distinction between a
theme, a slogan, or a message. For example, George Bush ran as a "compassionate conservative" in the 2000 presidential campaign. The Bush campaign, led by speechwriter Michael Gersen, who coined the term, sought to
persuade voters to "feel" that Bush had an empathetic trait and cared about
their needs and social programs (Riley 2006). The theme, compassionate
conservative, was supposed to change the public perception of Republicans,

who in the eyes of the voters were the party of cold businessmen and elites who did not care about the poor or working class (Mitchell 2000; see also Thompkins 2004). Some, however, viewed "Compassionate Conservatism" as merely a "slogan," which has a slightly less respectable connotation. Slogans are campy, fun, and seen as overt ways of selling a product. So when policy proposals offered by George W. Bush seemed to contradict his empathy-filled slogan, the phrase became something of an insult. In fact, then-governor Bush's fellow Republicans used the phrase as a means to attack him during the 2000 presidential primary.

In writing for the *Wall Street Journal*, one of the originators of the concept of compassionate conservatism, Myron Magnet, defended the slogan or theme, stating, "Last week a trio of outraged Republican presidential contenders dismissed the idea of 'compassionate conservatism' espoused by Texas Gov. George W. Bush as hot air at best and, at worst, a slur on past Republican accomplishments. They are half right: Compassionate conservatism does represent a break with national Republican programs of the past. But far from being an empty slogan, it is a well-formed domestic policy agenda" (1999). Others saw this phrase as a message. By naming himself a compassionate conservative, Bush was explaining why he should be elected in addition to contrasting himself with Al Gore, who was seen as stiff, less empathetic, and liberal.

Ironically, the phrase, whatever the initial intent, ended up being a millstone around Bush's neck by the 2004 presidential election. Not only had much of the public begun to question whether his policies and actions matched up with his former theme/slogan/message, but the public also began to question why he abruptly changed the justification for his presidency after the September 11 terrorist attacks. *Washington Post* writers Dana Milbank and Richard Moran, citing recent polls showing the public doubted whether Bush was governing "compassionately," said the following: "Bush came to office three years ago with a message that he was different from traditional Republican conservatives because he was promoting programs for the poor and disadvantaged. But with his presidency dominated by foreign policy issues and such traditional conservative favorites as tax cuts, he has dropped from his speeches the compassionate conservative moniker that was his trademark in 2000" (2004). Political scientists and political operatives may not have a working definition of the difference among a message, a slogan, and a theme, but ultimately not having a definition may not matter. The insight from the above examples seems to be that so long as a consistent idea is put across to the public and the press explains why a candidate is running, most parties will be satisfied.

Now that we have provided a differentiation among the concepts of a message, a slogan, and a theme, we must move to message creation. The questions answered in the next section are: How are campaign messages actually made, who makes them, and what goes into the process?

How to Make a Message

Ron Faucheux, former editor of *Campaigns and Elections* and a longtime political operator, laid out very clearly in one of his early books how to create a campaign message: "Campaign messages may be based on (a) the candidate's personal strengths and weaknesses (ex. experience, competence, independence, integrity, compassion, stability, preparation, etc.); (b) ideological and partisan differences (liberal versus conservative, moderate versus extreme, inconsistent versus consistent, pragmatic versus purist, etc.) or (c) the situational context (change versus status quo, right tract versus wrong track, reform versus the old way, etc.) or (d) a combination of any of the above" (2008). Faucheux more or less explicated each of the key elements in message creation. The next few sections delve into each of these elements to provide more specific context and examples.

Personal History

A candidate's personal history shapes the creation of his or her message. As I mentioned earlier, a good political consultant will spend time interviewing the candidate to learn about their background in order to make a message that sticks and to make a message that resonates with the public. If a candidate's life story serves as the impetus for their pursuit of office, as in the example of Emile DeFelice, the campaign is in great shape. However, candidates usually come from backgrounds that have to be constructed to make a strong connection with a distant public that is often apathetic and uninformed. In order to critically think about narratives that will ingratiate the candidate with the public, campaign operatives must ask questions such as:

- How do I connect being a retired public schoolteacher with a message to get the candidate on city council?
- What can be found in the background of a Gulf War veteran that would make them a good federal senator?

The more the public feels like it can identify with the candidate's background, the more the message created from the background will resonate. When asked why after only a couple of years in the Senate, North Carolina senator John Edwards decided to run for president in 2004, his campaign manager, Nick Baldick, went to Edwards's background to explain his message and intent: "I think it would go back to his life story and his message. Based on his background and the message that came from it, John thought that he could make a convincing case to be president and that he had the values and leadership to do so" (Institute of Politics at Harvard University 2006, 40).

Consequently, others argue that mentioning a candidate's background is part of creating an image message to the voters where they infer from this image ideas about the candidate's stance or beliefs on issues (Druckman et al. 2004; Haynes and Flowers 2003). Furthermore, Sellers (1998) notes that a candidate is more likely to use their background to create a message, whether that is personal or policy background, when they are in a certain position in the polls. The candidate's background is also a nice shortcut for message creators. Spreading a narrative of a hardworking woman whose father put her through college by working in the steel mills of western Pennsylvania is easier than explaining to the electorate that she cares about working-class voters.

Similarly, after interviewing dozens of consultants, Brian K. Arbour finds that a candidate's background helps in message creation by giving the candidate credibility as well as validating and legitimizing their issue positions. Going more in depth, he says, "The first reasons that consultants identify for the use of background appeals is its ability to demonstrate to voters their candidate's genuine concern with the issues of concern in the district. When discussing message with candidates, [Jara, a consultant] is looking for a story we can tell about a candidate that says 'I understand this. I can deal with this issue in a serious way.' . . . Because from their legislative leaders people want empathy" (2007, 11). This strategy extends beyond individual races into the national stage as well. In *The Thumpin'*, Naftali Bendavid's book on the Democratic congressional sweep in the midterms of 2006, background was key to the national Democratic campaign message. In the year heading up to the election, public sentiment toward the war in Iraq had reached record lows, and while voters were clearly unhappy with Bush's handling of the war, congressional Democrats were still seen by many as members of a left-wing antimilitary party with little credibility on foreign policy issues. To get out the message that "Bush and the Republican Congress were wrong on the war and Congressional Democrats would manage it better," several Democratic organizations banded together to recruit and run Democratic veterans for Congress in 2006. Nicknamed "the Fighting Dems" and recruited by Veterans for a Secure America and Rahm Emanuel, head of the DCCC, more than sixty Democratic candidates ran for House and Senate seats in the 2006 election, mostly in Republican or swing districts. While only six candidates won their races, the military background gave Democrats credibility in critiquing President Bush's policies on Iraq and reinforced their message (2007, 98). So, when creating a message, the more the campaign infuses its candidate's background into the campaign, the more the campaign makes the candidate palatable to the electorate. In addition, inserting the candidate's background eases voter concerns and mitigates cynicism toward campaigns in general.

Ideology and Context

The political environment and ideology can also help create messages for campaign teams, so long as the campaign managers keep both ideas in perspective. Discussing the messaging creations and strategies in the 2008 presidential campaign, Larry J. Sabato noted that time and place changed what messages would work. Bush's campaign message in the 2002 midterms—that the Democrats who voted against his policies should have their patriotism questioned—made sense when he had an approval rating hovering near 60 percent. Sabato continued: "In 2008, however, with the economy in crisis and President Bush's approval rating below 30 percent, far fewer voters were receptive to the McCain campaign's message that Barack Obama was an extreme liberal who enjoyed, in the words of Sarah Palin, 'palling around with' domestic terrorists" (2010, 98).

The campaign environment also influences the extent to which message creation derives from a particular ideology. Ideological messages are often set up as simple dichotomies between liberal versus conservative or moderate versus extremism. If the public extremely dislikes the state of the city, an extreme message that denotes change or reform might work well even if the changes suggested stem from ideological foundations. But a good campaign manager knows to properly temper the ideology with the political context to help their candidate. Voters tend to be wary of ideologically extreme messages and prefer those that seem more even toned. In relating some of his experiences as a message maker and speechwriter for many Republican candidates in the 1980s, Larry Speakes discussed several instances when containing hard ideological speech in messages was the order of the day: "We occupied a lot of time cutting hard-line stuff written by [Pat] Buchanan's people out of speeches, things that just would not do at all for the president to say. Pat should have learned some lessons from Tony Dolan, who was extremely right wing, but a very effective speechwriter" (1988, 100).

Candidates or consultants who are too ideologically driven often have trouble developing good messages. Their difficulty stems from a fundamental difference in how ideological strategists and many career political consultants see the creation of campaign messages. True ideologues do not believe that their message needs to be "sold"; the ideas should sell themselves. Most political consultants frequently subsume overt ideology in favor of winning. The question is how to create a message that is ideologically acceptable, fits the political context, and grabs public attention.

Polling and Focus Groups

The next method used to create campaign messages is polling. Polling the voters in the candidate's district or state or, in the case of a national campaign, across the country helps the campaign team find out what is important to them, which allows them to craft a message that addresses those concerns. Furthermore, polling also helps the campaign test several messages before the candidate hits the stump and starts using them. In various case studies from *Campaigns and Elections*, consultants offer advice about the value of polls and testing when coming up with campaign messages:

- "Good polling data enables the campaign to identify which messages are persuasive to which voting groups so they can be targeted for voter communication later in the campaign" (August 1998, 18).

- "The poll tested several messages, both for and against each of the candidates, to see what issues moved voters the most" (August 2000, 29).
- "Remember, as a political consultant, manager, or candidate, you will need to test messages in a real survey for the next campaign" (August 1996, 70).

Campaigns can also use focus groups to learn about the values of the public or to create campaign messages. Although focus groups do not necessarily have as wide a range as conducting a message poll, the campaign team might have more time to obtain more intimate responses from potential voters. However, the incredible expense of using polling to create campaign messages serves as a major drawback of the practice. Trent and Friedenberg note, "Polls are often just not practical for small campaigns for sheriff, or even county commissioner where the $10,000 to $20,000 price tag for a poll and subsequent interpretation might amount to upwards of 10% of a campaign's budget" (2008, 197). In the case of smaller campaigns, the message will simply be tested on friends, family, and even locally just to get an idea about how the public feels about it.

Words Matter

Messages express ideas, beliefs, and policies, but messages are composed of something even more intimate and manageable: words. The process of using words that make policies voters might otherwise reject seem more reasonable constitutes political message making. Two of the most important researchers and practitioners of the art of language in political campaigns are Dr. George Lakoff and Dr. Frank Luntz, who work for or with the left and the right side of the political spectrum, respectively.

Luntz (2007) argues exhaustively that political language must be clear and sincere on all levels, or else it is worthless. He provides specific playbooks on what words should and should not be used by Republicans in speeches and debates.[1] Although not a specific campaign example, Luntz is famous for encouraging the Bush White House to use the term *death tax* rather than *estate tax* when pushing through legislation. The estate tax, as it was known, taxed assets worth a certain amount at the time of death. For example, if a person had a million dollars in property and other assets to pass on to his or her children, those assets would be taxed when that person died. The rationale for the tax in the middle of the twentieth century was to even the playing field and prevent the robber barons of the day from avoiding taxes during life and rolling over their monumental wealth from generation to generation. President George W. Bush wanted to eliminate the tax, but much of the public wanted to keep it. In an interview with *Frontline* on PBS, Luntz explained why it was hard to repeal the tax and what he suggested politicians do to repeal it: "The public wouldn't support it [repealing the law] because the word 'estate' sounds wealthy. Someone like me comes around and realizes that it's not an estate tax, it's a death tax, because you're taxed at death. And suddenly something that isn't viable achieves the support of 75% of the American people. . . . I argue that is a clarification; that's not an obfuscation."

Both terms were accurate. The tax would apply only to those large assets passed along to one's children (perhaps $300,000 or more, depending on one's state or tax bracket), but at the same time the tax applied only after one died. But clearly one term is much easier to sell. Luntz encourages his political and nonpolitical clients to use creative language when attempting to deliver a message because he believes that the key to getting one's idea across has as much to do with *how* one makes his or her point as *what* his or her point happens to be. Other campaign messages from him include the use of *gaming* instead of *gambling* for statewide initiatives and *electronic intercepts* instead of *wiretapping* to discuss Bush's national security policy. Most recently, he encouraged Republicans to use the phrase *climate change* instead of *global warming* in the midterm elections of 2006, since the former term tested as much less urgent and dangerous in the minds of citizens than the latter.

The Left has also used consultants and campaign managers to develop its messages, although not often as effectively as its Republican counterparts (something that many Democrats will admit). There is, in fact, a leftist version of Frank Luntz, and that person is George Lakoff. Lakoff also researches messaging and has done a great deal of work with Democratic and left-wing political groups to change the terms of debate on gay marriage through the use of language. Lakoff suggests that Democrats use phrases like *same-sex marriage* instead of *gay marriage*, because *gay* is more provocative and more likely to engender fear or hostility from voters. Lakoff explains: "The radical right uses 'gay marriage.' Polls show most Americans overwhelmingly against anti-gay discrimination, but equally against 'gay marriage.' . . . 'Gay' for the right connotes a wild, deviant, sexually irresponsible lifestyle. That's why the right prefers 'gay marriage' to 'same-sex marriage'" (2004). Interestingly enough, Frank Luntz agrees with this assessment. He argued in his policy paper for the 2006 midterm elections that increasingly the term *gay* or *homosexual marriage* is linked to the hard Right and religious extremes of American society. Consequently, the crucial swing voter may have chafed at politicians who overused the phrase, posing a risk of alienating needed voters. Luntz suggested Republican candidates use the phrase *same-sex marriage* as an alternative but clearly for entirely different reasons.

We have now assessed how campaigns create messages using candidate background, polling, ideology, political context, and language in order to craft the right message that will put a candidate in the best position to win. Now that all of the pieces are in place, it is time to take the message out for a spin. In the following section, we will examine how political messages are actually used in the campaign environment.

How Messages Are Used

A campaign is ready to use its message when it has a credible speaker, has understanding of the electoral context, and has properly targeted both the persuadable voters as well as the opposition. Only when these three concepts are in play can a message work to its full potential.

Being a credible speaker is essential to how the candidate uses their message. If the candidate is not believable, for whatever reason, the public will not listen to whatever the candidate has to say, no matter how effective the message. This is why the candidate's background is so important in the creation of messages; the background should make the candidate credible to deliver their message to the public. If a candidate experienced a series of youthful indiscretions, a "tough on crime" message might not be the best message strategy. However, if the candidate lost their baby sister to gang violence, the candidate can be as tough on crime as the campaign manager desires.

The campaign's message should be targeted at specific members of the electorate with which the campaign seeks to communicate. Several political scientists have discovered that campaigns often create more personalized or less substantive messages to woo voters simply because those messages require less thought on the part of the electorate. In some cases, campaigns simply allow surrogates to deliver messages because they will be more readily understood and believed (Abrajano 2005).

Many campaigns employ more than one "message" when they speak to different groups. However, campaigns try to maintain the same theme, or slogan, no matter with whom they speak, according to Haynes, Flowers, and Gurian (2002a). While discussing the successful campaign of Mike Foster, a Republican who won the Louisiana gubernatorial race, Ron Faucheux makes the case for targeting and messaging over simple images: "In a more strategic sense, this election proved once again that just putting a pretty face on TV, especially for a long shot is not enough. Foster's upset win showed that the way to bag the big ones in today's politics is with a focused message targeted at identifiable voter groups" (Bailey and Faucheux 2000, 156). Furthermore, timing the use of the messages to coincide with a period when the press will notice proves very important (Bositis 1985). Also, the political messages provided by American campaigns vary depending on where candidates find themselves in the polls (Haynes, Flowers, and Gurian 2002b).

Haynes et al. list three types of messages that surface at different times during the race: those that are informative, comparative, and substantive. Candidates enjoying a comfortable lead tend to create informative messages, which explain, for example, where they will appear next and what will be their message of the week. Sometimes they even clarify issues. Challengers or candidates within striking distance of the front runner tend to deliver comparative messages to show the strength of their campaign compared to the front runner. They seek to lure the opposition into at best public debate or at least a response. Much to the chagrin of many political observers, Haynes et al. find that "substantive" messages tend to come from candidates who have little or no chance of winning. Third-party candidates or far-left or far-right candidates in primaries tend to have the most substantive messages, since they aspire to steer the discussion in one direction more than highlight their own chances at succeeding.

Message Consistency

Assuming that a campaign team has developed its theme, slogan, and message and has a candidate who has established enough credibility to deliver all three to the press and the targeted public, the campaign still has not completed its message strategy. A candidate must deliver their message with consistency, according to many political operatives, or all of the previous work could amount to nothing. Consultants and political analysts speak in grave tones about whether a candidate tends to speak "on message" or "off message" and the potential impact this has on a campaign's long-term success. Academics often suggest that staying on message through the inevitable distractions and unexpected events determines the success or failure of a campaign (Lodge, Steenbergen, and Brau 1995; Rahn, Aldrich, and Borgida 1994).

Consultants know that if the voters are not hearing the same message over and over, they will likely forget what the campaign is about, let alone why they should vote for the candidate. This does not mean that campaigns do not have several messages, as discussed above, but it does mean that even when tailoring messages to an audience, campaigns must push the same idea. In describing a dark-horse candidate who defeated an incumbent in a closely fought race, consultant Tom Russell stated, "Faced with an ideologically similar opponent who had landed nearly every endorsement and created a strong fundraising operation, a simple, visual message played a decisive role in ex–White House aide Michela Alioto's victory in the first District Democratic Congressional primary in Northern California. . . . The well focused Alioto campaign only veered from its tight message once" (1996). This focus on message consistency runs through all campaign levels (Stanley 1992; Yang 2000; Kumar 2009; Roe 2010).

One of the most noted praises and criticisms of the Obama presidential campaign in 2008 was his dogged commitment to his message. This is where our previous discussion of the difference between themes, slogans, and messages is crucial. The theme of the Obama campaign was "Hope and Change," the slogan was "Yes We Can," and the message was that McCain would be a third Bush term. Now, the differentiation among these elements is often conflated by consultants and political observers, but for our purposes distinguishing these elements is very important. While the Republican Party and media pundits across the political spectrum often mocked "Hope and Change," the mockery effectively hammered Obama's theme into the public's consciousness throughout the campaign. Meanwhile, McCain's message tended to change depending on the poll numbers (Elder 2008; Dickerson 2008; McGirt 2008). Political pundit and host of *Public Affairs* Jeff Berkowitz described the 2008 McCain campaign for president in these terms: "McCain's campaign had no central positive theme. What was Mc-Cain's message? 'I am not Bush'? Kind of like saying, 'I am not a crook.' Hardly words of inspiration" (2008).

Being off message is almost as bad as having a bad message or not having one at all. The campaign team has to constantly remind the candidate that the public has a relatively short attention span, and more specifically the campaign is targeted at swing or persuadable voters who are even less plugged into the contest than partisans. No matter what happens after defining, making, and using a message, the candidate must stick with it.

Staying on Message in the Worst of Times

Staying on message is not easy, and despite how much help a campaign team may provide, in many cases staying on message ultimately falls upon the candidate. He or she is subject to answering questions from reporters, the public, and the opposition for months on end, and the slightest slipup or well-intentioned tangent can irreparably damage a campaign. During the Ford-Dole campaign for president in 1976, consultant and speechwriter Larry Speakes spoke about vice presidential candidate Dole's refusal to stay on message. The *New York Times* had reported that Dole received illegal campaign contributions from an oil company, and Dole insisted that this charge was not true. Speakes wrote, "The White House told him to make sure he didn't talk about it anymore . . . but Dole insisted he had nothing to hide, and every time a reporter raised the Gulf [oil] issue, Dole would make an angry reply, which led to more and more stories" (1988, 56). Speakes further states that it was almost impossible to win an election campaign when there was no message consistency from a vice presidential nominee. He eventually lashed out at Dole during a tense message meeting, saying, "Senator if you don't get on the ball, you're going to be making American Express commercials for the rest of your life" (ibid.). The irony of this statement is just how prescient Speakes was. Almost twenty years later, after Bob Dole lost his presidential challenge to Bill Clinton in 1996, one of his first endorsement deals after retiring from public office was American Express.

Of course, being off message is not always campaign specific; sometimes an entire party can be off message, especially when it does not run the White House. A few months after failing to make any major ground during the

2002 midterm elections, Democrats in Congress attacked President Bush for copiloting a navy Viking jet onto the USS *Lincoln* and delivering a speech declaring "mission accomplished" in Iraq. Despite Democrats in the press and public office decrying this display as staged and premature, it did not have much of an impact on the president, and a Democratic strategist made it abundantly clear why: "We look petty, and why we're way off message." *Newsweek* reported one strategist as saying, "We should be roasting them on their tax plan. Instead we're talking about how much less it would have cost to fly him in a helicopter" (Clift 2003). The same phenomenon occurred with the Republican Party in the years after the 2008 presidential election. The leadership and the party grassroots spoke off message and, even worse, delivered conflicting messages. Early in 2010 when asked about whether his party could retake both houses of Congress in the fall midterms, then RNC chairman Michael Steele clearly stated, "Not this year," which differed completely from what grassroots party leaders had been telling donors since 2009. Furthermore, *ABC News* blogger Rick Klein noted, "Steele's comments were met with grumbling among national Republicans including many who have long been critical of Steele's leadership at the RNC as a chairman who was again going off-message" (2010). During midterm elections, party members often rely on the national party for a message to run their campaigns on, especially when a nationally driven message will help them win as opposed to a locally driven message. Arguably, there was not a coherent national Republican Party message in the 2010 midterm elections, yet they still won. Nevertheless, a party's leadership must speak with one voice regarding party goals and aims.

Message Consistency in the Survey

We now know that campaign messages are crucial, that they differ from slogans and themes, and that campaign managers and consultants spend a long time working on them. We also know that staying on message is viewed as important for both campaign managers and political scientists. Campaigners know that the lack of a consistent message will make it hard to convince voters of their legitimacy. Common wisdom in political science is that for uninterested voters to pay attention, the candidate must stay on message. The question now is whether these theories and beliefs held true in our survey

TABLE 2.1 Did your candidate stay on message?

	Frequency	Percentage
Mostly off message	6	3.4
Slightly off message	20	11.2
Mostly on message	66	37.1
Slightly on message	86	48.3
Total	178	100

sample. Again, whereas much of the existing work on campaign messages in political science examines polls or is based on interviews with consultants and managers, there is no comprehensive survey of political operative attitudes on message consistency. In the next section we will examine how consistent campaigners felt their candidates were on messaging during the campaign and what variables might impact whether they felt their candidate stayed on message. In our first survey question the campaigners were simply asked, "Did your candidate stay on message?"

More than 80 percent of campaign managers in the survey sample (Table 2.1) responded that their candidate was either mostly or slightly on message throughout the campaign, which suggests several things. First, the statistics show that message discipline was deemed important by campaign operatives. Second, the statistics reveal that the campaigner's candidate appeared at least slightly to stay on message.

The campaign world is a crazy place, and one never knows what can happen from day to day, making message discipline difficult. Campaign managers cannot predict when a candidate's old fraternity brother will do an interview stating that they did drugs together in the 1980s, nor can they know in advance that a candidate's husband will be investigated for tax evasion. However, there are other elements that can be predicted and tested to determine what influence they have on message consistency. As mentioned earlier in this chapter, some academics differentiate between image messages and verbal or written messages. While image messaging includes how a candidate dresses or looks (skin tone, losing weight, and so forth, as discussed in Chapter 1), image messaging is also interpreted as background, back story, and candidate demographics (Arbour 2007). For this analysis we will extrapolate from this basic concept on the two main factors that might influence whether a candidate can stay on message: contextual and demographic

TABLE 2.2 **Impact of contextual campaign variables on consultant views of candidate message consistency**

Dependent variable	Independent variable	Impact on message consistency
Did candidate stay on message?	Challenger, incumbent, or open seat	None
Did candidate stay on message?	Executive or legislative position sought	None
Did candidate stay on message?	Position in polls at midway of campaign	None
Did candidate stay on message?	Urban versus rural campaign district	None
Did candidate stay on message?	Education level in district	None
Did candidate stay on message?	Which candidate had more money	None

factors. Contextual factors include where the candidate stands in the polls, the type of candidate (challenger, incumbent, or open seat), and a host of other variables that are unique to the campaign environment.

Demographic factors are similar to "image" messages in that they represent unchanging elements to the candidate such as his or her race, gender, and partisan identification. We will examine the "who you are" and "where you are" questions of the campaign season to determine if either question presents us with a picture of what influences a candidate's tendency to stay on message according to the political operatives in the sample. I created two different regressions, one for demographic factors and the other for contextual factors. Perhaps when controlling for other variables, we will see a clearer image of what it takes to actually have a consistent message during a campaign. Table 2.2 determines which of the contextual factors influenced whether the consultant felt their candidate stayed on message.[2]

The results show that none of the contextual variables about the campaign environment seem to have an effect on message consistency. This is surprising, given the existing political science literature that suggests campaigns develop different messages for different constituencies, which would likely lead to a campaigner's seeing their candidate going off message. One would predict that campaigning in an urban area versus a rural area, or to more educated voters who might be more demanding, would lead campaign managers

TABLE 2.3 **Demographic variable impact on message consistency**

Dependent variable	Independent variable	Influence on variable
Did candidate stay on message?	Challenger, incumbent, or open seat	None
Did candidate stay on message?	Partisan identification, GOP or Democrat	None
Did candidate stay on message?	Gender of your candidate	None
Did candidate stay on message?	Gender of opposition candidate	None
Did candidate stay on message?	Race of your candidate	None
Did candidate stay on message?	Race of opposition candidate	Consultant says candidate is less likely to stay on message when opponent is African American

to see that the candidate might veer off message a little, but apparently not. What does this tell us, then, about message consistency in campaigns? It shows campaign environment does not drive message discipline; the candidates and the campaign teams themselves determine message discipline.

Let's take a look at the demographic variables that a candidate might have or face and examine which ones influence how consultants view message consistency. A second regression was performed with the following variables: election type, partisan identification, and the gender and races of the candidate and the candidate's opposition.[3] As we see in Table 2.3, only one key variable proved significant, yet it provides grist for healthy discussion.

The only demographic variable that seems to have any influence on campaigners' views of candidate message consistency is the race of the opposing candidate. When controlling for all other demographic variables, those consultants who ran campaigns against white candidates seemed more likely to say their candidate stayed on message than those consultants who ran campaigns against black candidates.[4]

One interpretation of these results is that the vast majority of campaigners in the sample reported that their candidates stayed on message. Therefore, these results show that running against a minority candidate takes a small number of whites off message. Given the small population of minorities versus minority campaigns in the survey, we can safely assume this is capturing white candidates going up against black candidates. The other interpretation is that some of the hidden dynamics of race in political campaigns are often spoken of but rarely empirically proven. In Chapter 1, we discussed the conventional wisdom that says white candidates running for office will use racially coded language or messages to attack black candidates. This can range from intentional messaging, as in the case of Nixon's famous "Southern Strategy" to arouse white fears of integration in the South, to more subtle and perhaps even unintentional racial gaffes that are an all too common part of the lingering legacy of racism in America. The presidential primaries and elections in 2008 were rife with such off-message comments from white campaigners, as they either intentionally or unintentionally went off on racially tinged tangents when asked questions about or discussing the campaign of Barack Obama. For example, after Obama won a surprise victory over Hillary Clinton in the South Carolina Democratic presidential primary in 2008, *ABC News* political blogger Jake Tapper reported Bill Clinton went off message. "Jesse Jackson won South Carolina in '84 and '88. Jackson ran a good campaign. And Obama ran a good campaign here," said Bill Clinton, who was responding to a question from *ABC News*'s David Wright about its taking "two Clintons to beat" Obama—but Jackson had not been mentioned. The implication was simple. The Reverend Jesse Jackson is a polarizing figure, to say the least, among most white voters in America, and an attempt to link Jackson to Obama presented a clear example of race baiting, especially since no formal links existed between Obama and the Jackson campaign and in many cases Jackson was lukewarm to hostile toward Obama. Their only link was that they were both black men who sought the presidency, and Clinton was attempting to highlight negative associations with a "black man" having that position. This was completely off the message that Clinton had been attempting to stick with since her victory in the New Hampshire primary, namely, that Obama was an idealist and a dreamer and she was the realist prepared to do the job.[5] Clinton's statement, combined with previous comments from Hillary regarding Martin Luther King, caused her campaign to wander off into racial gamesmanship that did not help her moving forward.[6]

However, the prominence of Barack Obama might influence these results, given that many of the consultants who responded to the survey detailed their experiences with his campaign in 2008. But if we rerun the regression excluding all respondents who ran against Barack Obama, we achieve the same results.[7] Consultants find that white candidates running against African Americans are less likely to stay on message. Apparently, the temptation to use race as a wedge issue in campaign messaging will always be an option. The role of race in electoral politics continues to have a persistent if somewhat complex role in strategy and messaging.

The Five Messages You Meet in a Campaign

Aristotle stated that all literature must have *agon*, a central conflict, in order to hold the audience's attention and passions. Over the years literary scholars have surmised that all fictional conflicts can be boiled down into three basic types: man against man, man against nature, and man against himself. Within just about any movie, story, or book, the main conflict falls into one of these three categories directly or indirectly. The same concept can be applied to political campaigns. While most consultants and observers will focus on the unique nature of every political contest, the fact is that when it comes to campaign messages, and how one chooses to define oneself and the opposition, there are only a few themes upon which a campaign can draw. Political consultants, academics, and marketing scholars have boiled down marketing and messaging to a few key concepts: change versus status quo, old versus new, idealism versus pragmatism, and fear versus security. These are some of the more common messages used to define a campaign environment or an opponent (Rothberg 2009; see also Baker 2009).

At the same time, political operatives frequently explain the importance of defining a campaign and the opponent early in the race to secure victory. If the campaign does not define the opponent quickly, the opponent or the press will define himself or herself for the voters. The opposite is also true. The candidate must define his or her campaign. If he or she does not define the campaign, the opposition and the press will define the campaign, which will not be positive. Once a definition of one's campaign sets in—be it as a hero or a crook—it is unlikely that a campaign will be able to decouple itself from the definition. In the days after Republican Scott Brown shocked the political world by winning the Senate seat held by liberal Democrat Ted Kennedy for almost forty years, Robert Menendez, chairman of the Democratic senatorial campaign, explained the key strategy that his party failed to enact: "Define your opponent early, define the race" (Rowland 2010). Spreading the definition of one's campaign and keeping a consistent definition of one's opponent, and by extension the race, are critical to running a successful campaign. Moreover, the less one's campaign is known by the public, the more important it is to define the opposition. In open-seat campaigns and campaigns against an incumbent, it is vital for the campaign to get out early and consistently. Joe Garecht of the *Local Victory* campaign-advice site explains it clearly: "When challenging an incumbent, it is imperative that Your campaign defines Your opponent before he gets a chance to define himself. Carefully research his record and develop Your message early. Get out ahead of the curve and define Your opponent in terms that are favorable to you."[8]

When developing a campaign message to define the campaign's opponent, the campaign must use basic messages, which are often organized into what political operatives call a message or a SWOT box (SWOT stands for strengths, weaknesses, opportunities, and threats). The message box is the invention of the late Paul Tulley, a Democratic campaign strategist who developed a simple way for campaigns to visualize what they stand for, where the opposition stands, and how to properly target messages. A basic message box looks like this:

TABLE 2.4 Message box example

What you say about yourself	What your opponents say about you
What you say about your opponent	What your opponents say about themselves

Variations of this concept exist in marketing, businesses, and political campaigns. These boxes or grids (Table 2.4) are used to lay out what the basic messages are that one's candidate will direct at the opposition, what basic messages the opposition will likely aim at the candidate, and how the campaign team will respond.[9] One side of this grid is usually dedicated to what messages one's campaign will deliver and the other side to the likely response. What is important about these strategy constructs is the realization that how the candidate chooses to respond or inoculate themselves from definitions is as important as the definitions that they put out (Burgoon, Pfau, and Birk 1995). Kathy McShea, a consultant for Emerald Strategies, provides an example of a message box to potential campaign clients and discusses how defining the opponent automatically defines one's campaign as well. McShea recalls when 7-UP marketed itself as "the un-cola" in the 1980s, which sent two distinct messages: First, 7-UP was a change from the Pepsi-Coke duality that had dominated soft drink discussions for years; second, "cola" itself was not such a good thing anymore (2008a; see also McShea 2008b). The same applies to political slogans. If a candidate runs as "Candidate X: For people who care about the issues," the candidate is sending out key ideas. The first idea is that the candidate cares about the issues of the campaign and the opponent does not. Second, every voter wants to think of him- or herself as caring about the issues, so voters are automatically drawn to the candidate who cares about the issues on the minds of the electorate. Strategy to define one's opponent operates by the same logic. If Candidate A argues that Candidate B is "out of touch," the immediate correlation is that Candidate A must be more "in touch" with the common man.

This next analysis of consultants combines and looks at the three ideas we have just reviewed: There are some basic messages that are used in all campaigns, it is crucial that a campaign develop a message to define the opposition, and these messages can be expressed in a box or table that directs a campaigner on how to initiate and respond to attacks. I took on the daunting task of seeing if there are basic defining messages used in political campaigns (specifically, messages that the campaign team tells the candidate to target at the opposition). We are looking at only the bottom half of the SWOT box, that is, what you say about the opponents and what the opponents say about you. The goal is to see if there are a few basic defining messages, and if so, if we can place them in a SWOT box that explains consultant messaging behavior. In the grander scheme of things, can combining several existing theories and areas of research teach us even more about one of the more elusive aspects of campaign strategy, namely, consultant views on messaging?

To figure out what the basic messages are that campaigners used, I had to find out what campaigners thought. Whereas many researchers ask or interview consultants, if these were to be overall themes that were fundamental to campaign definition strategy, a wider net had to be cast. I performed a content analysis of case studies from *Campaigns and Elections* over several years to figure out what concepts were most important to campaigners. Then I reviewed the case studies again to see what definitions appeared most often throughout the analyses. The results were five basic defining messages that are used against an opponent in a campaign.[10]

Out of Touch: Campaign after campaign featured examples of candidates defining the opposition as out of touch. In fact, this theme appeared more often than any other in the review of the literature. Perhaps it is because this theme can work with just about any type of election; challengers, incumbents, and even open-seat candidates can claim their opponents are out of touch. Common variations on this theme are defining the opposition as an *outsider* or a *carpetbagger*.

- A Democratic candidate for U.S. House [Lois Murphy] says Republicans are "out-of-touch and out-of-sync," leading to a series of problems from Iraq to ethical lapses. (United Press International 2006)

Incompetent: The incompetence definition was fairly common in the review of campaign definitions as well, although there was a wide range of ways in which it was employed by candidates during campaigns. Directly defining one's opponent as incompetent usually requires a large public or private example of their failure. But in many campaigns, incompetence was used to define candidates who failed to articulate a specific goal or message to the voters. The implication was that if they could not adequately explain who they were or what they intended to do, then they would not be able to perform well in elected office. On the policy level, this definition can be seen clearly in the example below, which occurred during a senatorial debate between Ted Kennedy and Mitt Romney during the 1994 election:

- In a vivid piece of political theatre, Senator Edward M. Kennedy of Massachusetts attacked his Republican challenger, Mitt Romney, tonight for his views on abortion, health care, and Social Security. "I am pro-choice," Mr. Kennedy said during an exchange on abortion. "My opponent is multiple choice." (Apple 1994)

Inexperienced: This is the second most common campaign definition discovered in analyzing the literature, especially from incumbents. Claiming the challenger has a lack of experience and may not be prepared to face the rigors of Washington or the state capital is a consistent and effective way for Goliath to knock out David before he puts a rock in his slingshot. However, this definition is not limited to incumbents. If there is a salient issue in the minds of voters—the war in Iraq, business corruption, or environmental issues—it is possible for an outside challenger with skills in those particular areas to define the incumbent as inexperienced in the face of what the public is concerned about. This can even occur in primary elections. When Joe Lieberman (I-CT) faced Ned Lamont in the Democratic primary in 2006, Lieberman rolled out the *inexperienced* argument in a style similar to most incumbents:

- Lieberman, as savvy a political pro as there is, hopes to make sure that media saturation doesn't do its job of raising Lamont's profile. In a full day of campaigning last week, he talked about his inexperienced, uninformed "opponent" without ever uttering his actual name. (Bacon 2006)

Too Old, Too Long in Office: Although at first blush this definition seems similar to defining a candidate as "out of touch," the difference is the type of campaign and candidate to which this definition is usually applied. "Too old, too long in office" is the common campaign definition used when a candidate is seeking to replace someone in their own party as well as the opposition party. This definition is usually targeted at an incumbent who may have served their constituents well in the past, but now it is time for fresh ideas and bold new directions. (Think of Elliot Close's campaign against Strom Thurmond in the last chapter.) The target of this definition might actually still be very much in tune with the community but has not developed or passed any new ideas or legislation in years. This is a common message for intergenerational challengers, and variations of it include calls for "change" or "new blood." In the example below a long-serving district attorney was removed from office based on the "too old" definition lobbed at him by his opponent:

- People were asking last week how long-term Bristol County District Attorney Paul F. Walsh Jr. could lose to a virtual unknown, C. Samuel Sutter. The answer is in the word "long-time." After 16 years, the public was tired of Walsh, and Sutter did an excellent job of pointing out all the mistakes and enemies Walsh made over 16 years. It must have been déjà vu for Walsh, who was first elected to office in a similar fashion, after people got tired of 12 years of Ronald Pina as DA. ("Walsh Stayed in Office Too Long" 2006)

Corrupt: Defining the opponent as corrupt during a campaign is a powerful if not volatile definition. In many cases, it is a message definition that is easy to recognize because usually a candidate has already been mired in some type of public scandal covered by the press, so defining the opponent as corrupt when he or she has already been associated with some misdeed is a safe and powerful move. However, this is a difficult definition to manage in the modern twenty-four-hour press cycle. By Candidate X defining Candidate Y as corrupt, Candidate X is implying that he or she is not corrupt. Therefore, if anything less than ethical is uncovered during the election by the press or the opposition, this definition can have serious blowback on a candidate, which is one of the reasons this definition is used so rarely. Consultants generally advise portraying a party or statehouse as corrupt rather than an individual because it provides some cover for the definer just in case some surprise occurs during the campaign. In the example below, one can see how this definition was used in a general sense during an election in New Jersey:

- The TV commercial, produced by Jamestown Associates, featured one greedy politician after another in what was termed the "Conga line of corruption," with hands full of greenbacks in front of the state house. Forrester then comes out with a broom to sweep Trenton clean. The ad's effectiveness is attributed to its use of vitriol. ("Campaign Studies" section, *Campaigns and Elections*, August 2002)

Testing the Message Definitions

The defining messages above appear to be reflective of most political campaign messages, but we are relying on a content analysis of campaign trade magazines from the past several years and coding various articles. Perhaps I missed some important defining messages, and these are simply the ones that jumped out most from the content analysis. To test this possibility, I took the defining messages from the analysis and put them directly to the campaign operatives in the survey, asking, "Which of the following best describes how you defined your opposition?" and "Which of the following best describes how your opposition defined your candidate?"

Out of Touch
Incompetent
Inexperienced
Corrupt
Too Old, Too Long in Office

TABLE 2.5 Messaging SWOT box

	How your opponent defines your candidate				
How you define your opponent	*Out of touch*	*Incompetent*	*Inexperienced*	*Corrupt*	*Too old, too long in office*
Out of touch	13 (17.8)	*9 (12.3)*	*42 (57.5)*	*8 (11.0)*	1 (1.4)
Incompetent	**12 (41.4)**	4 (13.8)	4 (13.8)	5 (17.2)	4 (13.8)
Inexperienced	*21 (53.8)*	2 (5.1)	2 (5.1)	6 (15.4)	*8 (20.6)*
Corrupt	**11 (52.4)**	2 (9.5)	5 (23.8)	3 (14.3)	0 (0.0)
Too old, too long in office	0 (0.0)	1 (16.7)	**4 (66.7)**	1 (16.7)	0 (0.0)
Total	57 (100)	18 (100)	57 (100)	23(100)	13 (100)

Note: Chi-square: .0000; the **bold** and *italic* responses are what your OPPONENT will say to define YOUR candidate in response to YOUR definition of THEM.

The results of these questions were analyzed together in a crosstab. The crosstabulation should provide us with two important answers. First, are the five definitions presented reflective of the definitions that consultants actually used in their political campaigns? Second, if the themes we have lifted from our analysis are reflective of the campaign themes used in day-to-day races, there should be a strong, statistically significant relationship between how consultants defined their opposition and how the opposition defined them. If the themes of definition and counterdefinitions do not have a statistically significant correlation, then our definitions are likely common but perhaps just random noise in the campaign machine. If they are strongly correlated, then we have discovered the backbone of most political communication during political campaigns among our sample of consultants. Aristotle would be proud. Table 2.5 should be read and interpreted from left to right. Begin with how "your" (from the operative in the sample) candidate chose to define the opposition and then compare that to how the opposition chose to define them. The number in bold print indicates that this is how opposing campaigns will respond when *your* campaign attempts to define them with the concept on the left.

To begin, the results are impressive from a statistical point of view. There is a perfect correlation in the sample between how campaign managers defined their opposition and how they perceived the opposition responded to their definitional attack.[11] Therefore, not only is the grid empirically solid, but it also comports with a great deal of existing campaign and academic work. This table essentially creates a universal message SWOT board for all campaigns seeking definitions and counterdefinitions during a campaign. The one potential drawback is that we cannot determine the order of these attacks or timing at this point. For example, we cannot tell how long in the campaign consultants took between definitions and responses, but we can say that this presentation of the chart operates from the campaign message staff initiating the definitions. This grid is not only proscriptive, providing suggestions for future campaigns, but also descriptive, explaining campaigns that have already elapsed.

When consultants said they defined their opposition as out of touch, the most common response was that they were in fact inexperienced. This correlates easily with an incumbent-versus-challenger campaign, but might actually apply to other scenarios as well. Out of touch does not imply simply being in office; it can also suggest a candidate who is not in touch with the needs and feelings of the average voter. Throughout this chapter we have seen how consultants try to create messages that connect and show empathy for the public's needs, so the suggestion that a candidate cannot feel the public heartbeat is a damning one. The most common response by far is to suggest that the attacker just does not know the complications of the job, but the second likely response is telling as well. Many consultants responded that the opposition struck back with the same charge. Perhaps the real test of the effectiveness of this definition lies with which speaker the public finds more credible with the charge.

When consultants say that they tried to define the opposition as "incompetent," the most common counterdefinition was "out of touch." Might the suggestion here be that when a campaign charges its opponent with not knowing how to do his or her job, the opponent's counterdefinition is that the other candidate is too far away from the public to know how complicated the job really is? There is, however, another interpretation to this definition battle that played out in a major way during the midterm election of 2010. Marc Ambinder, White House correspondent for the *National Journal*, wrote an appropriately titled article for the *Atlantic Monthly* describing the message definition strategies of the Democrats during the 2010 election. "We May Be Incompetent: But They're Crazy!" Ambinder goes on to describe how the Republican Party had been pushing a message all summer that the

Democrats in Congress were "incompetent" and had not managed to fix the economy, which was the most important issue in the minds of the voters. Faced with the harsh reality, fair or not, that the economy had not demonstrably improved in the eighteen months of Democratic White House and congressional rule, the Democrats responded by saying the Republicans were crazy. This is a pretty good corollary for "out of touch" with the mainstream due to the Republican Party's embrace of the Tea Party movement. Ambinder colorfully described the value of the "out of touch" message response to the "incompetence" definitional attack:

> The Democratic strategy in a nutshell is small enough to fit in one but has the protein of a good, tasty nut. The Republicans want to be mayors of crazy-town. They've embraced a fringe and proto-racist isolationist and ignorant conservative populism that has no solutions for fixing anything and the collective intelligence of a wine flask . . . and the more Democrats repeat it, and the more dumb things some Republican candidates do, the more generally conservative voters who might be thinking of sending a message to Democrats by voting for a Republican will be reminded that the replacement party is even more loony than the party that can't tie its shoes. (2010)

The above example is valuable not just as an affirmation of the message box created, but it also shows us that defining messages can come from general parties or individual candidates.

When consultants define the opposition as "inexperienced," the most common response is "out of touch," with "too old, too long in office" at a distant second. Again, we see how the "out of touch" definition remains popular for both attack and defensive message definitions. We also see the first likely use of the "too old, too long in office" definition. In some cases "inexperience" may be seen as "youthful exuberance" and a welcome antidote to an official who has been in office for a long time. This again could apply to individual campaigns or an entire party in the statehouse or Congress.

If the opposition tries to define the incumbent as corrupt, the best option according to consultants is to define the opposition as out of touch. This makes sense strategically because rather than accepting the corruption charge, the campaign response should be to highlight how the opposition spends so much time at the state capitol that they do not understand the complexity of the issues the incumbent dealt with, because if they did, the opposition would understand the incumbent broke no laws and did nothing wrong. In another example, if the opposition calls the candidate inexperienced, the newcomer's best response is to define the incumbent as out of touch. This is excellent strategy for taking down an incumbent, since challengers or open-seat candidates could likely never claim more experience, but they can argue that the candidate has lost touch with the common man. If the opposition attempts to define the candidate as too old, or too long in office, the grid suggests that the campaign defines them as inexperienced. This strategy was put into action in one of the most famous political exchanges in campaign history, the 1984 presidential debate between Ronald Reagan and Walter Mondale. Reagan was the oldest man to ever be elected president, and his age became an issue pushed by the Mondale campaign. When asked by debate moderator Edward Newman if he believed age would be an issue in the campaign, Reagan responded with wit: "I want you to know that I also will not make age an issue of this campaign. I am not going to exploit, for political purposes, my opponent's youth and inexperience." In one politically ingenious move, he inoculated himself from a negative definition, defined his opponent, and for the purposes of this research behaved in a strategy completely congruent with the message-definition grid. Although it would appear that the charge of being "out of touch" is fairly consistent throughout campaigns, the fact remains that there is enough consistency between answers to see that these are the strategies that consultants seem to feel work best when battling in the world of definitions.

In the final two message definitions, "corruption" led to the common response of "out of touch," and "too old, too long in office" led to a response of "inexperienced." The few responses to "too old, too long in office" might indicate that this definition can be used on only certain candidates and those who should be negatively defined in a careful manner. Overall, we can see that among these consultants, suggesting that someone is "out of touch" is the most effective and common definition. What we have seen thus far is only an examination of a crosstab of the two definition types. What other factors might influence which of these messages are employed by candidates under the advice of their consultants? To answer this question, I performed regressions that looked at contextual and demographic variables. Would context drive message definition strategy, unlike message

TABLE 2.6 **Significant contextual predictors by defining message of campaign from logistic regression analyses**

Model	Significant predictor	Interpretation: This message is used if
Your candidate defines opponent as out of touch	Party identification	you are a Democrat
	Challenger	you are a challenger
	Open seat	you are in an open-seat race
Your candidate defines opponent as incompetent	War chest	you have more money
	Open seat	you are not in an open-seat race
Your candidate defines opponent as inexperienced	Challenger	you are not a challenger
Your candidate defines opponent as corrupt	None	None
Your candidate defines opponent as too old, too long in office	None	None

discipline? Would demographic variables have similar influences? See the results in Table 2.6 above.

Who Defines Who by Campaign Context

In Table 2.6 I looked at contextual variables that drove campaign operatives' responses to what kind of message definition they used against their opponent as well as what definitions they felt were used against them. The first column, moving from left to right, is the message definition that the respondent's campaign employed or the opposition employed against them. The middle column shows that variables or predictors were actually significant in influencing how consultants felt about the use of that message definition. The final column shows the impact that variable had on the use of that definition. The table looks at how the campaign environment affected these feelings on strategy.

The biggest contextual drivers for message definition strategy among the campaigners were party identification, the campaign war chest, and what position they were in at the start of the campaign. Consultants working for challengers were much more likely to suggest their candidates defined the opposition as out of touch and not inexperienced. This is sound strategy, because if the candidate is a challenger, the candidate is usually not going to be able to make a credible argument about being more experienced than the incumbent, but he or she can make a greater case for having been among the people more than the incumbent can. Consultants working for open-seat candidates were also more likely to use a definition strategy of "out of touch" against the opposition, but not "incompetence." When a new challenger runs for an open seat, it may be harder to make a claim of incompetence since the seat is open unless the candidate makes a stretch and blames the exiting party. Those consultants who reported having more money than the opposition were more likely to make the charge of incompetence—something that many political operatives have implied has a connection to negative definitions. Going negative actually requires more research than going positive, and in turn requires skilled campaigners and a lot of money. So a well-funded candidate might have a greater chance of looking up the opposition's background and finding examples of incompetence than a poorly funded candidate. Finally, we see that being a campaign operative for a Democratic candidate leads one to be more likely to use the "out of touch" definition. As we have seen in this chapter and the last, Democratic candidates are often more sensitized to empathy as a character trait, which finds its way into their messaging. This is a definition that they likely have more credibility in lobbying than Republican consultants. No contextual variables had an impact on the consultants' views on defining the opposition as corrupt, too old, or too long in office.

Next, we look at how contextual variables influenced how consultants saw the opposition defining their candidate (Table 2.7). It is significant to point out that these are self-reported views from consultants. They believed this was how their candidate was defined, and thus these results show what environmental factors may have influenced how they believed their candidates were defined by their opposition.

The forces driving what consultants think about their opposition's message strategy are slightly different from what they reveal drives their strategy. Consultants believed their candidates were defined as "out of touch" because they had more money than the opposition. When incumbent Scott Murphy (D-NY) boasted a huge war chest heading into the final weeks of the 2010 campaign, his opposition, Chris Gibson, quickly used it to paint Murphy with a nasty definition and contrast his own grassroots financial

TABLE 2.7 **Significant contextual predictors by defining message of opposition from logistic regression**

Model	Significant predictor	Interpretation: This message is used if
Opponent defines your candidate as out of touch	War chest	you have more money than your opponent
Opponent defines your candidate as incompetent	None	None
Opponent defines your candidate as inexperienced	Open seat	you are in an open-seat race
Opponent defines your candidate as corrupt	None	None
Opponent defines your candidate as too old, too long in office	Polls at midway point	your candidate is ahead at the midpoint

support. "The groundswell of support from individuals around the district continues to build because people know Washington is out of touch and we need new leadership in Congress," Gibson said (Dlouhy 2010).

Consultants also believed that when they were in open-seat races the opposition was more likely to define them as inexperienced. What is interesting about this result is that it comports very well with the campaign message definitions that consultants use themselves as they state that they are more likely to define someone as inexperienced if they are incumbents or in an open-seat race. For the first time, polling becomes significant in definition strategy in our study, since consultants believed that the opposition was more likely to define them as too old, too long in office when they were ahead in the polls. While polling drives message strategy in many academic works, this is the first time consultants in our sample seemed to have their message strategy driven by polls. There were no variables that drove consultant feelings on why they were defined as incompetent or corrupt.

So far, we see that several contextual variables seem to influence message definition strategy from a consultant's perspective. And many of these variables—partisan identification, position in polls, and campaign type—are mentioned in political science theory as influencing message strategy. To this end, theory and practitioners appear to be in agreement in many areas. Table 2.8 examines the influence of demographic variables on the campaigner's views on message definition strategy. Similar to the tables above, I

TABLE 2.8 **Significant demographic predictors by defining message of campaign from logistic regression**

Model	Significant predictor	Interpretation: This message is used if
Your candidate defines opponent as out of touch	Challenger	you are a challenger
	Open seat	you are in an open-seat race
Your candidate defines opponent as incompetent	Open seat	you are not in an open-seat race
Your candidate defines opponent as inexperienced	Open seat	you are not in an open-seat race
	Challenger	you are not a challenger
Your candidate defines opponent as corrupt	None	None
Your candidate defines opponent as too old, too long in office	None	None

divide the results between what drove the consultant's advice to their candidate and what drove how they interpreted the opposition strategy.

When we examine demographic variables that drove how consultants saw their own messaging strategy, the election type proved most significant. When controlling for demographic factors such as race and gender, what drove consultants to define their opponents as "out of touch" is the same for contextual and demographic variables. Being a challenger or in an open-seat race drives this message type. The same applies to consultants defining their opponents as incompetent. The "incompetent" strategy is a favored message strategy to challengers and incumbents, but not those running open-seat races. War chest (the amount of money campaigns possess) was not a part of the demographic analysis, yet it does not seem to influence the fact that the results are the same. When it comes to defining the opposition as "inexperienced" when controlling for demographics, the results show that being an incumbent is the driving force. Intuitively, this was the most reasonable driver for this type of message, as an incumbent is more experienced in a job than just about any challenger, but the demographics tease out this factor. Finally, we see that no variables drive the consultant's use of the "corruption" or "too old, too long in office" message.

As the table turns to how consultants felt they were defined by the opposition, however, we see again where perception and results perform an intricate dance (Table 2.9). Although the results show that consultants did not

TABLE 2.9 Significant predictors of defining message by demographic variables: How the opposition defines your candidate

Model	Significant predictor	Interpretation: This message is used if
Opponent defines your candidate as out of touch	Your candidate's race	your candidate is white
Opponent defines your candidate as incompetent	None	None
Opponent defines your candidate as inexperienced	Your candidate's race Challenger Open seat	your candidate is black you are a challenger you are in an open-seat race
Opponent defines your candidate as corrupt	None	None
Opponent defines your candidate as too old, too long in office	Your candidate's gender Challenger Open seat	your candidate is female your candidate is a challenger your candidate is not in an open-seat race

believe that the race or gender of their candidate had any impact on how they defined the opposition when controlling for other factors, they clearly felt that their candidate's gender drove how the opposition defined them. Some of this, of course, captures the consultant's own biases, but the consistency of the results across all consultants regardless of party still gives us a glimpse into how definition battles truly play out during a campaign. Consultants of African American candidates saw themselves as being defined as inexperienced more than any other definition when controlling for other variables. Consultants for white candidates reported being defined by the opposition as out of touch when controlling for all other variables.

Some of these results may capture much of the message dynamics from the presidential election of 2008, since many consultants in the sample were working directly or indirectly with the Obama campaign. So I removed Obama from the regression, as I did earlier. Interestingly enough, the results were the same: Consultants of African American candidates still reported being defined as "inexperienced" more than any other message definition during the campaign, even controlling for all other variables. There does appear to be a consistent racial component in message strategy that candidates both experience and participate in during campaigns. Is *inexperienced* a racial code word for "blacks aren't intellectually capable or qualified" in political campaigns, much the way *arrogant* was a code word for "uppity black" in references to Barack Obama in 2008? Are political consultants working for minority candidates against white candidates more racially sensitized than consultants in races where the candidates are of the same race? The obvious answer is that survey respondents answered the questions as honestly as possible and could not have had any idea how these dozens of variables would come into play in demonstrating racial bias in campaign messages. Consequently, we can stand by these results because they are consistent. Recent work by McIlwain and Caliendo (2011) on the role of race in campaign messaging seems to affirm the conclusions reached here as well. Their work demonstrates that there are distinct messages employed in black-versus-black or white-versus-black campaigns that are measurable and influential. In addition, we can interpret those facts as a confirmation of the persistence of racial bias in message consistency in the campaign and know how consultants feel that candidates are defined by messages. Capturing another interesting demographic result, we see that consultants for female candidates, controlling for other demographic variables, felt their candidates were defined mostly as too old, too long in office. There are more men in elected office than women, and by extension more incumbent males, but in some respects this definition might reflect gender language coding in the way that "inexperienced" reflects racial coding. Many campaign operatives in writing and in interviews express concerns about going "too hard" after a woman during a campaign and having to straddle that line between defining an opposing female candidate in a negative way without coming across as sexist, condescending, or, worst of all, misogynistic. Kahn (1993) noticed that male candidates are more reluctant to attack female candidates, and when they do the focus tends to be on policy. Kelly Dittmar's (2010) survey of campaign consultants also found this tendency to shy away from strong attacks on women. Overall, 67 percent of consultants agree that male candidates need to "tread more carefully" in criticizing female opponents instead of male opponents. Republican and Democratic consultants are unified in this position (Dittmar 2010). Although we are not dealing specifically with attack ads at this point (that comes in Chapter 4), we are dealing with messages intended to define the opposition in a negative light. How does one reconcile the need to negatively define an opposing woman candidate while not angering or alienating the public or the press?

The defining message "too old, too long in office" is arguably the gentlest definition to respectfully and quietly escort the opposition out of office. Thus, it is a highly effective way to define a female candidate without engendering hostility (no pun intended). Inherent in this definition is that this candidate at one point did in fact serve the constituency well but has outlived her effectiveness. Perhaps it is this kind of soft touch that is used against women candidates at times rather than a more directly caustic definition like corruption or incompetence, which carry potentially damning gender stereotypes.

Message Discipline: A Case Study

This chapter has shown us a great deal about the messaging process from start to strategy to finish. With all of this knowledge, some new and some old, how do the message strategy and the ideas presented thus far play out in explaining a real-world campaign? In order to answer this question, we examine the case of the 2009 Virginia governor's race.

When Republican Robert F. McDonnell decided to run for governor of Virginia in 2009, he had a pretty big challenge ahead of him. The state had just gone for Barack Obama by seven points in the 2008 election and had elected consecutive Democratic governors who were very popular. To top it off, the demographics of the state were changing in ways that usually did not bode well for Republicans. The youthful, educated, and extremely diverse counties of northern Virginia that border Washington, D.C., had grown so much that they were now the highest population centers of the state. So how did he manage to win almost 60 percent of the vote and win nine out of eleven congressional districts in the state? The answer, according to McDonnell's own campaign staff, was strong message discipline.

McDonnell's campaign slogan was simple and witty, and he stuck to the accompanying message through thick and thin in the campaign. His Democratic opponent, Creigh Deeds, seemed to move from message to message, never homing in on one long enough to connect with voters. By 2009, the recession had hit the booming state of Virginia hard, and Robert McDonnell knew that focusing on a jobs message through the campaign would serve him well. He defined himself with the slogan "Results-Oriented Conservative" (which created the catchphrase "Solid as a ROC"), put out bumper stickers with the message "Bob's for Jobs," and used the defining message that Democrat Creigh Deeds was out of touch with the real concerns of regular voters. "He's talking about former governors and divisive social issues," McDonnell said. "He's talking about things people don't care about" (Kumar 2009). McDonnell had a great slogan (two, depending on who you ask), a message on jobs that addressed voters' fears, and as an open-seat candidate defined his opponent as "out of touch," conforming with all the research shown thus far in this chapter. Then a scandal hit the political environment.

A series of graduate papers that McDonnell had written at the age of thirty-four expressing controversial opinions about women and minorities surfaced, threatening to rock the campaign. But according to McDonnell's manager, Phil Cox, the campaign team remained on message. "We would address the charges but turn our message back to those issues that voters cared about." In contrast, the Deeds campaign seemed incapable of sticking to a message and tried to define McDonnell based on scandals and events as they occurred as opposed to having a coherent message box to which they would adhere. Deeds tried to paint McDonnell in a negative light by focusing on a graduate thesis he had written where he stated that working women are detrimental to the family and advocating government discrimination against "fornicators, co-habitators, and homosexuals." The problem was that voters had no idea what message to glean from this scandal, and Deeds did not give them one. Did this mean McDonnell was corrupt? Was he out of touch with the mainstream voter of the state? The message was never clear (Gardner 2009). In the end, Phil Cox summed up his candidate's key to success: "The message throughout was straightforward and consistent" (2010, 3).

As is the case in all campaigns, messaging is just one part of an overall strategy. However, it is obvious in the previous example that clear messages can mean the difference between success and failure, especially when unexpected events strike campaigns. When we look at how demographic variables play a role in messaging strategy in the real world, we move to another hotly contested campaign in the same year, this time just a few hours south from Virginia to North Carolina.

Race and Messages in the Queen City

Sometimes even when the field is unnaturally even, candidates can still fail to take advantage of a good message strategy. When Republican John Lassiter and Democrat Anthony Foxx ran for mayor of Charlotte in 2009, no one quite knew what to expect. The outgoing Republican mayor, Pat McCrory, had served for fourteen years but had established a reputation among Republican voters as a RINO (Republican in Name Only) who was not a true ideological conservative. John Lassiter, who was a close friend of McCrory, had been tainted by the same identity and needed to define himself and the opposition to voters. Anthony Foxx came from a long line of political power in Charlotte, had been mentored by powerful congressman Mel Watt, and had served four years as an at-large member of the city council after working in Washington, D.C., for a few years. Lassiter had more money in the bank, but only 25 percent of registered Charlotte voters are Republican. Foxx had the upper hand in registration but was not seen as a charismatic candidate and was viewed by some in the African American community as a career politician who had been groomed for the job since birth. Two candidates with problems connecting with voters were going to need excellent message discipline to pull out a victory.

In Lassiter's primary victory speech, the *Charlotte Observer* made his message clear as well as how he planned to define the opposition: "Lassiter said his message rang resonant with voters, and he vowed to continue the same message against Foxx. . . . 'We made sure we got our message out about experience and leadership, creating jobs, getting repeat criminals off the street, and keeping taxes low and services high,' Lassiter said" (Lyttle 2009).

Foxx's slogan of "One Charlotte, One Future" sought to create a feeling of togetherness for voters and promoted a theme of "unity" that would be crucial for an African American Democrat to have success in a citywide election. Foxx's message was simple: "It was time for Charlotte to change and accept its new role as one of the shining beacons of an economically vibrant and growing American South." In contrast, he painted Lassiter as the old guard, incapable of understanding what Charlotte residents needed in order to move the city forward. Local newspapers quickly picked up on Foxx's theme, slogan, and message. "Lassiter, a lawyer and businessman, campaigned on experience. He brought a long resume of community service—as a neighborhood leader, planning commissioner, school board member and a City Council member since 2003. He said all that offered a stark contrast to Foxx, a council member for four years. But change trumped experience for many voters" (Morrill 2009).

Two points are worthy of note about this campaign. Although there was an age difference between the two candidates, their actual years on city council were fairly similar, with Foxx only serving a year less on city council than Lassiter. On the other hand, Lassiter had more than fifteen years of public service, serving on planning boards and the powerful Charlotte School Board. So while Foxx was technically less experienced than Lassiter, in their immediate positions from which they sought the mayor's office they were fairly equal. The second point is that Charlotte was the last major city in America with a black population of more than 25 percent that had a white mayor in 2009.

The race was tight all the way until the end, despite the inherent structural and demographic advantages that Foxx seemed to have going in. In the end he squeaked by with a 51 percent to 48 percent victory over Lassiter. A race this close under those circumstances likely could have been won by John Lassiter, so what does our chart say about the message strategies that both sides employed? Our research suggests that when you are running for an open-seat position, you should define your opponent as "out of touch." Anthony Foxx did this well with his theme, slogan, message, and direct definitions of Lassiter as a man who did not know what Charlotte truly needed. What about Lassiter? Consultants in our sample reported that they were more likely to be defined as "inexperienced" when they ran campaigns for African American candidates and during open-seat races. So where was Lassiter's messaging mistake? Falling into a consistent racial pattern, he chose to define Anthony Foxx as inexperienced instead of defining him as "out of touch," which is a stronger message in an open-seat race, according to our message box. But the weakness in Lassiter's messaging goes even further. According to Lenny McAllister, author and former political commentator for the Fox affiliate in Charlotte, uneasiness in the black community about Foxx's political ambitions and his relatively short time in Charlotte would have made a defining message of "out of touch" more effective from the Lassiter campaign. In an argument of two candidates defining each other as "out of touch" for an open-seat race, Lassiter with fifteen years of public service on the city council and school board could have made a much more compelling argument than Foxx, who essentially moved back to Charlotte to run for public office. Given how close the race was, had Lassiter done a better job of using his money and resources and chosen the right defining message, he might have pulled out a victory that was clearly within his reach. McAllister stated: "Foxx leveraged his connections, the Charlotte grassroots community, and social communications channels (television, media) more consistently, and Lassiter's inability and unwillingness to do so made the difference in a razor-thin mayoral race because Foxx was able to put these factors into play through his campaign messaging."[12]

Too Old, Too Long in Office: The Gender Message

Finally, we look at one of the most prominent examples of our research results regarding the message definition of "too old, too long in office." As stated before, this is a definition that differs from "out of touch" in that it suggests a candidate is past their best years as opposed to not connecting with voters. The statistical analysis shows that consultants felt this message was most often directed at them when they were running campaigns for female candidates. There is no clearer example of this theme in play than George W. Bush's campaign for governor of Texas against Ann Richards in 1994. Richards was well liked among the voters in the state, and her sassy style and honesty about her own personal and professional failings made her resonate with Republicans, Democrats, and many races and ethnicities of the highly diverse state of Texas. Despite a far greater and more respected political career than Bush and more money at her disposal, Richards lost 46 percent to 53 percent in an upset. Although clearly some contextual variables were at play, namely, that 1994 was a terrible year for many incumbent Democrats at all levels of government, Richards was victimized by a stellar message campaign by Bush. In an interview on PBS's *Frontline*, Mark McKinnon, a former consultant for Richards in 1994 who then worked with Bush in 2000 and 2004, succinctly described how Bush managed to beat the popular incumbent. When asked why Bush beat Richards, he said:

> Incredibly focused candidate. And I think he made a fundamental decision, which was the right one, which was he never attacked her personally. I think that what he did was, he said: "Here's what I stand for. Here's my vision for Texas." And he said: "Gov. Richards—a good woman, good person, just not in line politically with Texas anymore. Let's give her a gold watch, give her a

hand and send her off." So he was very deferential. He was not disrespectful, which was the right thing to do, because people liked her.

The gold watch, the deference, and the subtle implication that Richards should be escorted out the door instead of thrown out of office were the key differences in the campaign. Richards, whose razor wit had been targeted at the Bushes for years, could not seem to focus on whether W. was a dunderhead, a spoiled rich kid, or just an unpleasant guy. During her speech at the Democratic convention in 1998, she famously chided the elder Bush's occasional verbal snafus by saying, "Poor George, he can't help it—he was born with a silver foot in his mouth," and continued that same tact against the younger Bush, referring to him as a "shrub" and "some jerk" on the campaign trail. It is highly unlikely that Bush could have gotten away with such vitriol against a beloved female candidate like Richards in Texas, so his calm but moving message that maybe Richards needed to be put out to pasture was the perfect antidote.

Conclusion

Roger Ailes, the author of one of the most important messaging books in political history, titled *You Are the Message*, argues that no matter how good a message is, or how consistently the candidate sticks to it, the message is really just an extension of the candidate. The better the candidate feels about himself or herself, the more powerful and authentic the message will be to the public. In this chapter, we have seen how once we disentangle what a message actually is, there are various ways that a campaign uses messaging to get a candidate off on the right foot and toward success. As discussed, voters often want candidate messages that show a connection or empathy toward their lives. Political consultants desire and encourage candidates to stay on message, but ultimately it is not them or the environment that drives message consistency. Indeed, the candidate drives message consistency. We have also demonstrated that some of the main drivers of message strategy in political science, that is, demographic and contextual factors, do have an impact on how political consultants behave, thus demonstrating again that existing theory has a role in explaining political professional behavior. However, we now know that current political science work lacks substantive discussions of message consistency and what accounts for it. While existing theory may address why voters need consistent messages, little work addresses how and why candidates stay on message, and this chapter demonstrates that consultants have unique insights that need to be explored further. Finally, we now see that there is a manner in which the majority of political defining messages can be distilled to create a valuable message box to describe and explain political consultant behavior.

Absent in this chapter's discussion of political messaging is what a large number of messages in campaigns are about, namely, policy issues. From the perspective of many campaign operatives, messages are simply a means to discuss policy issues and positions for the candidate. In *Campaigns and Elections: Contemporary Case Studies*, the relationship between messaging and issues is clear: "The essence of political strategy is to concentrate Your greatest strength against the point of Your opponent's greatest weakness. This is done through positioning which is the development and delivery of messages that present the voters with a choice based on candidate differences that are clear, believable and connected to reality" (Bailey and Faucheux 2000).

In summary, we first learned how campaign operatives worked with political candidates, we have seen how they create the principles behind message strategy, and now we can move on to what messages are about: issues. In the next chapter, we will analyze how political consultants manage issues and their candidates, and how all of these previous elements blend together in the wake of existing political science theory.

3

The Issues

"I voted for the 87 billion before I voted against it." When Republican campaign consultants captured Massachusetts senator John Kerry uttering those words about his votes on the crucial issue of Iraq War funding, they knew they had struck messaging and policy position gold. Bush's head campaign manager, Karl Rove, once referred to the quote as the "gift that keeps on giving,"[1] because despite wide-scale business scandals, an unpopular war, and an approval rating hovering just under 50 percent, George Bush managed to beat John Kerry in the 2004 election by tagging him with the most onerous of political labels in the past ten years: "flip-flopper."

Both of the campaign factors discussed in previous chapters—the importance of a candidate's traits and their ability to use and stick to a specific message—are used to express and sell a candidate's policy positions. A candidate's policy positions matter in a political campaign; the voters use them to judge character, commitment, and what the candidate will bring to the table once in office. If a candidate changes positions on an issue, or takes a stand on an issue that they do not appear capable of tackling effectively, the change in position or the indefensible stance can have serious consequences for the election. Taken in full context, John Kerry was explaining why he had voted for an early version of a bill but voted against final passage because of changes that had been added. Nevertheless, the modern world of American political campaigns offers little time to present lengthy explanations to the public. Ever since Kerry's infamous somersault in 2004, which earned him the label of flip-flopper (someone who changes policy positions either for political expediency or for lack of commitment), the phrase *flip-flopper* has proven to be one of the most onerous charges levied against a candidate.[2]

History shows us that appearing to "flip-flop" on an issue, and being attacked for flip-flopping by your opponent, can be campaign kryptonite. However, this phenomenon does not quite explain what and how issues come into play in political campaigns or the role consultants play in the process. "Issues" do not just randomly appear during a campaign cycle; political consultants, managers, and strategists work long and hard with their candidates to find just the right set of issues to draw the public's attention.

A Matter of Choice

In "High Priesthood, Low Priestcraft: The Role of Political Consultants," N. J. O'Shaughnessy stated, "There is a misconception often perpetuated by political commentators and occasionally some academics that candidates are pawns in the games that consultants play especially on issues, positions, and stances" (1990, 8). The reality is much less cynical; political consultants are more ideologically committed than one might expect. In their work on political consultants, Medvic, Nelson, and Dulio (2002) found that "not only are they dedicated Republicans or Democrats, but some work only with candidates of their own particular ideology, such as conservative Republicans, liberal Democrats, pro-choice, pro-life—wherever their own beliefs happen to lie on the ideological spectrum" (102). With that in mind, it is often their job to help the candidate sort through the myriad issues that they already care about and lead the candidate to focus on those issues that will paint them in the best light to voters. Managing candidate issues is not easy. In fact, it is one of the hardest jobs for a campaign manager or consultant to perform. Hundreds of issues arise during every election season that might matter to voters. Even more, consultants must manage the positions that candidates must take when events occur that the campaign does not control. Analyzing the evolving roles that campaign managers play, Grossmann noted that "practitioners often discuss which issues should be the focus of a candidate's campaign, even sometimes thinking in the same terms as scholars about whether to emphasize issues where the other party has a built-in advantage in public opinion" (2009). When evaluating this quote, we are struck by a question: What is a built-in party advantage on an issue? And second, how does this process play out in campaigns? To fully understand this, we embark on the following discussion of the most influential theories dealing with issue positioning in political campaigns.

Valence Issues, Issue Ownership, and Deliberative Priming in Campaigns

Raise your hand if you are in favor of crime. No? What about child abuse, or poverty, or communism? Still no takers? There are some issues in American politics that are just universally liked or disliked by a huge portion of the population. These are referred to as "valence issues" and were first identified by political scientist Daniel Stokes when analyzing what drives voter behavior when issues become central in a political campaign. Valence issues are often those general issues that everyone in the voting public agrees need to be addressed or a condition that everyone feels should be sought. For example, Stokes found that during the presidential campaign of 1960, both Kennedy and Nixon spent a great deal of time talking about improving American prestige abroad, a valence issue since everyone, Republican or Democrat, likes the idea of America being revered and respected abroad (1963, 373). Campaign managers love valence issues because it gives them an opportunity to guide their candidates toward speaking on something that will please their base and not anger or excite the opposition. The catch is that valence issues can eventually turn into "issue positions" once the campaign gets more intense.

While it is fine for a candidate to speak about ending crime, stopping communism, or improving public schools, there is a point at which he or she may actually have to provide policy *solutions* for those valence issues, and that is where things get complicated. Perhaps a candidate believes that the best way to improve public schools is through voucher programs or subsidizing single-sex education for elementary school students. Now you might have a fight on your hands because there are bound to be some voters who disagree with these solutions, and your opponent is likely to pounce on that opportunity to propose their own solutions. While the voting public may agree on the importance of a particular issue, the solution proposed by a campaign team and how effective the public thinks the candidate will be in implementing that solution are all influenced by the concept of "issue ownership."

In political science the concept of "issue ownership," developed by John Petrocik as well as researchers Budge and Farlie, refers to the way in which the voting public and consequently political practitioners view certain parties to have a built-in advantage when it comes to dealing with specific policy issues. Many scholars have noted that issue-ownership research argues that over time, political parties become so closely associated with certain issues that citizens come to take for granted the party's competence in handling those issues (Holian 2004; Ansolabehere and Iyengar 1994; Budge and Farlie 1983; Mair 1983). Clearly, a point exists at which voters assume one party deals with an issue better than other parties. So, while the valence issue of a "clean environment" might be on the minds of the electorate, voters might believe Democrats will do a better job than Republicans at finding solutions. Competence plays a role in issue ownership as well. Candidates cannot simply talk about an issue; they or their party must be able to demonstrate their ability to solve or at least limit the problem. In general, voters see Republicans as "owning" issues such as crime, national security, and taxes. In contrast, the voters see Democrats as "owning" issues such as education, health care, and race relations. Some researchers have argued that issues like the economy and foreign policy are never truly "owned," only "leased," depending on how well that particular party seems to have dealt with that issue over the past several years (Petrocik 1996; Kaufmann 2004).

So what is a campaign manager to do? How do you handle a valence issue that turns into a policy issue when your candidate's party may or may not even "own" the issue but you still have to run the campaign? Some political scientists have shown that you can circumvent "issue ownership" that works against your candidate by showing that the candidate has a strong background in that particular policy area, by promoting policies that prove to be effective, or in some cases by trusting voters to differentiate between your candidate and whatever reputation your candidate's party happens to have on the issue (Kaufmann 2004; Holian 2004; Egan 2006). Of course, all of those suggestions are good, but consultants are brought into campaigns to make sure things happen in favor of the candidate, so they often provide a more direct approach to issue strategy than the suggestions above.

Political consultants employ "deliberative priming" to make sure that the issues that paint their candidate in the best light are the issues that drive voters' opinions and judgments. Deliberative priming, according to long-term consultant researcher Stephen Medvic, is the process by which campaign managers make sure that the press and the public are paying attention to select issues, so that their campaign is driving the campaign narrative rather than being run over by it. "Consultants," according to Medvic, "help a candidate select the issues that give the candidate the best chance of winning. These issues will be ones that the public cares about; they will also be issues in which the candidate has a competitive advantage over his or her opponent" (2001, 433). Thus, deliberative priming solves the problems (and benefits) of valence issues and issue ownership. A campaign manager will help a candidate find a valence issue that their particular party is seen as more effective in handling, and then the campaign manager will work the press, the public, and the opponent in order to make that issue the central issue to evaluate both candidates in the campaign.

How does theory explain what campaigns do during a heated election, especially when issues are bound to crop up that no one expected? To find out we take a look at the Elian Gonzalez story from the early 2000 presidential election. In that campaign a crucial issue literally emerged from the ocean and brought valence issues, issue ownership, and deliberative priming into full view.

Elian Gonzalez and the Challenge of Unforeseen Issues

The issues that become prominent during a political campaign are not always anticipated. The ability of a team of political operatives to figure out the impact of an issue and advise its candidate to take the right position or pivot from a position can be the difference between a bounce in the polls and looking for a new job in November. One such example, the Elian Gonzalez case, impacted the closest presidential race in American history.

In November 1999, six-year-old Elian Gonzalez along with his mother and ten other Cubans attempted to escape to the United States on a ramshackle boat. The boat capsized, and everyone but Elian and two others drowned off the coast of Florida. The Coast Guard rescued little Elian and gave him to relatives in Miami, which set off a chain of events that grabbed all of America's attention in the early part of the 2000 presidential campaign. Elian's Miami family did not want to return him to communist Cuba, even though the boy's father wanted him returned and claimed that his wife fled with Elian without telling him. When media attention of the case grew because of the fact that it was taking place in the critical swing state of Florida, the media publicity forced front-runners in the presidential contest of 2000, John McCain, George Bush, and Al Gore, to take a public position on the issue. There seemed to be two potential "valence issues" at play during the event: Most Americans believed communist Cuba was not a good place to live, and a boy who had lost his mother and gone through a horrible tragedy should be reunited with his father. When the choice between advocating freedom (let the boy stay in the United States) or family (let the boy return to be with this father) confronts a candidate, how should a consultant advise his candidate?

From a valence-issue standpoint, the options were mixed. Nationally and throughout most of Florida, voters favored sending Elian Gonzalez home to his father. Gallup Polls showed that over the months of the crisis, about 60 percent of the U.S. public favored sending Elian back, and about 51 percent were against giving the six-year-old or his father permanent residency. Of course, on the ground, the local Cuban population staunchly favored keeping Elian in Miami.[3] As far as issue ownership, Republicans Bush and McCain were in pretty good shape. Republicans "owned" the issue of fighting communism and were longtime supporters of the anticommunist Cuban community in South Florida. So both Bush and McCain quickly spoke out in favor of keeping Elian Gonzalez in the United States rather than return him to a communist dictatorship. They even attempted to soften the separation idea by suggesting alternatives by which Elian's father could join him in the United States. Democrats did not really "own" any issues relating to the Elian Gonzalez case, either the family-values angle or the anticommunist angle, which actually should have given Al Gore more room to maneuver policywise. The Clinton administration and Attorney General Janet Reno had long advocated sending Elian back to his father, but Gore broke with them, initially favoring sanctuary for the boy, a plan similar to the Republican candidates'. But as the story and legal battles dragged into the spring, Gore remained silent on the issue. At one point, Gore went more than fifty-four days without a press conference addressing the subject.

The dithering noncommittal statements by his campaign managers and spokespersons in the meantime were not helping the campaign, either. Comments issued by one Gore campaign official characterized Gore's lack of commitment to one position. *Los Angeles Times* reporter Esther Schrader reported that spokesperson Doug Hattaway said, "Gore has made his position clear in the Florida case—he thinks it's important to let the talks happen and let the process play out. . . . He understands that people disagree with his position, but he thinks it's the right approach and you have to let the chips fall where they may." Yet in another instance, Hattaway seemed to distance Gore from the situation by rejecting any solution when he said, "The situation in Florida is so volatile that we don't want to be dragged into it" (*CNN.com* 2000). To make matters worse, Gore trailed Bush in the state, and he believed Florida would be critical to his campaign's success in the fall election. Attorney General Reno then moved ahead with plans to send Elian back, and a point of no return was coming. By mid-April, the Bush campaign deliberately tailored its message to prime the public into using this issue to evaluate Gore on his leadership ability (a key trait in candidate evaluation, as discussed). Ari Fliescher, campaign spokesperson and consultant for the Bush campaign, never missed a chance to knock Gore for his lack of leadership on the issue. He commented, "If Al Gore doesn't have the leadership to take on Janet Reno, how can we expect him to stand up to Fidel Castro? . . . Perhaps he'll hold a news conference tomorrow, when there's less heat in the kitchen."[4]

Bob Shrum, a Gore 2000 campaign consultant, wrote extensively in his memoir about how the Bush campaign effectively used the Gonzalez case to prime voters to see Gore's handling of this issue as reflective of his ability to lead:

> The arrival of a six-year-old Cuban boy in Miami was a matter of fate and the way Gore handled the controversy about sending him back to Cuba became more proof, in a Bradley phrase that the Bush campaign soon picked up, that Gore would do "anything to get elected." . . . Three weeks later the surprise raid that whisked Elian out of his great uncle's home and onto a plane to Cuba enraged Miami—and let the Bush campaign mock Gore, who claimed to be the most influential vice president in history as "ineffectual." (2007, 331)

New York Times journalist Adam Clymer reported, "After Elian was forcefully taken from his home by federal troops on April 22nd, and the courts made it clear he was going home, even the Bush campaign had cooled some of its rhetoric about the case" (2000). We all know that eventually the election of 2000 came down to chads and fights in November, but how did the positions on the Elian Gonzalez case come into play? Bush beat Gore among Cuban Americans 77 to 13 percent. While Cuban Americans in Florida tend to lean Republican, Gore lost close to twenty points of support with that constituency since Clinton's reelection in 1996.

Many local political leaders, journalists, and academics agreed that the Gore team's poor issue strategy played a role in his losing Florida. He initially favored a position that would help him with the passionate Cuban minority in South Beach, but then he backed off the issue and eventually took a different position. This reinforced the message that Gore would change positions for political expediency among the public at large and angered the local Cuban community, who felt that he betrayed them with his position change (Brookings Institution 2000; Adams 2000). Bush, on the other hand, managed the valence-issue and issue-ownership concepts much better. In the words of Gore campaign consultant Bob Shrum, "George Bush took the same position as Gore; but he got a free ride. Everyone expected him to side with a Cuban exile community that was heavily Republican" (2007, 331). Then the Bush campaign team deliberately primed the public to focus on this issue early in the campaign as a lesson on Al Gore's leadership skills. Had Gore simply stuck with his initial policy stance, or primed the public to view Bush's stance to keep a boy away from his father as antithetical to "compassionate conservatism," he might have not suffered so much at the ballot box among swing voters and conservative Democrats in Florida.

That the role of voter intensity on issue positioning played a significant role in the Elian Gonzalez crisis interested and instructed campaign managers and campaign theorists. While the public at large supported sending Elian home, the public did not feel strongly about it. In contrast, the Cuban community in Florida—a critical constituency to align with in order to win the state—passionately favored Elian's staying in the United States. This issue most certainly served as the driving force in the Cuban vote choice in South Florida. How does a campaign manager account for voter passions or population size in issue strategy? Does the manager take policy stances to stand with the majority who are simply paying attention to an issue or a passionate minority whose entire vote may be centered on that issue? What theories might explain when, where, and why campaign managers advise campaigns to take the positions they take? To answer these questions, we have to delve into one of the most contentious debates in modern political science.

Assume Which Position?

There are many choices that have divided American society—Coke or Pepsi, Quizno's or Subway, even Lakers or Celtics—and political science is not immune to these never-ending debates. One of the longest-running debates in political science deals with candidate positioning, namely, what is the best way for a candidate running for office to position herself or himself on issues in order to win an election? While we have just discussed how owned issues and priming play a role in what political consultants will advise their campaigns to focus on, there is still the matter of the voter. Where are the voters on the issues, and how do you position yourself in a way that your candidate's policy stance is closer to the voters' than the opposition's stance? Or does issue-position strategy revolve around a small passionate group of voters who may swing an election (conservative Cubans in Miami in 2000) over a larger group of voters who are less intense in their feelings (everyone else in America at the time)? The battle over the proper way to position your candidate on the issues to get the most votes is encapsulated in the debate over the "directional" and "proximity" theories in political science.

Anthony Downs's seminal work *An Economic Theory of Democracy* (1957) suggests some basic rules for when, how, and why a citizen decides to vote in an election, and by extension how a smart consultant should be telling a candidate how he or she should position himself or herself. First, voters consider the benefits they will get from reelecting the sitting elected official (incumbent) versus what they would expect to get from electing the other party (challenger). Part of how this is accomplished is by looking at where the candidates stand on particular issues. Most voters imagine every "issue" in an election to be a straight line from one extreme end to the other extreme, preferring to stay in the center. Therefore, the position strategy for most consultants would be to try to place their candidate as close to the median on any given issue because voters will vote for whichever candidate stands nearest to them on the issue continuum. This concept is referred to as the "median voter theory," or in this analysis the "proximity model," since citizens vote for the candidate whose position stance is in closest proximity to their own. So how might the application of this theory play out in the real world? Abortion is a good example.

The extreme Right has the position that abortions should be illegal under all circumstances including cases of rape or incest. Consequently, the extreme Left holds the position that abortions should be available to anyone of any age, for any reason, as a matter of personal choice. Very few voters, let alone candidates, would ever take either position—certainly not publicly. The majority of the public is comfortably in the middle on abortion, wanting to keep it legal as an option but not wanting it to be available to anyone under any circumstances. During the 1992 presidential election, the abortion topic sparked much debate. The issue polarized the Republican Party with pro-life and pro-choice Republicans unable to see common ground. The Democratic voter fared only slightly better, with about 60 percent of Democrats favoring to keep abortion legal and the remaining 40 percent either opposing it or desiring the party to not take a position. The Clinton campaign is credited by many political observers as having struck the perfect medium pitch with the abortion debate (Cohen 2006; Neumayr 2006). Jefferson Morley of *Slate.com* argued: "One small but essential part of Bill Clinton's two victories over Republican foes was to turn the abortion issue into a Democratic advantage. He accomplished this with his formulation that abortion ought to be 'safe, legal, and rare.' In simple positive language, Clinton framed the pro-choice position in a way that was firmly liberal yet appealing to voters uncomfortable with the inescapable reality that abortion involves ending a potential human life" (2002). Clinton's issue position on abortion during the campaign neutralized the issue in the Democratic Party. While some criticized "safe, legal, and rare" as linguistic gymnastics rather than the expression of a policy position, it became clear to the electorate that, one, Bill Clinton would keep abortion legal, and, two, he acknowledged the moral conundrum of the existing laws. This allowed him to focus on other policies during the summer of 1992.

Since we are dealing with theory, it is important to note that the proximity model makes several key assumptions that may or may not reflect the realities of the modern-day political campaign. First, the model assumes voters have "perfect information" and thus know exactly where candidates stand on every given issue. Second, the model takes for granted that the electorate will eventually vote sincerely based on what they believe about an issue. Last, it assumes that positions taken by politicians during the campaign will not change during the campaign period. In the real world of political campaigns, most of these assumptions do not really hold up. Voters are not always particularly informed about how candidates stand on issues and are often wrong or project their own policy beliefs upon the candidates they like. Also, many voters are strategic, that is to say, they vote not just for the candidate whose position is closest to theirs but for the candidate who they believe can actually accomplish something on that issue. However, the last assumption does hold true: More often than not, consultants want to avoid telling their candidates to change positions on issues during campaigns because changing positions sends a confusing and potentially disorganized message to voters. However, the key assumption of the proximity model for the purposes of this research is this: The majority of voters are in the middle on most issues, and the candidate who places him- or herself closest to that median has the best chance of winning in any campaign.

Directional Model

The directional theory is the Sprite to the proximity model's 7-UP. It is the most prominent alternative theory on candidate positioning in political science literature. The directional model incorporates two elements in campaign position theory and argument that are missing from the proximity model: direction and intensity. Political scientists Rabinowitz and MacDonald argue that successful positioning in a campaign is taking a policy stand on the right "side" of key issues: "If we think in symbolic politics terms, the directional prediction makes sense. The voter who prefers one side of a debate to the other but cares little about the issue would not generally be expected to support the candidate who favors the opposite side and says little" (1998, 97). Whereas the proximity model argues that the distance between the voter's position and the candidate's stance is the ultimate determinant of vote choice, the directional model argues that direction and intensity of the stance that both the voters and the candidates show for a given issue are the determinants of vote choice. The median voter remains important in the directional model but in a different way. The goal of a campaign following the directional model is to capture the median voter by being intense in the direction of that voter without moving outside of the "region of acceptability" where they would be perceived as being too extreme. Rabinowitz and MacDonald also state, "The more intense a candidate is on an issue, the more the candidate generates intense support or opposition with regard to that issue. Candidates can make an issue central to judgments about their candidacy by taking clear strong stances" (ibid., 98). If we look again at the Gonzalez case, candidate George Bush boldly announced his views, which had the effect of attracting those voters in the passionate minority who felt the same way. Conversely, Gore took a much more tepid stance, which had the effect of alienating many voters when he eventually switched positions.

The directional and proximity models are just the opening salvo for the position discussion in political campaigns. While most academics would say that these theories represent the two main theories that explain political positioning in campaigns, some political scientists criticize both plans as incomplete, or downright wrong.

Critiques of the Proximity Model and Electoral Position Taking

Gershtenson (2004) and Ansolabehere, Snyder, and Stewart (2001) argue that the level of competition in a Senate race in particular has an impact on the likelihood of the proximity model explaining candidate positioning. Gershtenson asserts that other factors may make the proximity model more or less effective in explaining candidate positions during campaigns. He initially states that in competitive races, where there is high information being presented by both candidates (usually open-seat races), candidates are more likely to move to the median voter preference. He goes on to say:

> Essentially these other factors have to be taken into consideration when studying electoral competition because positioning alone is not sufficient. First, the effects of candidates' positions vary across a number of dimensions such as party affiliation and election competitiveness. Second, and more importantly, candidates' ideological locations are less meaningful in determining the outcomes of congressional elections than are many other variables. As a result, Downsian conceptions of electoral competition and representation are unlikely to reflect the reality of American politics. (2004, 11)

Ansolabehere, Snyder, and Stewart suggest that the campaign district and the competitiveness of the race have a vacillating effect on candidate positions over time. They find that from the 1940s to the 1970s, candidates were much more likely to take positions based on district interests, but through the 1980s and 1990s national party positions became more of the norm. This is particularly interesting given that the power of political parties was seen as being at a bit of a nadir through the 1980s and resurfaced only in the mid- to late 1990s. The conclusions that they come to are in marked contrast to those of Gershtenson regarding the influence of open-seat or competitive races: "Open seats are widely conjectured to exert a moderating influence on Congress. . . . Our results suggest that the opposite is typically true. Open-seat contestants are on average more extreme than other challengers. This is true even controlling for district partisanship" (2004, 153).

Continuing with the theme of electoral and district competition on the median voter theory, Francis and Kenny contend, "Candidates shift positions as they move from lower offices in pursuit of higher office (House to Senate)." They find that rather than simply seeking the median voter, candidates shift their positions from the district-median position on issues to the state-delegation median on most issues. Whereas the previous authors look primarily at competition as a mitigating factor on the power of the proximity model, Francis and Kenny find that the district itself can also influence the strength or power of the proximity model to explain electoral positions. Candidates who change their positions on issues as they move through the campaign process seem to be more successful in elections. "Among candidates, winners are more likely than losers to have moved closer to the state party position" (1996, 780). Winning candidates are those who shift positions on key issues, which suggests that simple maintenance of the median position does not work on large-scale campaigns. Moreover, across states movement varies depending on party, Francis and Kenny report: "Movement away from the center, to the left for Democrats and to the right for Republicans, occurs as consistently, if not more so, than movement toward the center than the wings. As such, the findings confirm that in most states members do not behave as if there were only one winning position (i.e., the median voter position), but rather as if there were two divergent winning positions, one for Democrats and one for Republicans" (ibid., 783).

Finally, Moon, nodding to campaign managers and political operatives, offers the "resource-constrained election model," in which the need for campaign resources and party activities makes political moderation of the Downsian kind a pathway to electoral failure. Moon, using the Clinton impeachment hearings as a backdrop, argues that candidates are dependent on party activists for resources, money, campaign expertise, as well as votes, and activists are much more ideologically extreme than your average voter. If candidates for office fail to appeal to these activists, by trying to stay in the middle on key issues, they will eventually lose elections. Due to such party pressure, candidates cannot, as a simple Downsian analysis would expect, reliably gain popular votes by becoming more moderate, according to Moon (2004, 629). If candidates moderate, they lose the passion and support of the party faithful, which means a loss of campaign resources, which in turn means that whatever vote gains that are captured from moderation are lost due to a weaker campaign team. In the end the author suggests that incumbents, who can collect a team of campaign activists who are more loyal to them than any particular party of position, can afford to be more proximity oriented than challengers or those in open-seat races.

These authors provide us with a valuable set of questions with which to analyze consultant positioning behavior and the validity or power of the proximity model to explain electoral behavior. Ansolabehere, Snyder, and Stewart (2001) find that highly competitive races elicit extreme candidate positions, whereas Gershtenson (2004) finds competitive races to have a moderating influence. Francis and Kenny (1996) find that the position being sought by candidates can also influence whether they seek the median voter, and moreover that median is influenced by party. Interestingly enough, the case studies do not seem to explicitly address the role of race intensity on the positions being taken. While some cases discussed races that were competitive, others discussed races where one candidate was in the lead the whole time. Therefore, a series of questions on this notion could be illuminating for both academic and consultant perspectives.

Finding the "Acceptable Region": Critiques of the Directional Model and Candidate Positioning

In addition to district size and composition, candidate position may be a simple element of realizing the "passionate minority." While Downs discusses the notion that this passionate minority may trump an actual majority of voters, McGann, Koetzle, and Grofman reinforce this point in their analysis of candidate positions under various electoral systems. This is an important element for the overall research because consultants are not always working for candidates in a two-person winner-take-all format; multi-candidate nonpartisan mayoral races and run-off elections, for example, do occur across the nation. McGann, Koetzle, and Grofman discuss how in plurality elections, or sequential run-off elections, the winning candidate's position may be the model voter position instead of the median. This essentially explains how many minority coalitions have managed to win mayoral contests in major cities despite not always having a pure majority. "Regions of the distribution that are dense will be advantaged over less dense regions and may prevail even if the less dense regions are broader and have greater population. It is possible that a concentrated minority may have its way over a more dispersed majority" (2002, 145). This notion is particularly important in analyzing consultant strategy in city council or some mayoral elections where plurality votes and sequential elections are more common.

Claassen argues that when you put the two models up to each other, the directional model simply does not hold up. He argues that essentially intensity is much more important than distance and shows through various methodological changes over existing theories that even extreme voters, part of the core of directional theory, have their limits, and thus proximity still captures their voting behavior more effectively. "Furthermore even extreme individuals seem to like moderate candidates who are closer more than they like extreme candidates who are more distant" (2007, 271). In many ways his work seems to show that personal affinity can also play a role in ideological vote choice, a concept other analysts have assessed yet come to a different conclusion as far as the value of the directional-versus-proximity models.[5]

Most of the previous analyses of candidate position were direct or indirect discussions or refutations of the proximity model; however, there is an analysis that is a variation of the directional model that has relevance to this overall project. The directional model is based in large part on the "region of acceptability," a concept that is critiqued on multiple occasions by Westholm (1997, 2001). However, the basic notion of a region of tolerance that includes winning policy positions during a political campaign was approached by another researcher at the same time, although from the perspective of the candidate and their handlers. Wuffle et al. created a "finagle point" wherein it is possible for a candidate to find a position such that without having to move radically from their initial starting point, they can take a position that will always beat a potential challenger. "Nonetheless, we claim that we can find a point, which we shall call the finagle point, which has the property that every point in the space is defeated by some point very near the finagle point, and no point with a smaller radius can be found" (1989, 349). This theory is valuable for several reasons. First, it finds that the campaign itself can be viewed as a game with successive movements on key policy issues, the incumbent's stance on most issues being known, and the challenger then moving to a counterposition until election day. This idea is missing from most discussions of candidate position, which seem to imply fairly static campaign positions on issues. Moreover, Wuffle et al. consider the fact that candidates have a minimal amount of time that they can move, since moves that are too radical or shifting positions may cause voters to doubt a candidate's consistency or integrity.[6] Keep in mind, the power of this theory is that it demonstrates it is theoretically possible to find the perfect undefeatable position in a multipositioning game between two candidates. Nevertheless, finding out what that position is is a process of trial and error and a great deal of work for political consultants. In many cases, rather than trying to find the perfect position, consultants suggest to their candidates that they avoid getting into specifics about how they will solve issues and instead allow other factors such as looks, personality, or longevity in office to fill in the blanks for the voter's policy doubts.

Directional Versus Proximity

When consultants advise their candidates how to stand on certain issues, how do they envision that stance affecting the voters they want to target during the campaign? In most political campaigns the goal is to take a public stand on an issue that will excite your base and then gain a certain amount of undecided or swing voters in order to win the election. But if you have to target one group with an issue stance, which do you want, the swing vote or your base? Do consultants see tension between positions chosen to please the base and the swing voter? This fundamental question has a great deal to do with whether consultants' positioning suggestions to their

TABLE 3.1 **Responses to survey question: In general, how much tension do you feel there is in developing a strategy that pleases the base and developing a strategy to win over the swing voter?**

	Party		
	Republican	*Democrat*	**Total**
Survey Option	*N (%)*	*N (%)*	**N (%)**
No tension; these goals are entirely compatible	7 (10.9)	10 (8.3)	17 (9.2)
Little tension; trade-offs exist, but by and large the goals are compatible	23 (35.9)	47 (38.8)	70 (37.8)
Modest tension; clear trade-offs exist, but they are not severe	22 (34.4)	50 (41.3)	72 (38.9)
High tension; strong trade-offs exist	11 (17.2)	14 (11.6)	25 (13.5)
Incompatible; if one pleases the base, one alienates swing voters	1 (1.6)	0 (0.0)	1 (0.5)
Total	64 (100)	121 (100)	185 (100)

Note: N = actual number of responses. (%) = percentage of total.

candidates can be explained by directional or proximity theory. The less tension a consultant sees between pleasing the base and seeking the swing voter, the more likely they are actually using the proximity model in their positioning strategy. If they see a great deal of tension, they are likely operating under more of a directional model for candidate position strategy. For the issue section of the consultant survey I asked Republican and Democratic consultants how they viewed position strategy with an eye to directional and proximity theory[7] (Table 3.1).

When asked how much tension they felt between pleasing their base and the swing voter in general, Republican consultants in this sample were slightly more likely to say they saw more tension than Democratic consultants. Of the Republican respondents, 18.8 percent expressed that it was either very tense or entirely incompatible to develop a strategy that pleases their base and the swing voters, whereas only 11.6 percent of Democratic consultants in the sample felt the same way. However, this survey question asked respondents to think of campaigns in general. Perhaps theoretically, Republicans consider pleasing the base and the swing voter to be more complicated than Democrats, but what happens when we ask them about their own unique campaigns? It is perfectly possible that in the abstract the concept is more difficult than what consultants and managers actually experience on the ground. Therefore, I

TABLE 3.2 Responses to survey question: Now consider your campaign. How much tension did you feel there was between pleasing the base and winning over the swing voter?

| | Party | | |
Survey Option	Republican N (%)	Democrat N (%)	Total N (%)
No tension; these goals were entirely compatible	7 (11.3)	19 (16.2)	26 (14.5)
Little tension; trade-offs existed, but by and large the goals were compatible	27 (43.5)	46 (39.3)	73 (40.8)
Modest tension; clear trade-offs existed, but they were not severe	16 (25.8)	35 (29.9)	51 (28.5)
High tension; strong trade-offs existed	10 (16.1)	15 (12.8)	25 (14.0)
Incompatible; any effort to please the base alienated swing voters	2 (3.2)	2 (1.7)	4 (2.2)
Total	62 (100)	117 (100)	179 (100)

Note: N = actual number of responses. (%) = percentage of total.

asked the same question but asked consultants to consider their specific campaign in their answers. The results were almost identical (Table 3.2).

The responses of the political consultants in the sample are similar, whether they were talking about their own specific campaigns or campaigns in general. Again Democratic consultants in the sample stated that they saw much less tension in coming up with a position strategy that appeals both to the base and to the swing voter (14.5 percent) than Republicans in the sample (19.3 percent). So in both cases consultants seem to see a slight difference in how they organize their campaign strategies on issues based on party.

Some might argue that the questions were a bit more complicated than needed for political practitioners, that concepts like "tension" between strategy types might be so nuanced that we would not truly capture what consultants felt about issue strategy for the base and the swing voter. To address this I asked our "rough" version of the question, basically asking if the consultants developed strategies targeting the swing voter or the centrist voter. This "rough proxy" question served as a way to determine in part if the previous questions were complicating or confusing the question to consultants. Those consultants who responded that they were more likely to cater to their base in strategy were more likely to have their strategies explained by the proximity model, and those consultants who responded that their strategy

TABLE 3.3 Did you seek your base or the centrist voter by party?

| | Party | |
| | Republican N (%) | Democrat N (%) |
Position		
Seek the centrist voter	21 (42.0)	68 (70.1)
Cater to the base	29 (58.0)	29 (29.9)
Total	50 (100)	97 (100)

Note: N = actual number of responses. (%) = percentage of total.

sought out the centrist voter were more likely to have their strategies explained by the directional model.

When we look at the rough proxy results, the differences in Democratic and Republican issue strategy are both stark and unmistakable (Table 3.3). By very similar margins Democratic consultants in the sample sought out the centrist voter during the campaign (70.1 percent), and Republicans in the sample sought out their base with policy positions (58.0 percent). There are several conclusions and discussions we can draw at this point in our discussion.

First, it seems consistent in the sample that Republicans' and Democrats' policy position stances and the strategies they used to sell them can be explained by the two major positioning strategies in political science. Republican consultants by and large seek out their base and create policies to excite and motivate that base. Democratic managers, on the other hand, focus on and promote those policies that are likely to engage and entice the swing voters. The survey responses did not change when we looked at political practitioners on the local, statewide, or national level, so perhaps the directional and proximity theories are fairly consistent explanations for issue strategy. To see how these theories might play out in the real world, we look at the hard-fought political campaign for governor of South Carolina in 1998.

David Beasley and Jim Hodges: Directional Versus Proximity Versus Climbing the Political Ladder

The gubernatorial election of 1998 in South Carolina should have been a shoe-in for Republican David Beasley. David Plotz, a political writer for *Slate.com*, at the time summed up the race perfectly:

I cannot state this too emphatically: This should not be a race at all. Republicans dominate South Carolina politics demographically and do so even more today than when Beasley was elected in 1994. A Christian conservative in a state where that helps (and a Bruce Willis look-alike in a state where that can't hurt), Beasley seems to have everything going for him. South Carolina is booming. Under him, as he declares in his stump speech, "South Carolina is No. 1 in the nation in job creation. It is No. 1 in the nation in personal income growth. And its unemployment rate is the lowest in its history." Poverty is down, welfare rolls have shrunk by 75 percent, and violent crime has dropped. And Beasley's Democratic opponent, former state legislator Jim Hodges, is little known statewide. (1998)

So how did Beasley end up losing a race that was not only supposed to be a cakewalk but also propel him into being a 2000 presidential hopeful for the Republican Party? It is very easy, and all too common, to try to sum up the events of a long campaign season with one seminal event or theory. However, in this case the directional and proximity models of candidate issue positioning provide some insight into how one set of factors in this race led to Beasley's surprising defeat. We will focus on these factors to illuminate how and why this race transpired the way it did. There were two major policy issues that inspired voter passions in the gubernatorial race in South Carolina that year: the introduction of a state lottery and the positioning of the Confederate flag.

On the lottery issue each candidate initially took the stand that is consonant with the strategies we have discussed thus far. Jim Hodges based his campaign on proposing a statewide lottery where the funds would be used to improve public schools in South Carolina. Generally, Democrats and independents were ambivalent about the lottery itself, but the fact that South Carolina's public schools were consistently ranked fiftieth in the nation made any policy suggestion to improve schools a winner with swing voters. Hodges went so far as to run a series of very successful "Bubba ads." These ads featured a convenience store owner over the border in Georgia who got a lot of his business from South Carolinians driving a couple of miles to buy lottery tickets. He "praised" Governor Beasley for helping make sure that the Georgian lottery put computers in every public school. True to form, Hodges the Democrat sought out the swing voters.

Governor Beasley adamantly opposed creating a state lottery and framed the issue as not just public policy but one of morality as well. Refusing to "gamble on children's future," Beasley tapped into the conservative base of the state that disliked the idea of gambling in general and found the mixture of gambling and children to be distasteful at best. Already an opponent of the video poker industry, which thrived in South Carolina, Beasley made his antigambling position even more clear to the public when he refused to even allow a state referendum on the issue of a state lottery. This clear appeal to his base seemed to be working for Beasley initially; even some conservative Democrats came out to support him, which was the norm in South Carolina (Associated Press 1998).

The second issue, the Confederate flag, drove the election in 1998. The controversial symbol of the Old South had flown on the capitol building in Columbia, South Carolina, since the 1960s. Politicians placed the flag there as a defiant symbol against the civil rights movement and integration in general. The issue of whether the flag should have any place in or around the state capitol had already become an issue in Georgia, but it looked to be a pivotal issue in the South Carolina governor's race.

Conservative whites in South Carolina viewed the flag as a symbol of southern heritage and a proud history that should be respected in the state. Many of the state's new residents from the rest of the country and the sizable African American population of the state saw the flag as a relic of a racist and violent past and an anachronistic symbol that helped keep South Carolina's reputation as part of the "Old South." The symbol was not just cultural, however. The NAACP had imposed a boycott on the state that had cost millions of dollars as prominent entertainers and conventions avoided South Carolina until the flag issue was resolved.

Jim Hodges sought the swing voter again, proposing a compromise in the statehouse that would move the flag from the top of the capitol to somewhere else on the capitol grounds. In an interview with *Stateline.org* taken after the election, he laid out his position during the past campaign carefully and pointed out all of the swing groups and middle-of-the-road voters he had hoped to court:

Well, it's a tough problem. I think we have made some progress over the course of the last month. I laid a plan out several weeks ago that enjoyed the support of a substantial number of members of the African-American Caucus, along with Democrats and Republicans in the Senate, and a large number of business and political leaders in South Carolina. I think it's a good plan, it meets the concerns that were raised in the original resolutions by a number of groups, including the NAACP. But it also continues to place the flag in a historically appropriate place on our (Capitol) grounds. ("On the Record" 2000)

Beasley, following proper Republican strategy, chose to support the flag. He consistently said that the flag should remain on the top of the capitol building throughout much of his term in office, and his conservative base warmly appreciated it.

So far it would seem that everyone was following the proper plan, the Democrat seeking the centrist voter, not seeing much tension between the base and the swing voter, and the Republican candidate seeking out the base, which makes sense in a state that leans heavily Republican. So how did Beasley lose? One reason is that he did not follow the right position strategy. David Beasley, perhaps thinking past his own reelection and more to the national stage, made the awful strategic misstep of changing his position on important issues.[8] First, his hard stance on the lottery turned out to anger not so much his base but actually one of the more important business segments in his state as a whole. The $2.5 billion video poker industry in the state gave millions of dollars to the Hodges campaign and supported a very popular "Ban Beasley" series of billboards and ads. The implications of his stance on the issue resounded on the national political stage. The Republican governors' association that was strongly allied and received millions of dollars in contributions from the gambling industry dropped a plan to spend $500,000 on ads to help Beasley. In attempting to please his base, Beasley ignored the fact that more than 60 percent of state voters favored the lottery, and what's more voters cared more about education than the lottery. He took a strong stand on the wrong issue to please a base that he would have carried regardless. Eventually, on the eve of the final debate between Beasley and Hodges, he switched positions and agreed to support a referendum on the issue, a reversal of more than four years of stated policy positions. His base was furious, the swing voter was not moved, and Beasley looked weak on all sides. It might have been too early to be dubbed a "flip-flop," but it sealed Beasley's fate.

The same can be said for the Confederate flag issue. The two sides that felt strongly about the issue would not be happy with any form of compromise: Black and liberal voters wanted the flag gone, moderate voters wanted the issue resolved, and conservative voters were apoplectic about any changes at all. Realizing that on the national stage an issue like the Confederate flag would bury him, Beasley changed his position on the issue in 1996. Appearing on ABC's *Nightline*, an appropriate springboard for a governor seeking the national stage, Beasley claimed that God had come to him in a dream and told him to remove the flag from the top of the capitol. The base was incensed. Conservatives felt betrayed. Even when Beasley attempted to change his position again, the damage was done. Changing one's public position on cultural issues is often the death knell in politics. A scathing editorial published by an Augusta, Georgia, newspaper right after the first flip-flop foretold Beasley's future: "Having campaigned as a 'read my lips' supporter of the Confederate flag, he opens himself to the kind of charges that ultimately brought down George Bush's presidency. When will conservatives learn that appeasement never wins them new friends on the Left? It only loses them friends on the Right" (*Augusta Chronicle* Editorial Staff 1996).

The eventual result? Jim Hodges beat Beasley 53 percent to 45 percent in the election, carrying independents and his base by a wider margin than Beasley carried his own base. He faithfully followed the proximity model the whole time and sought the swing voter, while the Republican candidate consistently sought his base. Hodges also chose to prime the voters toward those issues that would be to his benefit rather than those that would benefit Beasley in a statewide election. The problem ultimately was that when Beasley attempted to expand from his base, he not only alienated it but also took strong stands on issues that ultimately ruined his chances for success. This analysis would suggest that had Beasley taken a softer stand on the lottery early in the campaign, it likely would not have become the lightning rod that it did and moreover led to the financial support that took his opposition over the top.

Directional and Proximity Theory over Time

A major theme in this book is that campaign strategy and consultant behavior are dictated as much by the conditions on the ground as any sort of universal theory. So this begs a question. Having analyzed directional and proximity theory in action, and seen an example of how the Beasley and Hodges campaign played out, have we seen a universal lesson or a situational event? More specifically, Republican political operatives' strategies for issue positions seem to be better explained by directional theory, and Democratic political operatives' strategies seem to be better explained by the proximity model. The question is, do these tendencies hold over time? Could Beasley have tried the same strategy in 2004 and been successful when he was not in 1998? And even more generally, is the issue really about directional or proximity theory or perhaps simply who is in the White House? To examine this question we will look back at an older set of data on political consultants and compare it with the results used as the primary basis for this analysis.[9]

Researching the Old School

The survey of political consultants that is the backbone of this analysis is primarily composed of campaigns and consultants who have worked in the 2008 to 2009 election cycles. Consequently, they were operating under unique national circumstances that may have impacted how they viewed directional or proximity theory in campaign position taking. Nationally, Democrats retook the House of Representatives in the 2006 election and then in 2008 won the White House and expanded their leads in Congress. When we combined all of the years that consultants reported running campaigns in this survey, about 75 percent of them ran campaigns under a Democratic administration, with the vast majority of the respondents reporting on campaigns that they ran in the 2008 election year and the 2009 off-year elections. It is under these conditions that we acquired the results above: Democrats are concerned with the centrist voter, Republicans cater to their base, and Democrats experience a little less tension between catering to their base and pleasing the centrist voter than Republicans. But what happens if we take a look at consultants who ran campaigns under different circumstances, perhaps when the nation had mostly Republicans in power nationally and in the White House?[10]

To do this I examined previous consultant survey data and discovered some interesting results.[11] In the previous data set conducted primarily in 2006 and 2007, more than 90 percent of the survey respondents wrote about

TABLE 3.4 Consultant response to general amount of tension between pleasing the base and winning over the swing voter by party and time period

Republican N (%)		Democrat N (%)	
2006–2007	2008–2009	2006–2007	2008–2009
High tension to incompatible	High tension to incompatible	High tension to incompatible	High tension to incompatible
10 (11.9)	12 (18.6)	22 (16.0)	14 (11.6)

Note: N = actual number of responses. (%) = percentage of total.

campaigns that took place under a Republican administration (George W. Bush). When we compare directional and proximity responses for Democrats and Republicans during these eras, the results demonstrate a slight trend.

As you can see, when responding about the general campaign environment, there appears to be a marked difference in the reactions of Republicans and Democrats in our sample under the final few years of the Bush administration and the first years of the Obama administration. The number of Republicans expressing high tension to incompatibility between satisfying the two constituencies almost doubled from the 2006–2007 survey to the 2008–2009 survey. At the same time, there was a precipitous drop in the number of managers for Democratic candidates who saw tension between pleasing the base and seeking the centrist voter. What might this mean, given the relatively close proximities of the two survey cycles? Perhaps the level of tension felt by consultants is related to their perceived power and thus responsibility to the voters. Consider that only about 10 percent of Republicans and Democrats reported high tension when they were the ruling party in the White House and at least one house of Congress (2006 and 2008, respectively). However, when you are the "out party," in many cases your base becomes more radicalized, and pleasing them becomes more difficult. The Tea Party movement in the past two years is a clear example of this. Tea Party groups, whether they are the Tea Party Patriots, Express, or local organizations, consist of disaffected Republicans and right-leaning independents who, disgusted with the bailouts late in the Bush term and Obama's spending policies in early 2009, formed these organizations. The base of the Republican Party, having long been catered to, chose to strike out on its own rather than continue to feel abandoned by the mainstream party.[12]

TABLE 3.5 Amount of tension between pleasing the base and winning over the swing voter by party and time period in your campaign

Republican N (%)		Democrat N (%)	
2006–2007	2008–2009	2006–2007	2008–2009
High tension to incompatible	High tension to incompatible	High tension to incompatible	High tension to incompatible
8 (9.5)	12 (19.3)	16 (11.6)	17 (14.5)

Note: N = actual number of responses. (%) = percentage of total.

When asked to discuss their own specific campaigns in regards to tension over time, the responses from consultants were a bit more muted (Table 3.5).

When asked to express how much directional tension they felt in their individual campaigns, the trends for Republicans and Democrats in the samples were the same, though to different degrees. Both Republican and Democratic consultants felt that they faced more tension between the base in the swing voter in the 2008 sample compared to the 2006 sample, but the degree of increased tension varied. For the GOP the amount of tension more than doubled, which explains the rise and political influence of the Tea Party movement in America. There is an increase in Democratic tension in their specific campaigns as well, but this suggests an entirely different phenomenon. Moving from the party on the outside looking in to being the party that controls the White House and both houses of Congress brings with it a new type of responsibility and frustration on the part of voters in a constituency. When Democrats came into power under Barack Obama, their long-suffering base had expectations that the party would deliver on long-promised but seldom-delivered policy goals, such as universal health care, ending the wars in Iraq and Afghanistan, and a host of other issues, again demonstrating the fundamentally different approaches and strategies needed to appeal to each party based on consultant beliefs.

I performed one more test on the directional and proximity theories with the rough proxy question to see if the Republican and Democratic consultant views stayed consistent over time. I compared the basic "cater to your base or seek the centrist voter" question across the two surveys as well.

Table 3.6 shows the surprising stability of the consultant responses over time on the most basic of questions about political position strategy. Repub-

TABLE 3.6 Did you seek your base or the centrist voter by party and year?

| | Party | | | |
Position	Republican N (%)		Democrat N (%)	
	2006–2007	2008–2009	2006–2007	2008–2009
Seek the centrist voter	24 (38.1%)	21 (42.0%)	65 (61.3%)	68 (70.0%)
Cater to the base	39 (61.9%)	29 (58.0%)	41 (38.7%)	29 (29.9%)
Total	63 (100%)	50 (100)	106 (100%)	97 (100%)

Note: N = actual number of responses. (%) = percentage of total.

lican consultants barely moved, expressing that they primarily catered to their base in their candidate campaign positions, dipping a mere 4 percent, from 61.9 percent in 2006 to 58 percent in 2008. Democrats changed more noticeably in the survey, but with results going in their general strategic direction. They catered to the centrist voter even more in their 2008–2009 responses, increasing by 10 percent over the previous survey and dropping by an equal amount in seeking their base. In the short term, what this likely means is that while Democrats eat further and further into the political center in order to expand their campaign opportunities, Republicans remain steadfastly focused on turning out their base, even if that base had been dwindling in voting strength since the 2006 midterm elections.

The Campaign Environment and Directional and Proximity Theories

Although the theories above may give us an idea as to how to explain some consultant theory, the fact remains that the final piece of the campaign issue puzzle is all about the campaign environment. While the environment can be rocked by something as unpredictable as a six-year-old boy coming out of the ocean, it can just as easily be influenced by partisan identification in the district, winning or losing, or a whole host of other campaign-specific events. For that reason I performed a regression analysis with the consultant results on directional and proximity theory. Using a series of district and campaign environmental factors I attempted to discern if they had an impact on whether campaign consultants were more likely to engage in strategic behavior explainable through the directional or proximity model.

TABLE 3.7 Significant predictors by which issue position strategy consultants are most likely to use: Cater to base or seek centrist voter

Model	Significant predictor	Interpretation: More likely to use this position strategy if
Cater to your base (directional proxy)	Party preference in district	Democratic-leaning district
Seek the centrist voter (proximity proxy)	Party identification	you are a Democrat

I used the following variables: Party identification; Type of election; Executive or legislative race; Federal or state; Won or lost; On or off year; Election before 9/11; Poll midway; Urban or rural campaign; Minority percentage; Education level, District income; Party preference in the district; and Your candidate's race and sex.

When we include the various elements that create a campaign environment and control for other factors, we see that, again, partisanship comes into play for issue positioning (Table 3.7). When we control for other variables, consultants running in Democratic-leaning districts are more likely to cater to their base with issue positions than those running in Republican-leaning districts. When we consider our previous question of issue ownership, this result sheds even more light on the complexities of district preferences that campaign managers face.

At first glance, these results seem contradictory. On the one hand, consultants in Democratic-leaning districts cater to their base even when controlling for party identification. On the other hand, consultants for Democratic candidates seek to find the centrist voter with their position stands even when controlling for district-party preference. Actually, the two results are congruent with each other if you think like a campaign manager instead of a theorist. Imagine that you are a Democratic consultant; in general, you seek out the centrist voter, taking most other options into consideration. As a Republican consultant, you tell your candidate to position himself or herself with the base, all things considered. But what happens when the district has a strong party preference? Well, for a Republican it does not make a difference because you are going to stick with your base, win or lose, because that is how you tend to campaign, but a Democrat might actually choose to look at seeking their base if he or she is in a heavily Democratic district. So in

TABLE 3.8 **Significant predictors by directional or proximity model within your campaign logistic regression analysis**

Model	Significant predictor	Interpretation: More likely to use this position strategy if
Little or no tension between pleasing the base and seeking the centrist voter	Win or lose	winners say less tension between the two
	Education level in district	the more educated the district, the less tension between the two
Moderate tension to incompatible to cater to the base and seek the centrist voter	None	None

TABLE 3.9 **Significant predictors by directional or proximity model in general logistic regression analysis**

Model	Significant predictor	Interpretation: More likely to use this position strategy if
Little or no tension between pleasing the base and seeking the centrist voter	Win or lose	winners say less tension between the two
Moderate tension to incompatible to cater to the base and seek the centrist voter	On or off-year election	it is a presidential election year

general, as the second model demonstrates, Democrats are going for the median voter with "Don't Ask, Don't Tell" policies and speaking out against "partial birth abortion" but not abortion in general, no matter what. But in the instances when they are in their home districts, they will seek out the base, since that is the one area where they can rely on turnout and voter attention to stay consistent until election day. When we look at the full directional-versus-proximity models we see the trend continue.

Two points stand out when you look at the logistic regressions for policy strategy both within consultants' campaigns and in general (Tables 3.8 and 3.9). Consultants who do not find a lot of tension between catering to their base and seeking the center are more likely to win their campaigns than those who see a great deal of tension. Does that mean the directional model works better for position strategy? Not necessarily, but it might mean that you have to pick and choose very carefully which issues you will take hard public positions on.

We also see that the district plays a role in that level of tension as well. Consultants in districts where the voters were more educated stated that it was a bit easier to thread that needle of policy issue stances than those in less-educated districts. Consider John Kerry's infamous "I voted for the 87 billion before I voted against it." This statement does not sound good to most voters, but a sophisticated and educated constituency might understand the nuances behind it. The infamous quote used by Bush was right on the money: Kerry did vote for and against the $87 billion for the war in Iraq but under completely different circumstances. What was on the table was $87 billion in emergency funding for troops and reconstruction in Afghanistan and Iraq. Bush wanted senators to simply vote the money up or down; an alternative bill was proposed that would have granted the $87 billion for the war effort under the condition that Bush's tax cuts would be repealed. The alternative policy that Kerry voted for failed fifty-seven to forty-two. So when the vote for President Bush's unconditional use of $87 billion came up, John Kerry along with twelve other Democratic senators voted against the bill, even though it passed. Now, is John Kerry still a flip-flopper, incapable of taking the tough policy stands and making the tough decisions one needs to as president? That was for the voters to decide, but the intricate policy scenario was one that only politically aware, educated, or sophisticated voters might have been able to comprehend, let alone consider when looking at the candidate's policy stances. In general, consultants believed that at least in their own campaigns, the smarter the voters, the more nuanced policy positions and arguments they could make.

Finally, whether it applied to their campaigns or not, in general consultants felt that there was a lot more tension between pleasing the base and seeking the center when running during a presidential election year. This is because, generally, when a presidential election is going on, it is very difficult to set your own local policy agenda. The nominees for your party are setting the agenda in the press, which trickles down to even local races, and suddenly while you want to run on a policy of increasing farm subsidies in rural Iowa, you are answering questions about gay marriage and homeland security because of the previous night's presidential debates. If your candidate is in agreement with the policy positions of your party's nominee, this works to your advantage, but depending on your district's leanings, your own position stances, and other factors, this might cause complications. Examples of this have been seen in most midterm elections in the United States. During a presidential election year a candidate is obligated in most cases to follow the party leader on major policy issues, no matter the cost. During midterm elections, congressional candidates in particular often experience the tension of running with the president's national agenda or running on local issues, depending on which one is more likely to please the constituency.

In our previous case study, the roles of issue ownership and to a lesser extent priming were intentionally downplayed in order to highlight the potential explanatory power of the directional and proximity models for consultant strategy behavior. But now let's return to the concept of issue ownership and see what ways, if any, that we can determine if current theory explains or is in concert with the beliefs of political operatives in the sample.

Issue ownership studies thus far are based almost exclusively on the opinions of voters. Voters are asked in surveys or in focus groups which parties they believe are the most concerned with and the most effective at solving or mitigating certain problems. What do political operatives think about issue ownership? Clearly, as organized partisans they would believe that their candidate or by extension party has an effective plan for any political problem, but as we discussed earlier in this chapter, consultants consider issue ownership when advising candidates about what positions they should focus on during the campaign. We have also seen in the case-study examples that movement on critical issues during a campaign can have negative electoral consequences. Combining these two ideas, I developed a series of questions for consultants in the sample to assess the theory of issue ownership. First, I examined if shifting position on policy issues is common in a campaign, according to the political operatives. Then I asked them if there were particular issues that they viewed as being more problematic to shift on than others. The assumption was that in the minds of political managers, changing positions during a campaign should be exceedingly rare, and in particular, the more problematic a consultant viewed changing positions, the more likely it was they considered that issue to be "owned" by their party.

Throughout the sample you can see that the vast majority of political operatives reported that their candidate did not shift on any policy issues

TABLE 3.10 **If your candidate adjusted policy positions during the campaign, which of these policy areas did they shift positions on?**

Policy-area shift	Frequency	Percentage
Foreign policy	4	2.4
Education policy	3	1.8
Jobs	9	5.4
Taxes	7	4.2
Social/cultural issues	18	10.8
No position changes	126	75.4
Total	167	100

TABLE 3.11 **What were the main reasons your candidate shifted on issues?**

Reason	Frequency	Percentage
Presented with new information that changed our position	19	11.4
The opposition took a new position, and we changed to counter it	8	4.8
Our stance was unpopular and hurting us in the polls	19	11.4
My candidate did not shift on any issues	121	72.5
Total	167	100

(Table 3.10). While generally more than 70 percent of respondents said that their candidate did not change positions on any issues, in the few instances where positions did change, the trend falls into three areas. Consultants usually admitted that their candidates moved slightly to the right on issues, or moved only when their stance was killing them in the polls or new information forced them to change (Table 3.11). These were rare instances overall, however, which helps us to establish within this sample the rarity of issue changes.

With the rarity of issue-position changes established, we now take a look at specific issues that different political parties are said to "own" according to existing research. I used foreign policy, taxes, social and cultural issues, education, and jobs as the policy areas. I then performed a regression analysis wherein I attempted to discover what factors in the campaign environment or within the candidate himself or herself influenced how problematic political consultants found it to change positions on certain issues (Abbe and Hernnson 2003; Druckman, Jacobs, and Ostermeier 2004).

I used the following variables: Party identification; Type of election; Executive or legislative race; Federal or state; Won or lost; On or off year; Election

TABLE 3.12 **Direction of policy-stance adjustment**

Policy-stance adjustment	Frequency	Percentage
Moved far left	1	0.6
Moved slightly left	6	3.6
Stayed the same throughout the race	134	80.2
Moved slightly right	25	15.0
Moved far right	1	0.6
Total	167	100

before 9/11; Poll midway; Urban or rural campaign; Minority percentage; Education level; District income; Party preference in the district; and Your candidate's race and sex.

Table 3.13 establishes what policy areas consultants considered "owned" by a particular party. The first column on the left is the policy-issue area. The second column shows the characteristics or variables in the district that had an impact on how the consultant felt about that particular policy area. The final column on the right shows how the absence or presence of that variable impacted consultant feelings on changing positions on that policy issue.

The most consistent variable and result from the analysis is that consultants for Republican candidates were much more likely to see it as more problematic to change positions on issues than consultants for Democratic candidates. Although it is not surprising Republican consultants saw it as problematic to move on issues that they "own," such as taxes and foreign policy, education (a typically Democratic issue) and the economy (an issue that fluctuates in ownership between the parties) were still seen as problematic. What might this tell us about the Republican consultants in our sample? First, perhaps ideological consistency or even stubbornness are viewed as positives by Republicans, and compromise and flexibility on policy are viewed more favorably by Democrats. If you remember in our previous chapter on candidates, it was Republican consultants who often cited "position on issues" as the strength for their candidates. Further, most polls show that Republican voters are much less in favor of political compromise on policy than Democratic voters. In a Gallup Poll taken right after the Republican sweep in the 2010 midterm elections, when asked about "the best approach for leaders to follow in Washington," 41 percent of Republicans

TABLE 3.13 **Significant predictors by difficulty of changing policy stances model from logistic regression analyses**

Model	Significant predictor	Interpretation: Very problematic to change policy if
Foreign policy	Party identification	Republican candidate
	Minority percentage	large-minority population
	District income	lower-income district
	Party-preference district	Republican-leaning district
Taxes	Party identification	Republican candidate
	Party-preference district	Republican-leaning district
Social/cultural issues	Open-seat election	you're in an open-seat election
	Win or lose	you won your campaign
	Minority percentage	higher minority percentage
	Race of your candidate	your candidate is white (instead of black)
Education	Party identification	you are a Republican
	Federal or state election	state-level election
	Minority percentage in district	higher minority percentage
Jobs	Party identification	you are a Republican

responded, "It is more important for political leaders to stick to their beliefs even if little gets done," compared to only 18 percent of Democratic voters holding the same belief (Kilstein 2010). It is also worth noting that whereas Republican consultants appeared to see position change as more problematic than their Democratic counterparts, this research does reinforce existing results on issue ownership. Consultants viewed campaigning in a Republican-leaning district, regardless of party, as more problematic if the candidate changed positions on foreign policy and taxes.

On the other side, being a consultant for a Democratic candidate did not have an impact on how consultants in the sample felt about changing positions on key issues, but perhaps we did see some impact through other variables. Democrats are much more likely to represent districts that have higher minority populations, be they African American, Latino, or even Asian in most parts of the nation, and the size of the minority population in the district influenced consultant attitudes on issue change on foreign policy, social and cultural issues, and education. In terms of foreign policy, these results may be an indicator of certain trends in the African American and Latino communities regarding the armed forces. The war in Iraq is extremely unpopular with African Americans, and that conviction combined with the unpopularity of George Bush have led to a record drop in African American recruitment to the armed forces since 9/11 (Asch, Heaton, and Savych 2009; Williams and Baron 2007). During this same period, however, there has been a marked increase in the number of Hispanic recruits. Perhaps the sensitivity of the wars in the Middle East and their perceived disparate impact on minority communities account for this result.

The other areas where having a larger minority population influenced how likely consultants were to say that moving on policy issues was problematic, social and cultural issues as well as education, are all in some respects "owned" or "leased" by the Democratic Party. Democrats are viewed as being the more successful party in dealing with intergroup relations as well as education, and social and cultural issues like language integration, school diversity, and the like are more important in districts with large minority populations than those with small minority populations. It should be noted, however, that these results, like others in this book, may be influenced by the interpretations and self-reporting of the respondents in the sample. Social and cultural issues, for example, could mean anything from family values, an area in which Republican strategists may believe they have a lead, to immigration and school integration issues, in which Democratic strategists may believe they have a comparative advantage. What's more, these results can be considered both time bound and generalizable. Although there appears to be a confirmation that existing issue-ownership theories are consonant with how campaign managers in the sample view their own parties and candidates, one has to accept the other theoretical tenet—that "leased" issues change over time. Depending on the progress of the war in Iraq or the economy, it is possible that survey results in a future analysis could change.

Conclusion

When a candidate is running for office, they often seek out a political consultant to help them figure out exactly what issues are important to the voters and how best to present their views on that issue to win a campaign. This is a challenging process, and in some cases the campaign can successfully make the case about their policies, and sometimes it cannot.

In this chapter we learned that political consultants look at a variety of factors when coming up with a campaign strategy for policy. They have to consider what issues are "owned" by their party, what issues the voters care about, and what issues they are going to "prime" voters to pay attention to. On top of that, they have to figure out if they are targeting the centrist or swing voter with their policy stances and how much or how intensely they will take a stand on whatever issues come into play during the campaign. Our results show that some issues really are "owned" by Republicans and Democrats, according to consultants in our survey sample. Republican consultants are much more anxious about coming up with ways to please the base and attract swing voters, and they feel less flexible in changing positions on most issues they seem to "own," such as foreign policy and taxes. Democrats, on the other hand, usually try to target swing voters in their policy-position strategy, and while perhaps education and cultural issues are very important to their base, they will consider altering their positions on policy if that is what it takes to win or get policy through.

We also saw in the cases of John Kerry's presidential bid in 2004 and the South Carolina governor's race in 1998 that it is very important for candidates and their campaign teams to choose wisely which issues will be the focus of their campaigns. If and when they feel forced to change positions, either through changing circumstances on the ground, new information, or polls, the smart consultant has to prepare their candidate for potential backlash. The perception that a position change was made lightly or just to pander to the voters might get your candidate labeled a "flip-flopper," and that might end your race long before election day.

4

The Negative Ad

There are very few areas in political science campaign work that elicit more research, more discussion, and more analysis than negative advertising. Unlike candidate analysis, messaging, or even issue positions, negative advertising is one of the areas in political science that receives almost equal attention from the voters, the press, and academics. Why? Not everyone understands issues, or policy, or the complexities of government, but everybody understands it when someone else is getting slammed on national television. Negative advertising is primal, exciting, and one of the reasons so much time and money are raised and spent on television during campaigns. The truth, however, is that those same intense, negative mudslinging ads might also be one of the more problematic parts of political campaigners' behavior and American politics in general.

In this chapter we will discuss the state of negative advertising research in political science and how this work may or may not capture what is happening in the minds of political professionals. Then we will examine the existing theories about how, when, and why negative ads are used with the input of political professionals from the sample. Finally, we will take a look at the content of political ads and see exactly what campaigners are putting on the airwaves and why it matters.

Political Science Goes Negative

Political advertising, specifically negative advertising, is really an extension of messaging strategy with more focus on the opponent and their policies.

As we learned in Chapters 2 and 3, messages are used to explain why a candidate is running for office, what they stand for policywise or personally, and why you should not vote for the other person. Sometimes, however, just saying why a voter should choose one candidate and not the other is not quite strong enough; a candidate needs to hammer the point home even more intensely. That is where negative advertising arrives. In political science, the study of negative advertising often focuses on two areas of research, the implementation[1] and the effect.[2] Implementation work looks at when, how, and why campaigns tend to go negative, based on where the candidate is, the race they are running, or other factors. Studies of negative advertising on "effects" look at what supposedly happens to voters who are exposed to negative ads. There are a few main drivers of negative advertising behavior that are worth pointing out at the beginning of this discussion.

Implementation

Position in Polls

Not surprisingly, most research shows that polls are a major driver of negative advertising strategy by campaign operatives. Candidates trailing in the polls attack a lot more than candidates who are ahead (assuming trailing candidates have the money to do so) (Skaperdas and Grofman 1995; Sigelman and Shiraev 2002; West 2005; Peterson and Djupe 2005). Of course, this tendency interacts with several other factors. For example, if the candidate trails by only a small margin, that candidate will attack more so than a candidate behind by large margins. Consequently, challengers will lob attack ads when they fall behind more than incumbents if an incumbent begins to falter (Haynes and Rhine 1998; Damore 2002; Hale, Fox, and Farmer 1996; Lau and Pomper 2002; West 2005; Peterson and Djupe 2005).

Party

Scholars have shown that the partisan identification of the candidate as well as their district leanings influence negative advertising strategy as well. Some researchers have shown that Republicans are much more likely to launch attack ads than Democrats, even when they have less money to spend, and regardless of whether they are incumbents, challengers, or in open-seat races (Theilmann and Wilhite 1998; Lemert, Wanta, and Lee

1999; Benoit 2004). Kahn and Kenney's book *The Spectacle of U.S. Senate Campaigns* (1999), however, shows that when they attack, Republicans are much more likely to use issue attacks. In addition, Theilmann and Wilhite find that Republican consultants and voters are much more accepting of negative advertising in general (1998, 1050). Damore did not find much of a partisan leaning in attack behavior and saw that both parties attacked based on a situational basis (2002, 670). Partisanship appears to have two roles in negative advertising strategy: an inherent partisan motivation that leads Republicans to be more aggressive than Democrats and the voters' party identification and beliefs (Ansolabehere and Iyengar 1994; Johnson-Cartee and Copeland 1997).

Type of Race: Open Seat, Incumbent, or Challenger

Conventional wisdom and political science say that the type of campaign a candidate runs impacts their negative advertising strategy (Haynes and Rhine 1998; Damore 2002; Johnson-Cartee and Copeland 1997; Peterson and Djupe 2005). Challengers attack more because they have to stake out a claim in a new campaign environment (Hale, Fox, and Farmer 1996; Hughes 2003; Lau and Pomper 2004). Some have argued that the most volatile races, however, are open-seat contests. The reason is that both candidates are trying to get the attention of the public and usually a public that is not all that interested in the campaign itself (Lau and Pomper 2002, 2004; Walker and Seacrest 2002; Beiler 2002). Finally, we find that incumbents' relationship with negative advertising is a mixed one in most political science literature. Incumbents are the least likely to attack in most political campaigns. In fact, when an incumbent goes on the attack, most voters see it is a sign of weakness in the campaign. Further, incumbents seem to be the most immune to attack advertising, seldom responding to attacks by the challenger unless they see significant slippage in the polls (Damore 2002; Sigelman and Shiraev 2002). West (2005) notes that researchers suggest that candidate position does not have much of an impact on whether and how someone uses attack advertising at all, but that view has generally been the minority.

Gender

Dittmar conducted interviews with political consultants and discovered that many of them were more worried or hesitant to run attack ads against women (2010, 18). Several researchers have found that women are less likely to attack, or at least less likely to attack an opponent's character, than are male candidates (Kahn 1993; Fox 1997; Herrnson and Lucas 2006). Women hold back, despite the fact that Dinzes et al. conducted research that showed crossing the gender barrier actually made negativity more effective. By and large, however, most research does not show a consistent relationship between going negative and gender for either candidate (Lau and Pomper 2001, 2004; Benoit 2007; Dinzes, Cozzens, and Manross 1994).

Das Effects?

Studies of negative advertising on "effects" look at what supposedly happens to voters who are exposed to negative ads. Many argue that negative advertising depresses the turnout of voters, while others say the impact depends on who is listening (Ansolabehere and Iyengar 1994; Stevens 2005; Iyengar 2006; Kolodny, Thurber, and Dulio 2000; Bailey and Faucheux 2000). The most famous detractors of negative advertising, Ansolabehere and Iyengar, argue that "negative advertising depresses turnout amongst voters by clogging the airwaves with attacks that turn people off and frustrate the public" (1994, 350). They are backed up by numerous political pundits and observers who pop up every election season to decry negative advertising. On the other hand, political consultants usually defend the use of such ads, since from their perspective they are necessary to get the message out. Political scientists in recent years seem to have backed up the practitioners, whether they realize it or not. Goldstein and Freedman (2002, 721) found that negative ads actually stimulated turnout in campaigns, whereas Wattenberg and Brians discovered that negative advertising actually made most voters more informed (1999, 891). Furthermore, Geer (2006) reported that not only do negative ads inform and stimulate the voter, but they do so much better than positive ads.

One of the reasons that negative advertising research can engender such fierce debate is that actual political practitioners are seldom included in negative advertising studies. Many political scientists assess campaign negativity through content analysis or coding of ads (Kaid and Holtz-Bacha 2006; Wattenberg and Brians 1999; Goldstein and Freedman 2002; Lau and Pomper 2001). College students or adults gather in a room to look at ads and then tell researchers what they do or do not think is negative. Ads themselves are sometimes coded based on what researchers think are "negative" words, which is how we learn about negative advertising. The few negative advertising studies that include political practitioners in the results are often much more nuanced and proscriptive, since the creators and implementers of the ads themselves are involved (Theilmann and Wilhite 1998; Grossmann 2009).

The other major complication in negative advertising research is that the majority of political science literature fails to provide any actual definition of negative advertising at all. Most political scientists acknowledge this deficiency and then attempt to create their own definitions. Niven exemplified this conceit in his discussion of the impact that negative advertising has on turnout: "While there is no consensus definition of negative advertising most researchers start with the notion that negativity involves the invoking of an opponent by a candidate . . . that is a negative ad suggests the opponent should not be elected rather than the sponsoring candidate should be elected" (2006, 203). Overall, however, political science literature seldom systematically addresses the actual lack of a definition for negative advertising. After acknowledging the lack of a functional negative advertising definition, and then providing one, Mayer blamed practitioners for the current state of ambiguity: "Not surprisingly, most journalists and political practitioners do not define the term (negative advertising) explicitly, but the above definition clearly fits the way that they use the term in their speeches and writings" (1996, 440).

Some of the most seminal works in negative advertising research do not contain actual definitions of negative advertising but simply continue with the research as if the definition is a given or come up with a definition "on the fly" (Geer 2006; Theilmann and Wilhite 1998; Schultz and Pancer 1997). Of the few political scientists who have offered their own definitions of negative or attack advertising, there is little or no consistency in their definitions, ranging from the very general to more specific (see Table 4.1) (West 2005; Skaperdas and Grofman 1995; Stevens 2005; Mayer 1996; Hale, Fox, and Farmer 1996; Damore 2002). As we can see from the table, there is a fairly wide range in academe about what actually constitutes a negative advertisement. Some suggest that it is about personal attacks; others define negative ads as anything that is actually "negative" at all, which is complicated, since in the minds of consultants, if they cannot criticize the competition, then how can they actually prove to voters they deserve the job?

TABLE 4.1 **Definitions of negative advertising**

Author	Definition
West 2005, 169	"Substantive manipulation, whereby leaders deceive citizens about policy matters."
Skaperdas and Grofman 1995, 49	"Adapting terminology from Surlin and Gordon, we use the term negative campaigning to refer generally to that which 'attacks the other candidate personally, the issues for which the other candidate stands, or the party of the other candidate.'"
Stevens 2005, 413	"Talking about the opponent—his or her programs, accomplishments, qualification, associates, and so on—with the focus, usually, on the defects of these attributes."
Mayer 1996, 440	"Most people who use the term seem to have in mind a definition such as the following: Negative campaigning is campaigning that attacks or is critical of an opposing candidate."
Haynes and Rhine 1998, 695	"We define 'attack' politics as a candidate's strategic use of intermediated anti-rival statements. The purpose of using such negative messages is to weaken support for and thus eliminate the targeted rival."
Lau and Pomper 2002, 48	"Negative campaigning is talking about the opponent—his or her programs, accomplishments, qualifications, associates and so on, with the focus, usually, on the defects of these attributes."

To find out how to define negative advertising specifically, one must use the language of the men and women in the field creating and presenting these messages. Whereas Lau and Pomper (2002) contend that negative advertising is in the eye of the beholder, political consultants draw a distinction between types of attack ads in a way that academics may or may not recognize (Nelson, Dulio, and Medvic 2002; Alvarez and Hall 2004). I took this question of negative advertising to the political practitioners in the study and found out how they defined this consistent controversy.

Consultants' Definitions of Negative Advertising

The survey asked consultants "What is your definition of negative advertising?" in an open-ended question, to allow as much expression as possible in the responses. It is important to note that this question was optional on the survey, which would likely lead only those respondents who felt knowledgeable or passionate about the question to respond.[3] From the beginning a few key themes stood out. The first was the distinction between "attack" and "negative" advertising, the second a distinction between "contrast" and "attack" advertising, and finally some divergence among consultants about what actually constituted a "personal or character" attack. Beyond these content themes, there were no differences in consultant attitudes based on political party, federal or state races, region of the country, or even the demographics of the candidate. Even more surprising was the similarity of these themes for the level of the campaign: Everyone from managers for local school board representative to presidential consultants seemed clear on what they thought negative advertising meant, even if they could not put their finger on the definition. For example:

- "You know it when you see it." (manager for female incumbent in state legislature in the West)
- "It's like pornography, I'm not sure, but I know it when I see it." (manager for male open-seat state legislature candidate in the Pacific Northwest)

The distinction between "attack" advertising and "negative" advertising is one that is not often specifically stated in the political science literature but was replete in the responses from the consultants. Consultants in the survey made a distinction between the two types of ads, although the distinction often fell on the same definition. For example:

- "Ads that emphasize negative attributes about one's opponent. I would not, however, characterize these as 'attack' ads, which stand on their own, attacking the personal character of a candidate." (media consultant for incumbent federal senator in the Northeast)
- "Negative advertising exists on two planes. The first is ads which point out negative aspects of your opponent—his stand on an issue, failure to address an issue, residency, etc. The second is attacks on the opponent's character, often twisting facts or only partially stating the facts to make the opponent appear other than he is." (campaign manager for challenger for federal House seat in the Midwest)

- "Negative advertising is anything that puts your opponent in a bad light. There are effective negative ads—ones that point out discrepancies in your opponent's record—and there are bad negative ads—ones that personally attack the morals, values, and integrity of your opponent. The former negative ads are more effective, but negative personal attack ads can be effective in very heated close contests like the one witnessed in VA between Sen. George Allen and Jim Webb." (campaign manager for open-seat race in state legislature in the South)

These responses are reflective of the general attitude expressed by consultants in the survey. Ads that make the distinction between the personal and the professional were critical in the minds of most consultants. Many referred to unethical ads as "attacks" or "attack ads" and acceptable ads as "negative." Regardless, the notion that there are acceptable and unacceptable types of ads is helpful in finding a possible definition. Most consultants viewed attack advertising as either attacking the personal life and character of a candidate or lying. For example:

- "Attacks on family members. Candidates character and voting record should be examined thoroughly." (manager for male challenger for city council seat in the Southeast)
- "Attack advertising dealing with personal (rather than political) issues. Often distorted or out of context." (media adviser for incumbent county register of deeds candidate in the Northeast)
- "Lies, distortion, smear tactics and fear mongering. Discussing your opponent's voting record or accurately disclosing your opponent's past statements in context is NOT negative campaigning." (manager for challenger for federal Senate in the Northeast)

A campaign can put many things in ads that are demonstrably true but personal in nature about the opposition. Although many campaigners seemed to believe this practice was unfair, there were at least a number who believed sincerely that personal behavior should be a significant part of negative advertising strategy, so long as the words were true. Jordan Lieberman, former publisher of *Campaigns and Elections*, pointed out that one of the most effective ads he had seen in recent years was purely personal and about character. He reported:

The best attack ad I've seen was for Pennsylvania's Tenth Congressional District. Don Sherwood, twelve-year incumbent, safe seat. It was 2006, not the best year for the GOP, [but] even in a bad year he should've won. Except that he was sued by his mistress for choking her. Rather than come clean, he just hid from the story, until ten days before the election, when his opponent Chris Carney ran an ad featuring the woman's dad telling the public he was a Republican but that Sherwood had no place in public life. (Johnson 2010a)[4]

The key here appears to be that as long as the ad is relevant and true, political campaigners will go for it. For example:

- "Negative Advertising is only 'negative' when it is untrue. Otherwise, it's all fair game." (GOTV organizer for incumbent president)
- "If an opponent has committed acts that are immoral or illegal, etc., then bringing that to the attention of voters is justified. Negative attack ads are otherwise immoral and corrupt the system. I would not use such false attacks in order to win votes." (candidate and manager for open-seat race in state legislature in the West)
- "There are two kinds of negative advertising: negative character ads and negative issue ads. Example, assailing an opponent because he slept with a prostitute. That's a negative character advertisement. The other is attacking an opponent because he came down on the unpopular side of a vote. Typically voters have more of a problem with the former than the latter." (GOTV coordinator for Republican federal senator in the Midwest)

It would appear that any other aspect of the candidate is considered fair game, from their past associations to their voting records, but personal attacks that are also untrue were deemed off-limits by just about all consultants.

Finally, consultants were adamant about explaining the difference between attack ads and contrast ads. Contrast ads were generally deemed as fine, no matter how harsh they became, because the ads included both candidates. In fact, when using contrast ads, personal character traits were often mentioned, as candidates attempted to define themselves as having shown more integrity or character throughout their careers. For example:

- "A negative advertisement would be an ad that attacks one's opponent on an issue not related to the election (i.e., candidate hates puppies). This is in contrast to an ad that makes the distinction, possibly in harsh tones, of the differences in the records of the candidates in question." (GOTV director for an open-seat race for state auditor in the Midwest)
- "There are many definitions of negative campaigning. Some would say anything that puts your opponent in an unfavorable light would be negative. I would not call going after your opponent on issues and votes or the way they run their office as negative. Some would disagree. I would say that is comparison. I would say that the only truly negative campaign would be personal attacks on your opponent, which I stay away from. Showing a difference between candidates on issues or how they would run their office is not negative. I would call it comparison. I would also say that I am answering your questions about 'negative' campaigning on what I believe you mean. I would not call the campaigns negative in nature, but more of a comparison campaign." (campaign manager for a challenger for city manager in a midwestern city)

Looking at these responses, we are taken back to our initial challenge of coming up with a more effective definition of negative advertising. First, we clearly have to decouple the terms *negative advertising* and *attack advertising* because they are used interchangeably by most of the public, but they mean entirely different things in the profession. Negative advertising is simply *any message criticizing your opponent, with whatever materials you have, with whatever evidence you have, so long as it is the truth and at least tangentially relevant to the campaign*. But this definition is incomplete without also defining attack advertising: *any messages in political campaigns that are factually untrue and that focus on issues that cannot be readily understood as relevant to the campaign*. Distinguishing between these two types of ads will not only clarify the discussion of campaign advertising in political science, but to the degree that these terms become adopted in our common political and journalistic discourse on campaigns, it will become easier to identify, through surveys, content analysis, or any of the prior methods of ad analysis, what is truly harmfully negative and what is simply a part of campaign politics.

There is understandable doubt about adopting these new definitions of negative advertising, even if they are actually based on consultants' views as opposed to academic opinion or public survey. One could logically question whether distinguishing between "attack" and "negative" ads is a question of convenience created by consultants to justify their activities. However, distinguishing between "negative" and "attack" advertising in public discourse is not an exercise in linguistic gymnastics, but actually a step in the right direction for consultants and commentators alike. Consider the word *steroids*, for example. When many sports commentators say *steroids*, the connotation is almost universally negative and implies wrongdoing on the part of some athlete and trainer. However, within the sports world most trainers are aware that there are many steroids that are legal, common, and part of regular medical care for professional athletes. The same applies for political consultants: *Negative advertising*, like the word *steroids*, has come to embody a whole slew of activities and content to which professionals in the field often do not subscribe. In their world there are differences in these loaded terms, and thus if we are to effectively discuss the concept and the practitioners of ads, we should employ vocabulary that is reflective of their work environment. Political consultants know that "negative" advertising works and that "attack" advertising is usually problematic and can backfire during the campaign, a concept we will address later.

Policy Versus Character

Political advertising regardless of whether it is defined as "negative" or "attack" focuses on one of two targets: the candidate's policies or their character (Benoit 2000, 274). Political scientists and social commentators decry the seeming imbalance in political advertising that focuses more on personality and character than policy positions. As Thurber, Nelson, and Dulio have pointed out, "This analysis demonstrates that the majority of verbal content in political advertisements is not discussion of policy" (2000, 60). Some analyses have shown that personal attacks can have as much influence on voters' evaluations as policy attacks and that voters can make informed policy inferences about candidates based on character cues they see in advertising (Hacker et al. 2000; Homer and Batra 1994).

No one knows for sure just how much of the mud being slung back and forth between candidates is personal or policy in nature, but there does seem to be a consensus among researchers as to who is throwing the first personal punch: Republicans. Research conducted at the University of Missouri by William Benoit dealing with presidential television campaign spots showed that "from 1952–2000, 44% of Republican attacks concerned character and 56% were about policy. For Democrats, on the other hand, only 33% of their attacks were on character and 67% addressed policy" (2004). This conclusion seems to be supported by most journalists and political commentators as well. Republican campaign professionals make no secret of their penchant for bringing up personal issues about the opposition during the campaign season. A *Washington Post* story before the midterm elections of 2006 noted, "Republicans are planning to spend the vast majority of their sizable financial war chest over the final 60 days of the campaign attacking Democratic House and Senate candidates over personal issues and local controversies" (VandeHei and Cillizza 2006; see also Walsh 1992; Berke 1996; and Crowley 2008).

So we have now set the stage to discover what political managers say about negative advertising. Thus far, the general consensus has been that many contextual factors like polls and partisanship play a role, although we are still not clear as to what role the ad content—policy or character—plays in a dynamic campaign. The results below take us step by step through the campaign environment of the survey respondents and paints a fairly vivid picture of what goes on in modern American campaigns.

Negative Advertising Results

The majority of consultants said that they were operating in an environment where negative ads were run (76.6 percent) (see Table 4.2), although not surprisingly they also claimed to be the victims rather than the perpetrators of such attacks (53.3 percent). Challengers and open-seat consultants acknowledged attacking first about a third of the time (28.8 percent), compared to incumbents, who reported attacking first only 9.8 percent of the time in the campaign. Of consultants, 39.7 percent of consultants reported outside groups running attack ads during the campaign against their candidate, and 27.4 percent of respondents stated that no negative advertising was run at all by outside groups.

Not surprisingly, few consultants admitted to attacking character during campaigns (16.4 percent said mostly or always, according to Table 4.3), yet

TABLE 4.2 Were any negative ads run during your campaign?

Question Option	Frequency	Percentage
No negative ads run	47	23.4
Yes, opponent attacked us first	106	52.7
Yes, attacked our opponent first	48	23.9
Total	201	100

TABLE 4.3 Frequency and type of attack ads run against your opponent

	Your attack ad	
Question option	*Opponent's character* N (%)	*Opponent's policy positions* N (%)
Never	48 (32.9)	16 (11.0)
Seldom	28 (19.2)	8 (5.5)
Sometimes	46 (31.5)	28 (19.2)
Mostly	17 (11.6)	49 (33.6)
Always	7 (4.8)	45 (30.8)
Total	146 (100)	146 (100)

Note: N = actual number of responses. (%) = percentage of total.

they were much more comfortable saying that the character of their candidate was attacked (51.4 percent said mostly or always, according to Table 4.4). Clearly, this suggests that attacks on character might be a matter of interpretation, or that consultants simply do not want to admit how they engaged their opponents. On policy issues, campaigners reported that opponents attacked their policy (41.7 percent said mostly or always) less than they attacked their opponent's policy issues (64.4 percent said mostly or always).

However, when we break down character versus policy attacks by political party, we run into a fascinating contradiction that implies interpretation might be more at play in campaign ads than previously expected. I broke down the tendency to attack an opponent on character and policy by the most consistent behaviors, "mostly to always," for both Republicans and Democrats. The results are shown in Table 4.5.

The first set of responses show that Democratic consultants admitted to attacking their opponents' character (18 percent) almost twice as much as

TABLE 4.4 Frequency and type of attack ads your opponent ran against you

| | Your opponent's attack ad | |
| | *Your character* | *Your policy positions* |
Question option	N (%)	N (%)
Never	14 (9.6)	20 (13.7)
Seldom	16 (11.0)	25 (17.1)
Sometimes	41 (28.1)	40 (27.4)
Mostly	46 (31.5)	50 (34.2)
Always	29 (19.9)	11 (7.5)
Total	146 (100)	146 (100)

Note: N = actual number of responses. (%) = percentage of total.

TABLE 4.5 Frequency of attack ads against your opponent's character or policy by political party

| | Democrat | | Republican | |
| | *Opponent's character* | *Opponent's policy positions* | *Candidate's character* | *Candidate's policy positions* |
Question option	N (%)	N (%)	N (%)	N (%)
Mostly to always	16 (18.0)	51 (57.3)	5 (10.2)	35 (71.4)

Note: N = actual number of responses. (%) = percentage of total.

Republicans said that they attacked their opponents' character (10.2 percent). Further, Republican consultants reported attacking Democratic candidate policies (71.4 percent) by a much larger margin than their Democratic counterparts (57.3 percent). Are Democratic campaigners in the sample just more honest about their character attacks than Republicans, or is something else afoot? We next take a look at how campaigners in the sample looked at how *they* were attacked on policy and character by their opponent.

When we look at how consultants perceived negative attacks against their candidates, we find a surprising result. The responses of the two parties' political operatives are almost polar opposites. Table 4.5 shows that 57.3 percent of Democratic political practitioners reported that they attacked Republicans on policy mostly to always, whereas Table 4.6 shows that 67.3 percent of Republican consultants reported that they were attacked on policy mostly to always. But whereas Republican practitioners in the sample

TABLE 4.6 Frequency of attack ads against your candidate's character or policy by opponent by political party

	Democrat		Republican	
	My candidate's character	*My candidate's policy positions*	*My candidate's character*	*My candidate's policy positions*
Question option	N (%)	N (%)	N (%)	N (%)
Mostly to always	54 (60.7)	28 (31.5)	18 (36.7)	33 (67.3)

Note: N = actual number of responses. (%) = percentage of total.

said they attacked policy 71.4 percent of the time, according to Table 4.5, Democratic consultants felt their policies were being attacked only 31.5 percent of the time, according to Table 4.6. So when Democratic consultants launched policy attacks at Republican candidates, it was perceived as such. But when Republicans launched character attacks at Democratic candidates (which they claimed to do only 10.2 percent of the time), Democrats still picked up vastly more character attacks (60.7 percent). Democrats contended that just about everything launched at them by conservatives was a negative character attack.

So what is really going on here? This is reminiscent of the work of Frank Luntz from our message chapter, whose book *Words That Work: It's Not What You Say but What They Hear* (2006) has become a bible of sorts for message strategy. There is a clear disconnect between what Republicans said they intended in their attacks and what Democrats said they heard. It is unlikely that only 10 percent of Republicans were going after Democratic character "mostly," and moreover there seems to be a much wider gap between Republican intent and Democratic reception than the other way around. Then again, this is a reflection of fundamental differences in issue strategy as well. We saw in the last chapter that the selection of issues and the messages that a campaign team will use to focus on those issues drive most campaign communication. Republican voters and by extension campaign operatives often view policies as reflections of character. In the candidate chapter we saw that Republican political operatives continued to point out that "taking a strong stand" on issues was actually one of the traits they liked best in their candidates. We have also seen that Republicans strategically focus more on strict policy positions and feel more compelled to "own" certain issues than Democratic consultants. When a Republican attacks a

Democrat on abortion, part of the intent may be policy, but part might also be a sign that the Democrat does not respect the life of the unborn. The Democratic target might be picking up on the character question more than the policy question.

Nevertheless, campaigns are all about combat. Neither Democrats nor Republicans are probably all that concerned about how the opponent views or interprets their negative ads, so long as the voters are moved in a direction that helps them win the race.

Predictors of Negative Advertising Use

At the beginning of this chapter we discussed how political science literature often looks at the difference between implementation and impact for negative advertising. We are now going to take a look at the implementation side of the analysis with input from our consultants. We will find out what they thought made a campaign more likely to go negative. We will employ many of the variables from existing political science literature and see if they still hold for driving campaign negativity when viewed through the lens of consultants. Moreover, we will take a look at the content impact as well, as we examine what variables drive character or policy attacks during campaigns.

The first three regression models focus on character attacks (Tables 4.7, 4.8, and 4.9). Table 4.7 shows what factors influence how likely a consultant is to attack their opponent's character with negative advertisements, controlling for other factors (see the Appendix).

Table 4.7 demonstrates that when controlling for other factors, a candidate's place in the polls at the primary is the biggest driver behind the decision to go negative, but not necessarily in the way that most political observers think. While political party and election type did not seem to drive the ad strategy in this sample, being ahead in the polls right after the primary had the most significant impact. Managers of campaigns that were ahead in the polls right after the primary were much more likely to report attacking their opponents' character than those who were behind right after the primary, controlling for other variables. Does that mean consultants want to bring out the big guns early, or is something else at play? Most likely, this is a reflection of "definition" strategy, discussed earlier. If you can come

TABLE 4.7 **Predictors for how likely a consultant is to attack their opponent's character**

Dependent variable	Independent variable in the regression	Impact variable
Likelihood of character attack	Being a challenger	None
Likelihood of character attack	Open-seat election	None
Likelihood of character attack	Executive or legislative position	None
Likelihood of character attack	Federal or state office	None
Likelihood of character attack	Southern region	None
Likelihood of character attack	Midwest region	None
Likelihood of character attack	West region	None
Likelihood of character attack	Poll position at primary	More likely to attack character if ahead in polls right after primary
Likelihood of character attack	Poll position midway	None
Likelihood of character attack	Education level in district	None
Likelihood of character attack	Campaign war chest	None
Likelihood of character attack	District party preference	None
Likelihood of character attack	Republican or Democrat	None

right out and define your opposition as a man or woman of low character through negative attacks, you have a better chance of setting the agenda during the rest of the campaign. During the hotly contested governor's race in Ohio in 2010, Democratic governor Ted Strickland came out swinging against his Republican challenger, John Kasich, launching his first negative ads against Kasich mere days after the Republican won his party nomination. The *Columbus Dispatch* noted:

> As Kasich and his running mate, state Auditor Mary Taylor, began a three-day "jobs tour" aboard a luxury bus to 13 staunchly Republican counties, Strickland posited the race as a choice between his Main Street values and Kasich's Wall Street values, dovetailing on TV attack ads he launched last week. "He's Wall Street to the core," Strickland said. . . . Kasich . . . labeled the attacks by an incumbent governor at the start of a campaign "pathetic and sad." . . . The rancorous exchange just eight days after the primary election set the tone for what portends to be an ugly five-month campaign. With polls showing Kasich is little-known by most Ohio voters, Strickland is attempting to define him negatively, a strategy that also could diminish the Democrat's standing in voters' eyes. (Niquette and Hallat 2010)

TABLE 4.8 Predictors for how likely a consultant is to attack their opponent's character when their character is attacked

Dependent variable	Independent variable in the regression	Impact variable
Likelihood of character attack	Being a challenger	None
Likelihood of character attack	Open-seat election	None
Likelihood of character attack	Executive or legislative position	None
Likelihood of character attack	Federal or state office	None
Likelihood of character attack	Southern region	None
Likelihood of character attack	Midwest region	None
Likelihood of character attack	West region	None
Likelihood of character attack	Poll position at primary	More likely to attack character if ahead in polls right after primary
Likelihood of character attack	Poll position midway	Less likely to attack if ahead in polls at midway point of campaign
Likelihood of character attack	Education level in district	None
Likelihood of character attack	Campaign war chest	None
Likelihood of character attack	District party preference	None
Likelihood of character attack	Opponent attacks character	More likely to attack if your opponent's character has been attacked
Likelihood of character attack	Republican or Democrat	None

Ted Strickland hoped that by pointing out Kasich's time at Lehman Brothers, one of the major Wall Street firms bailed out by the federal government, that he could portray him as a cold and heartless businessman not sensitive to Ohio's needs. While Ted Strickland still lost the election, the margin was much tighter than expected, which many attribute to his heavy attacks on Kasich early on.

In our next regression (Table 4.8) I looked at the factors that predict character attacks when an opponent attacks a candidate's character. Although not as prominent a predictor as some of the others mentioned earlier, if an opponent attacks first, or harder, it can impact the campaign negativity, as some political scientists have noted (Kahn and Kenney 1999; Haynes and Rhine 1998; Lau and Pomper 2001, 2004; Damore 2002).

In the second regression we begin to see the seeds of where heavy character attacks in ads come from. When a consultant felt that their opponent attacked their candidate's character, they were inclined to respond with character attacks themselves, although this was influenced by position in the

TABLE 4.9 Predictors for how likely a consultant is to attack their opponent's character when their policies are attacked

Dependent variable	Independent variable in the regression	Impact variable
Likelihood of character attack	Being a challenger	None
Likelihood of character attack	Open-seat election	None
Likelihood of character attack	Executive or legislative position	None
Likelihood of character attack	Federal or state office	None
Likelihood of character attack	Southern region	None
Likelihood of character attack	Midwest region	None
Likelihood of character attack	West region	None
Likelihood of character attack	Poll position at primary	More likely to attack character if ahead in polls right after primary
Likelihood of character attack	Poll position midway	Less likely to attack if ahead in polls at midway point of campaign
Likelihood of character attack	Education level in district	None
Likelihood of character attack	Campaign war chest	None
Likelihood of character attack	District party preference	None
Likelihood of character attack	Opponent attacks policy	None
Likelihood of character attack	Republican or Democrat	None

polls during the campaign. Those candidates who were ahead early started the campaign with negative character attacks, even controlling for if they were attacked on character. However, as the campaign moved on, if the candidate maintained their lead, the political professional was less likely to place negative character attacks, even when their candidate was attacked. This brings a very interesting element that is often overlooked in political science theories on negative advertising, namely, that the content of ads is driven not just by polls but perhaps by the timing within the campaign as well. Right after the primary or during the middle and end of the campaign, strategies may change the nature of ads.

We now look at the results of the table in a different kind of attack. What factors drive campaign professionals to engage in character attacks when their candidate is attacked on policy?

Even when attacked on policy grounds, consultants were still more driven by polling numbers in negative advertising strategy. What is also interesting to note is that policy attacks were not nearly as much of a driver of behavior as character attacks. Clearly, consultants feared and were motivated more by assaults on character over the airwaves than criticisms of policy positions.

TABLE 4.10 **Poll averages in late July and early August 2008**

Ap Ipsos (7/31–8/4)	Obama	47	McCain	41
CBS (7/31–8/5)	Obama	45	McCain	39
Time (7/31–8/4)	Obama	46	McCain	41
Gallup (8/3–5)	Obama	46	McCain	41

Note: The numbers represent where Obama and McCain were in the polls during that month in various national polls in 2008.

The results in the table add credence to the earlier discussions of messaging, namely, a consultant must define the opponent early, and character definitions might be much more powerful than policy definitions. To see an example of how character attacks played out nationwide, we look at the content of ads during the presidential election of 2008.

Celebrity Attack Ads and the Presidential Election of 2008

The timing of character versus policy attacks played out in a large way during the presidential election of 2008 between John McCain and Barack Obama. During the middle part of the campaign in late July, most national polls showed Barack Obama had led McCain for about a month. Even worse for McCain, although there remained a large number of undecided voters, Obama's lead was growing past the margin of error (Table 4.10).

After another month of relative stagnation in the polls, in the final week of August 2008, the McCain campaign launched its infamous "Celebrity" ad, comparing Barack Obama to Paris Hilton, and began a steady stream of ads intending to show that Obama was personally not fit to lead the nation.[5] After a steady stream of negative character ads directed at Obama from the McCain campaign throughout August, the impact began to show in polls. By the middle of September, John McCain had posted two consecutive weeks of leads over Barack Obama in Gallup Polls, the first time that had happened during the campaign. Gallup Polls for September 5–13 showed McCain with a small but consistent lead over Obama.[6] Prior to this point in the race, the Obama campaign had not directed many character attacks at McCain through televised ads, focusing instead on their message that McCain would be a third Bush term, essentially a policy message. But facing a tight race heading into the presidential debates, the Obama campaign swung back with some of their most intense character attacks of the entire election cycle. In an article titled "Obama Goes After McCain for Being Old, Incompetent," *Huffington Post* political writer Sam Stein described the Obama "Still" add directed at McCain right after the September 11 weekend in 2008: "Making overt references to McCain's age, the spot, titled 'Still,' calls the Republican nominee out-of-touch, showing footage of him from 1982 alongside screen shots of disco balls, a (Zach Morris–like) old school cell phone, a record player and a Rubik's cube. It even calls McCain out for his unfamiliarity with the Internet. And, as a parting jab, the ad uses footage of the Arizona Republican riding with George H. W. Bush in a golf cart" (2008).

There are several significant points to be made about what this article captures, our research, and the Obama campaign's intent. Although it is true that they also released the ad "Real Change" the same morning as the "Still" ad, the character-attack ad grabbed all the media attention. Further, notice how the terminology we discussed earlier came into play: The ad attacked McCain's competence, a key term, according to our own findings and ANES surveys, and the Obama team employed the "too old" message that we distilled from campaign strategies in Chapter 2. The ad, almost humorous in its music and imagery, fit in with the "too old" message of seeing McCain as a doddering old man, nice but no longer competent or capable of doing the job. It was a character attack and message definition all rolled into one. The result? Within a week Obama had bounced back to a five-point lead in the Gallup Poll and never trailed again during the campaign.

Continuing to affirm our research results, trailing by a widening margin heading into the final month of the election, the McCain camp did not just get more "negative"; it got more personal in their ads as well. By the final weeks the McCain-Palin ticket was openly discussing the "Nuclear Option" of going directly after Obama personally. Tim Shipman reported in the *Telegraph* that "John McCain's campaign has accused Barack Obama of consorting with terrorists, the first shot in a calculated program of character assassination designed to revive his flagging presidential prospects" (2008). This example shows the power of these survey results in not only revealing a little-known element of campaign strategy but how it played out in a larger political realm. Character attacks are driven by overall campaign negativity but in particular by polling position, with candidates using them to define the opposition early on and then often relying on character again only when trailing in the polls.

Now we look at the forces behind when and where political professionals engaged in policy attacks on their opponents.

Policy Attack Ads and the Power of Campaign Levels

The next three regression models focus on policy attacks (Tables 4.11, 4.12, and 4.13). The regression analysis was performed with essentially the same variables as those used for character attacks but with two significant additions. Policy arguments during the campaign are influenced by many of the same potential factors that might influence character attacks, but there are some environmental factors that should be taken into consideration. When analyzing consultants' tendencies to attack on policy grounds in negative ads, we will also add the variable of "on- or off-year election" and "rural or urban" campaign district. The reason for these two additions is both theoretical and practical. When running a campaign during a presidential election year, lower-ballot candidates are inevitably influenced by what the top of the ticket is taking on policywise. If you were a Republican running for state attorney general in 2004, you might have been attacked on your support or lack of support for President Bush's USA PATRIOT Act, whereas this was much less likely to be an issue in a 2005 or 2006 campaign. Therefore, it is more important to consider how the election year might influence what policy attacks a consultant makes or responds to. In addition, rural voters tend to be in smaller, more homogenous districts, and therefore policy stances are much less likely to be muted or hidden in the way that can occur in highly economically and culturally diverse urban districts. A small district in upstate Michigan where everyone is a farmer is much more in tune with a candidate's policy positions than in suburban Phoenix, where constituents with multiple employment areas and cultural backgrounds may each have their own policy niche. Therefore, I added this variable to see what, if any, impact it had on the policy attacks by consultants.

The results from Table 4.11 confirm our previous discussions about the role that partisanship can play in campaign strategy. Democrats by their own admission in the survey and through analysis were much less likely to

TABLE 4.11 **Predictors for how likely a consultant is to attack their opponent's policies**

Dependent variable	Independent variable in the regression	Impact variable
Likelihood of character attack	Being a challenger	None
Likelihood of character attack	Open-seat election	None
Likelihood of character attack	Executive or legislative position	None
Likelihood of character attack	Federal or state office	More likely to attack policy of opponent when seeking a federal position
Likelihood of character attack	Southern region	None
Likelihood of character attack	Midwest region	None
Likelihood of character attack	West region	None
Likelihood of character attack	Poll position at primary	None
Likelihood of character attack	Poll position midway	None
Likelihood of character attack	Education level in district	None
Likelihood of character attack	Campaign war chest	None
Likelihood of character attack	District party preference	None
Likelihood of character attack	Republican or Democrat	Less likely to attack opponent on policy when you are a Democratic consultant

attack on policy than Republicans. However, all consultants were much more likely to attack on policy grounds when they were seeking higher office. Although the regression shows that candidates seeking federal office were much more likely to attack policy than those seeking statewide office, we can safely assume this applies further down the ballot, with city council members attacking less on policy grounds than mayors and mayors less than county executives and so forth. When we look at how the type of attacks that candidates are subjected to influences consultants' policy attacks, we see even more how these factors come into play.

The trend showing the importance of seeking a federal position continues when we examine what influences the likelihood of a consultant getting the campaign to attack policy when their candidate's character is attacked. None of the other variables seemed to influence consultant thinking, even when considering a character attack, other than what level of office they were pursuing.

When we examine the impact of how being on the receiving end of policy attacks influences whether consultants drove their campaigns to attack

TABLE 4.12 Predictors for how likely a consultant is to attack their opponent's policies when attacked on character

Dependent variable	Independent variable in the regression	Impact variable
Likelihood of character Attack	Being a challenger	None
Likelihood of character attack	Open-seat election	None
Likelihood of character attack	Executive or legislative position	None
Likelihood of character attack	Federal or state office	More likely to attack policy of opponent when seeking a federal position
Likelihood of character attack	Southern region	None
Likelihood of character attack	Midwest region	None
Likelihood of character attack	West region	None
Likelihood of character attack	Poll position at primary	None
Likelihood of character attack	Poll position midway	None
Likelihood of character attack	Education level in district	None
Likelihood of character attack	Campaign war chest	None
Likelihood of character attack	District party preference	None
Likelihood of character attack	Opponent attacks you on character	None
Likelihood of character attack	Republican or Democrat	None

TABLE 4.13 Predictors for how likely a consultant is to attack their opponent's policies when attacked on policy

Dependent variable	Independent variable in the regression	Impact variable
Likelihood of character attack	Being a challenger	None
Likelihood of character attack	Open-seat election	None
Likelihood of character attack	Executive or legislative position	None
Likelihood of character attack	Federal or state office	More likely to attack policy of opponent when seeking a federal position
Likelihood of character attack	Southern region	None
Likelihood of character attack	Midwest region	None
Likelihood of character attack	West region	None
Likelihood of character attack	Poll position at primary	None
Likelihood of character attack	Poll position midway	None
Likelihood of character attack	Education level in district	None
Likelihood of character attack	Campaign war chest	None
Likelihood of character attack	District party preference	None
Likelihood of character attack	Opponent attacks you on policy	More likely to attack opponent's policy when they attack your policy
Likelihood of character attack	Republican or Democrat	None

policy, more trends become apparent. The first is that federal races tend to be more oriented toward policy attacks than nonfederal races; the second is that that there appears to be a "mirroring" process in the use and implementation of negative advertising campaigns. These results should actually encourage political scientists and political observers who express concern about the state of negative advertising in American politics. These results show that when pursuing higher office, campaign professionals tend to move their strategies more toward issues and policy than simply personality and character.

A Note on Race and Gender

I intentionally did not include race or gender of candidates or opposition in the initial regressions because I wanted to be as specifically focused on those two traits as possible. Existing literature speaks to the role of gender in who attacks and who is attacked, and our previous results on race indicate a strong possibility that the race of a candidate or the opposition could play a role in negative ad strategy. Although I performed separate regressions to assess the impact of these demographic traits on campaigners' views of strategy, the results were nowhere to be found. Existing research and various examples from individual races indicate that race still plays a role in campaigns when one of the candidates is a minority.

One of the most famous series of ads deemed racially provocative in the past twenty years was run by conservative Republican senator from North Carolina Jesse Helms against African American former mayor of Charlotte Harvey Gantt. Although ads were hard-hitting on both sides, two Helms ads in particular became famous among political operatives for their naked use of racial symbolism to stoke fears through a negative ad. Strickland and Wicker took note of one ad in their analysis of campaign strategies for African Americans in statewide races: "In the commercial a woman is lying on the ground apparently beaten and raped, the announcer asks 'The death penalty for rapists who brutally beat their victims?' Then he answers 'Gantt says no Helms says yes'" (1992, 206). Another famous ad featured a white man sitting at a table with a pink slip in his hand, an obvious job-rejection notice. The camera zooms in as the hand crumbles the letter, and the narrator states in a grave tone, "You needed that job and you were the best qualified. But they had to give it to a minority because of a racial quota. Is that really fair? Harvey Gantt says it is" (ibid.). More recent examples of elections where racially motivated ads came into play included attacks against Harold Ford Jr. when he ran for senator of Tennessee.[7]

Yet race played no role in campaigner strategy and beliefs in this sample. This contradicts some existing research but perhaps in a good way (Caliendo and McIlwain 2007, 2008, 2009). Is it not in the best interest of the nation to see that race and gender actually are not driving negative advertising attacks? Now this is not to say that race and gender do not matter in negative advertising, only that I did not find evidence of it in this study.

When we look at the overall results from both character and policy attack regressions, we find a narrative about how negative advertising works in campaigns and perhaps the motivations and the ordering of the campaign strategies. Although we may not know which campaign "started it," we do know that policy attacks are driven primarily by the level of the race, are more likely to come from Republicans, and are more likely to occur when the consultant believes that their campaign has been attacked on policy. In and of themselves, polling numbers do not appear to be much of a driving factor in when or how policy attacks are implemented. Character attacks, however, are a completely different matter. When a campaign is ahead right after the primaries, it is more inclined to attack an opponent's character and the opponent is less inclined to do so. However, once the first handful of mud has been slung, all bets are off. If a candidate is close in the polls or behind in the polls after the midway point and has been the target of any character attacks, they attack back with character. Although this may come off as a bit complicated, the scenarios described above are much more common in the campaign environment than most people realize. Much of the above research played out in the campaign of challenger Jim Webb against George Allen for a U.S. Senate seat in Virginia in 2006.

Allen, former governor of Virginia and a front-runner for the Republican presidential nomination in 2008, looked at his Senate reelection bid in 2006 as a stepping-stone more than a real contest. Extremely popular as governor and then senator, Allen had maintained high approval ratings for almost a decade. His opponent, Jim Webb, was a Vietnam veteran who had served as secretary of the navy under Reagan and had switched to the Democratic Party only after souring on Bush's polices and the second Gulf War. What's more, Webb had a bruising primary fight for his nomination and remained unknown to most Virginia voters, and those who knew him considered him to be gruff and aloof.

Right after the Democratic primary in mid-June, Webb trailed Allen by ten points (51 percent to 41 percent), and the Allen campaign, ahead in the polls right after the primary, launched the first subtle personal attack at Webb after he came out opposing an amendment to make flag burning illegal: "James H. Webb, Jr. continues to demonstrate he is totally beholden to liberal Washington Senators who dragged him across the line in the Democratic primary. . . . By announcing his opposition to the Flag Protection Amendment, James H. Webb, Jr. puts himself firmly on the side of John Kerry, Ted Kennedy and Charles Schumer" (*National Journal* 2006). The statement was a healthy mix of both policy and character criticism; being called a "liberal" in Virginia is not so much a policy critique, as the term carries with it all sorts of social and cultural connotations that are not viewed kindly by most voters in the state. Add to that the suggestion that Webb was "dragged" over the finish line by national Democrats, and the implications of this statement are clear. Consonant with our findings, Webb did not initially respond with character attacks against Allen; instead, he aimed negative advertising at the incumbent senator on his policies, support for the war in Iraq, and a host of other Bush initiatives.

Allen, still leading by double digits, ran his first two television ads in late June. Consonant with the research presented above, both the "Matters" and "Family" ads focused on his record of policy positions, from crime and improving education to national security. However, the campaign soon went personal, and with a vengeance. Allen was caught on tape by a Webb campaign "tracker" using an obscure racial slur against Indians, and that was followed by several former friends and football teammates of Allen's claiming that he consistently used the racial slur *nigger* to refer to blacks around them. Webb jumped on the opportunity, and once the campaign began to move into character attacks, even though it was a Senate-level race, both campaigns' negative advertising strategy followed the research results presented above with surprising consistency. The Allen campaign, clinging to a statistically insignificant lead after the midpoint of the campaign, went negative and used character attacks, accusing Webb of supporting sexual assaults of female naval cadets during the "Tailhook" scandal and suggesting various explicit sex scenes from books that Webb wrote were indicators of his attitudes toward women. The consultants in Webb's campaign responded with the "Truth" and "History" ads, referring to *Washington Post* articles that called Allen a liar and referred to his ads as "political sewage." The Webb campaign matched Allen's initial character attack statement for statement, commercial for commercial, throughout the campaign. In the end, the Allen campaign was undone by the constant barrage of criticism lobbed at him by Webb and the national press based on his alleged racist and hostile statements toward minorities. Webb's seemingly sexist or insensitive writings did not seem to carry as much weight as the racial monkey that had attached itself to Allen's back. Webb narrowly won the Senate election after trailing Allen for almost the entire summer by roughly .03 percent of the vote.

True to form, the leader after the primaries, Allen, started with character attacks, and while sticking to policy initially, Democratic candidate Webb quickly went personal against Allen, aided and abetted by some of his own public snafus. The race demonstrates again what appears to be the more consistent strategy by political consultants. Policy ads seem to be the refuge of those who are behind in the polls at first and in high-profile federal races. However, if the numbers do not improve, character attacks are next. Further, Webb's status as the challenger and Allen's status as the incumbent did not seem to have much of an impact on their negative advertising strategies, nor did their advertising focus on the position they sought. The research suggests that consultants for both campaigns were driven by poll numbers at the primary and midpoints of the campaign, demonstrating once again that the beliefs of consultants in the field provide a more authentic analysis of the world of negative advertising than content- or interview-based analysis alone.

Conclusion

There were two main research goals of this chapter on negative advertising. The first was to find a new, more functional definition of negative advertising that would satisfy both academics and practitioners, and the second was to determine what factors drive campaign strategy beliefs of consultants and whether those line up with existing political science theory. We met our first research goal of finding a suitable definition of negative advertising using the consultants' perspective. *Negative advertising* is an important and acceptable part of modern political campaigns, but *attack advertising* can offend politicians, anger voters, and in some cases cause a backlash that harms a candidate. Consultants see and operate under this distinction and understand the consequences of ignoring it. Matt Lewis, a longtime Republican campaign manager who worked on a hotly contested school board race in Frederick, Maryland, put it succinctly: "To win a tough race, challenger candidates simply must run aggressive, comparison-based campaigns. However there is a difference between running a tough campaign and spreading lies. We've all seen campaigns that crossed the line, and occasionally, it backfires" (2001, 3). His candidate, Linda Naylor, was subjected to attacks from outside groups about her character, child-rearing ability, and personal life. The attack ads against her were so personal, and so seemingly irrelevant to the position she was seeking, that voters eventually rejected the attacks outright and swept Naylor into victory almost in protest.

We also satisfied our other major research question, the discovery of negative advertising predictors for advertising strategy and content. Some of the results confirm existing political science theory in that poll position plays a major role in how consultants and campaign professionals envision their campaign strategy, as does the position sought by the candidate. But many of the other factors, such as race, gender, and party, did not have much of an impact on strategy, according to the survey results. In fact, the results show that campaigners are mostly driven by polls and polls only, except in a few circumstances.

An additional contribution to this chapter is the role that content types play on campaign strategy. While existing political science theory has looked at whether policy or character attacks have an impact on voters, this chapter demonstrates that political operatives do consciously decide when to employ different kinds of political content in ads. In fact, one could go so far as to suggest that if consultants were included in much of the existing political science work, many of the other driving forces in campaign negative advertising theory might turn out to be less significant.

We have seen that consultant views can play a role in candidates' messaging, issue-position strategy, and negative advertising, but what about all the ways that these concepts are delivered to voters? Of course, there has been a tangential discussion in the book so far about media, mostly television and occasionally newspapers, but those are not the new frontier of political campaigns. In the next chapter we will take a look at the Internet and find out how all of the changes that we have seen thus far in theory might be reenvisioned even more when we look at manager opinions on Internet use in modern campaigns.

5

The Internet Campaign

On January 3, 2008, the Barack Obama campaign had just secured an amazing victory. Obama shocked the political world by winning the Iowa caucuses with 38 percent of the vote to John Edward's 30 percent and Hillary Clinton's 29 percent. Hillary Clinton, the presumed front-runner, scored a "must-win" victory at the New Hampshire primaries just a week later, and then an Internet story broke that rattled both campaigns to the netroots. On January 14, 2008, the *New York Post* posted an online story titled "Hillary, Barack, Rap & Rock," citing an anonymous source who claimed the Obamas took their Iowa victory celebration just a little too far: "As Obama and his wife, Michelle, strolled triumphantly into his victory party in Des Moines, Iowa, on Jan. 3, Jay-Z's '99 Problems' was blaring. . . . Some listeners took it as a not-so-sly reference to Hillary." For those not familiar with rapper Jay-Z, his classic anthem "99 Problems" isn't particularly subtle or sly. The chorus of the song passionately intones: "If you're having girl problems I feel bad for you, son / I've got 99 problems, but a bitch ain't one!"

It would not take a music critic at the *Source* to figure out who the "bitch" being referred to at an Obama victory party was. Jay-Z was a known backer of the Obama campaign, and the story went viral on progressive and liberal sites, where fights about race, gender, Obama, Hillary, and primaries got very intense. This only served to exacerbate tensions between the two camps that lasted all the way until the nominating convention.[1] As much blog space and chatter as there was associated with the "99 Problems" story, the mainstream cable and network news shows never paid much attention to it, and neither did any major "old media" print newspapers. This was probably a good thing, since the story was totally false. Once the blogosphere started to investigate the story, the *Post* could not provide witnesses or evidence that the song was played either at Obama's main victory party or at a subsequent private party in Iowa. In fact, Ben Smith, a blogger for *Politico.com*, noted that the story had gotten out of hand online with little or no real evidence in the real world: "So I've now spent way too much of my morning trying to report out the *New York Post*'s item that Obama had sexist entrance music. . . . It's a provocative scene. But I can't find any evidence that it happened, though it does seem to have been the subject of chatter among staffers of both campaigns (12:28 p.m.)" (Smith 2008).

Later that same day, at 10:51 p.m., Geekesque (2008), a *DailyKos.com* blogger who had attended the Obama victory rallies, got involved in the discussion after both Smith's and the original *New York Post* pieces became a hot topic online. Geekesque posted video on YouTube showing that Obama did stroll onstage and music was playing, but it was not the music reported by various sources online.[2] Geekesque wrote:

> Well, the Clinton-supporting Rupert Murdoch publishes this BLATANT LIE in the scummy New York Post. Shocking! Not surprisingly, a number of dishonest, pro-Clinton/anti-Obama websites have latched onto this smear? The only problem with this outrageous tale being told by pro-Clinton propagandists.
>
> It isn't true.
>
> You see, when the Obama family took the stage, it wasn't Jay-Z that was playing.
>
> It was Stevie Wonder's "Signed, Sealed, Delivered." (*Update: Actually, it was U2. They left to SSD.*)
>
> Don't believe me?
>
> You don't have to.
>
> Here is *video footage of Obama* entering the room. (thanks to indefinitely)
>
> Here is *video footage of Obama taking the stage.*
>
> Turn up the volume on your computers. Tell me when you hear Jay-Z.

Links between the original *New York Post* story, Democratic blogs like *DailyKos*, and *DemocraticUnderground* flew back and forth, and reports indicated that both political campaigns were aware of the story. Although the story eventually blew over, it was pretty clear that bloggers and online supporters of each candidate were ready to fight it out online.

Now let's step back and consider the larger scene here. An unfounded rumor started on an online post of a print newsmagazine goes viral, is repeated across the blogosphere, and is finally debunked by a YouTube clip, but only after raising the blood pressure of Obama and Clinton supporters to condition red for almost twenty-four hours. This story is the epitome of the power of the Internet in modern campaigns. While the Web can provide campaigners with incredible freedom to share ideas with voters, organize, and raise money, it is also an untamed free-for-all where hidden videos, uncorroborated e-mails, and doctored pictures can derail campaigns at the click of a mouse.

Online campaigning, or e-campaigning as it is sometimes called, has become a standard part of every federal election in the country and increasingly a standard part of statewide elections over the past decade and a half. Internet habits and trends change rapidly, and so do the strategies of consultants who use this new medium to get votes for their candidate. All of the basic tenets of political campaigns—messaging, the candidate, negative ads, and positioning—have already been influenced by Internet politics, but political scientists have had a hard time examining exactly what consultants are doing with these newfound tools, and why. In this chapter we will look at what practices are most common among political operatives when it comes to Internet strategy, examine operatives' attitudes toward the Internet's overall influence on campaign strategy, and then explore what drives these strategies. We will then see if the current political science work on political campaigners and e-campaigns truly captures what is happening out in the field.

The History of the Internet in Political Campaigns

Before we get to the present, we have to understand our Internet past, and for that we take a look at the history of campaigning on the Internet. The Internet has been used in national political campaigns in some capacity or another since the early 1990s when then governor Bill Clinton's campaign team used e-mail to communicate rapid-response attacks during his presidential run in 1992. However, his "war room" mostly used the Internet among themselves, and voters were by and large not part of the equation. By the 1996 presidential election Republican nominee Bob Dole was actively asking voters to contact his campaign through his Web site during his first debate with then president Bill Clinton. Although hearing Dole belabor the entire address to the listening audience, "You can go to w-w-w-dot . . . " was distracting, it was also the first time a presidential candidate used a national debate as a means to promote his Web site for voters to donate to and communicate with his campaign.[3] By the late 1990s and early 2000s Minnesota governor Jesse Ventura and Republican presidential primary candidate John McCain were Web innovators on a grander scale. In the case of McCain, he broke records with online fund-raising and collecting volunteers in crucial primary states in his failed bid to win the Republican nomination for president (see Farnsworth and Owen 2004). This time period was really the "Stone Age" of the Internet in politics as well as the average American's life. American campaigns did not truly enter the next Internet age until the 2004 Democratic nomination run by former Vermont governor Howard Dean.

It is important to note that political consultants and the campaigns they run tend to be fairly risk-averse operations. The goal is to win an election, not necessarily rock the boat. In fact, oftentimes campaign technology is only equal to or even slightly behind modern marketing and sales technology (Semiatin 2007; Schneider and Foot 2005). So how did the Howard Dean campaign become such a powerful and transformative force when it came to Web campaigning during the 2004 Democratic presidential primary? It was through a perfect storm of cultural, demographic, and technical changes.

Penetration, Speed, and Comfort

Prior to the Dean campaign in 2004, the confluence of factors needed for most of the modern campaign uses for Internet technology was not in place. In order for the Internet to be a valuable resource for an enterprise as complex and expensive as a political campaign, you have to have penetration, speed, and comfort.

Penetration

Penetration refers to the number of Americans who actually had access to the Internet either in their homes or somewhere else. Only 18 percent of

American homes had a Web-connected computer in 1997; that number more than doubled to 50 percent in 2001, and by January 2004 three out of every four homes in America with a phone had access to the Internet. With 75 percent of the U.S. population online at home, let alone at work, school, or the local library, and burgeoning mobile Web access, Internet use had finally moved from the "Stone Age" to the "Wild West."[4] Those with Internet access in their homes tended (at the time) to be more educated, have higher incomes, and be more likely to vote. Therefore, campaign managers knew they were communicating with a likely voter demographic (Dulio and Nelson 2004; Howard 2006).

Speed

The next element that brought the perfect storm to bear on the 2004 election was speed. It seems like ancient history now, but there was a time when a majority of Americans knew they were connecting online by that loud screeching sound of the phone line opening up access to the Internet. Dial-up technology, accessing the Internet through home phone lines, was cheap, easy to use, but also incredibly slow. Your home computer had to get an open line to the Internet, and worse, during peak hours of the day, right after work and in the hours between dinner and bedtime, access was limited since everyone tried to dial in at the same time. Due to policies initiated by President Bill Clinton in the 1990s,[5] broadband technology was made more accessible to public facilities and eventually people's homes. By 2004 45 percent of U.S. homes with the Internet had broadband, which allowed for speedier exchanges of high-quality photos, downloads, and streaming videos (Thurber and Nelson 2004). These innovations made interactive elements of Web sites like blogs and videos much easier to run and access by reporters, partisans, and, most important, voters.

Comfort

Finally, you have comfort. Americans were gaining a level of comfort with the online world by late 2003 early 2004 that was unprecedented. You know people are becoming comfortable with a concept when they are willing to spend money on it, and that is exactly what we saw in the Christmas season of 2003. Internet sales jumped almost 25 percent on critical days, especially after-Christmas sales (Grant 2003). Americans, facing increasing gas prices and loss of jobs after the tech bubble burst, went online in record-breaking numbers to purchase everything from food to clothes, and they stuck around afterward to read a little news as well. Recent studies by the Pew Center on the Internet in American Life predicted that as Americans became more and more familiar with the Web, they would be willing to engage in more complex tasks online (Lee and Horrigan 2002). American comfort with the complexity and expansiveness of the Web, combined with increased comfort with spending money online, set the stage for Dean's incredible campaign.

The Dean Campaign and the End of the "Stone Age"

The Dean campaign is considered by many academics and political observers as the beginning of modern Internet campaign strategy. Political scientist Michael Cornfield says definitively, "For all campaigners, the year 2004 looms as the year 1 A.D." (2004; see also Semiatin 2007; and Oates, Owen, and Gibson 2006). Howard Dean's campaign to be the Democratic nominee against George Bush for the 2004 presidential election was a "long shot," and that was a generous interpretation. Very few people had heard of this medical doctor–turned-governor from Vermont advocating fiscal responsibility and universal health care. After announcing his campaign in June 2003, Dean's team of Internet experts, led by Joe Trippi and Larry Biddle, realized they could use existing Internet behavior by most Americans to organize and further a campaign goal. People were already socializing on Friendster and Meet-Up, so why not use those sites to recruit and organize Howard Dean supporters? Americans were already buying books online through Amazon and other sites, so why wouldn't they be willing to donate to a political campaign online? But Dean's contribution to e-campaigning was not only in the realm of technology but also in the overall attitude that the campaign managers and consultants had toward the Web and supporters. In his assessment of the campaign, Hindman noted that Dean's truly "bottom-up" attitude toward campaigning was a sharp break from previous wide-scale Internet campaigns for office: "Howard Dean did something that was smart, brave, and unprecedented—something only a candidate with little to lose would do: he created a genuinely interactive campaign Web site. Previous online campaigns—including those of John McCain and Jesse Ventura, the most celebrated antecedents to Dean's efforts—kept rigid control over their Web presence" (2005, 121).

While the Dean campaign staff is credited with many innovations, from a change in campaign philosophy to the creative use of "Meet-Up" technology and candidate blogging, they are remembered most for their groundbreaking moves in the realm of campaign fund-raising. During the "invisible primary," the months and in some cases years before the first actual presidential caucus, the Dean campaign revolutionized fund-raising. He raised more money than any other candidate (more than $24 million), shattering Democratic fund-raising records set by Bill Clinton in 1995, and was the first Democrat in thirty years to forego federal matching funds during a campaign because he believed he could raise more than the limits the federal government placed on him (Schouten 2006). Hindman pointed to how crucial the Internet was to Dean's cash flow success: "To paraphrase a previous presidential campaign, it's the Internet, stupid. There is strong evidence the Internet was an indispensable component of Dean's fund-raising success. Dean challenges nearly all of the conventional wisdom on political fund-raising: who gives, to whom, how much, and with what sort of underlying message" (2005, 127).

The Howard Dean campaign did not just raise money by driving people to their Web site or putting the campaign URL on bumper stickers. They found new and compelling ways to make the campaign fund-raising process interactive with voters. Michael Cornfield (2004) credited the Dean campaign with creating "news pegged fundraising appeals." These new appeals were e-mails sent to supporters with shocking or compelling news stories about the opposition that were going to get the blood boiling, and then at the end of the e-mail they encouraged the reader to donate and send that e-mail off to friends and family. The process was both interactive and passive at the same time and led to some impressive results. Cornfield recalled one specific example from the campaign:

> For example, in July 2003 the Dean campaign took advantage of news reports about an upcoming $2,000-a-plate Republican luncheon featuring Vice-President Cheney. Up, out, and around the Dean network went word of "The Cheney Challenge"—could Dean supporters raise more money than the luncheon by the time it took place?—accompanied by a web video of the

candidate munching on a "three-dollar" turkey sandwich. Cheney's lunch raised $250,000 from 125 guests. The online fundraising gimmick netted the Dean campaign $500,000 from 9700 people, and great publicity about its grassroots enthusiasm and prowess. (2005)

The idea of receiving a shocking e-mail with some brazen headline, such as "Democrats Have Plan to Take your GUNS!" or "Republicans Plan to Ship Teacher's Jobs Overseas!" followed by an appeal to send money to a random candidate is now standard campaign practice. In the past direct mail was used to excite voters this way, but direct mail has two major limitations that the Dean campaign sought to overcome with their Web strategy. First, it is called "snail mail" for a reason. By the time some compelling news item hits the airwaves, it is unlikely that even the swiftest of campaign teams can compose a quality mailer and send it out to potential voters, let alone make a real estimate as to when the money will trickle back in. With "news pegged mailing" whenever a story broke, it could immediately be sent out to donors, who would often donate right on the spot after reading the story. Moreover, if the story was sensational enough, they could be trusted to send the e-mail on to friends and family and collect even more funds. Using this methodology, individual online donations to the Dean campaign were fairly small (most were under one hundred dollars), but more people were willing to give since the process was so quick and easy. Plus, in the process of someone either donating to the campaign or receiving an e-mail, their information could be stored for future campaign mobilizations.

Staying true to the Dean campaign's "bottom-up" roots, many fund-raising ideas came from "Deaniacs" themselves (that is, fans of the presidential candidate). Deaniacs suggested the use of a bat-wielding Dean fan on his Web site with the bat's color indicating how well that week's fund-raising goals were met. It started off yellow, and the red line continued to go up until the fund-raising goal had been met.[6] This became the talk of major Internet sites on the Left all throughout the campaign season and was yet another sign of how the Web was used like never before for Dean in 2004. Between his own campaign team and suggestions from the netroots (grassroots organizers who commune mostly on the Internet) heading into the Iowa caucuses in 2004, Howard Dean appeared to be an unstoppable Internet-powered political juggernaut. He had been endorsed for the Democratic nomination by Al Gore, whom many Democrats still revered after the contentious presidential election of 2000, and he had thousands of supporters and more cash than anyone else (Pew Research Center for the People and the Press 2005). And then he lost. Big.

Howard Dean got trounced by John Kerry and John Edwards in the Iowa caucuses. He came in dismal third place with 18 percent of the vote. There are many reasons this happened. One reason is negative advertising between Dean and Dick Gephardt, who both considered themselves the front-runners and thus needed to define and attack the other.[7] Another reason was that John Kerry appeared to be the more electable candidate (as we discussed in Chapter 1). Some even argued that the Dean campaign "peaked to soon," one of the most overwrought political and sports analogies to come out of that campaign period (Sullivan 2003; Hines 2010; Nichols 2004). The reality is that Democratic primary voters wanted to beat George Bush in 2004, and they felt that of all of the Democratic candidates John Kerry, with his distinguished service in Vietnam and long-respected history in the Senate, had the best chance.

As a legacy the Bush and Kerry presidential campaigns adopted many of Howard Dean's e-campaign strategies during the subsequent general election, including fund-raising, meet-ups, and interactive media on their campaign Web sites (Semiatin 2007). However, Dean's loss put a damper on many political observers' and academics' expectations of the Internet's overall value in future campaigns.

Internet Optimists and Internet Pessimists

Political scientists have been analyzing the use of the Internet in political campaigns for years, and much of that work has centered on whether the Internet was truly transforming political campaign practices or was simply another vehicle for old campaign practices to be done online (Benoit 2000; Foot and Xenos 2009; Howard 2006). I categorized those who see the Internet as transformative versus those who see it as an extension of existing trends as "Internet optimists" and "Internet pessimists," respectively. The spectacular flameout of the Dean campaign only hardened the views of those who felt that the Internet was a new toy but not a "game changer." I defined these people as Internet pessimists. In general, they are political observers, academics, and sometimes political professionals who view the Internet as a useful tool but doubt whether it truly changes the nuts and bolts of how American campaigns are run. Many Internet pessimists even looked at the Dean campaign and questioned the Internet's long-term impact: "We would not go so far, in summary, to argue that presidential campaigning was completely revolutionized in 2004 . . . that sprawling databases provided access to large, differentiated political audiences even as blogs offered the digitally hip places for instant interpretation . . . that new teams of experts—the digital nerds—would be required if candidates wanted to play competently in the new campaign arenas" (Denton 2005, 228).

Even in the area of fund-raising, considered Howard Dean's most visible legacy, there remained questions about the value or long-term impact of the Internet compared to existing campaign practices. Joseph Graf, an analyst at George Washington University's Institute for Politics, Democracy, and the Internet, made this clear when he put the Dean campaign's 2004 fund-raising effort in the context of all fund-raising for elections that year: "So although new technology raised about $100 million, the 'old' technology shattered previous records with another $500 million. Great change but new technology did not displace the old methods" (Semiatin 2007, 49; see also Graf et al. 2006; and Davis 2005).

In terms of political communication, Internet pessimists often doubted that the new online world was actually improving American elections or politics in general: "Likewise, Web video and audio files do not appear to change the style or sound of what counts as a well spoken candidate. Instead the Internet complicates and thickens the communicative scene, requiring those running for office to quickly speculate and assess how messages in an off-line world will be picked up and played out in Web sites, message groups, and blogs. Despite its structural integrity, the Net is an unpredictable space" (Denton 2005, 227).

Finally, Internet pessimists often pointed to the fact that the Internet in and of itself could not actually put bodies into the voting booth. William Crotty (2008) attributed this to the fact that the Internet itself is not truly applicable to campaigns in general since it is a "destination tool." People have to want to find a Web site in order to use it, and therefore the Internet is a substandard campaign tool since the goal of a political campaign is to attract people who have never heard of you before. Others believe that the

Dean campaign just revealed the most basic of campaign truths, that ultimately door knocking, phone calls, and kissing babies are still the ways to win elections, and the Web is just a means to do those things. John Nichols, political blogger for the *Nation*, expressed this point of view in assessing then recent Democratic Senate nominee Barack Obama in March 2004: "There was a great deal about the Obama campaign that mirrored the most interesting and impressive aspects of the Dean candidacy. Obama made early and effective use of the Internet and drew supporters together using Meet Ups. He built an enthusiastic network of supporters that included college students, suburban liberals and veteran progressive activists in Chicago" (2004). But he went on to point out that it was Obama's commitment to organizing in the real world and the grassroots that won him the election, not the Web. Thomas Schaller, a political scientist and writer for *Salon.com*, essentially made the same argument in the months after Dean's failure in 2004: "The first mistake Trippi made was in confusing the qualitative value of Dean's political support with such quantitative indicators as the Dean Web site's ubiquitous fundraising 'bat' totals, the latest Meetup.com and house party attendance figures, or the campaign's growing list of official endorsements. These innovations did not enable Dean to translate his support into the only electoral commodities that ultimately matter: votes and victories" (2004).

This belief has extended into the modern campaign world, as many political commentators try to dissect the role of the Internet in Barack Obama's victory. In response to some of the more extreme Internet optimists who saw the 2008 election as a validation that Obama was (in a positive sense) an Internet creation, political analyst Craig Watkins tamped down the rhetoric: "Yes, new media technologies certainly aided Obama's historic run. But he was not successful because of the Internet. He was successful because of how he incorporated the Internet into his campaign. . . . From the beginning Team Obama understood that digital was not merely a tool to target young citizens but rather a medium to talk with them, open up to them, and interact with them" (2009, 198). Baumgartner and Francia also pointed out that it was Obama's use of the Internet to recruit on-the-ground volunteers that was the key to his success (2010, 156–157). Political observers are not the only ones expressing this point of view. Even as recently as 2009, Trent and Friedenberg stated that although they saw changes occurring in political campaigns based on their observations of elections in 2006, they quoted a consultant from *Campaigns and Elections* to express their lack of idealism: "While there are enthusiasts who predict an Internet revolution that will change the face of American politics by ending for example, the 'stranglehold' of media consultants over candidates and their campaigns . . . we believe that the 'revolution' will be markedly different than the pie-in-the-sky predictions made just a couple of short years ago" (2008, 408).

To examine this idea of Internet optimism or pessimism I posed a question to campaign operatives about the Internet's impact on campaigns. They were asked, "The use of the Internet in political campaigns changes rapidly in every campaign season. Sometimes these changes are positive, and sometimes negative. Briefly describe the most significant impact the Internet has had on your campaign work." Although by no means the majority, there were a number of Internet pessimists in the sample as well:

- "Candidates spend too much time and start-up money worrying about their 'virtual' presence and not enough time and money on fundamentals." (Republican targeting consultant for presidential campaign in mid-Atlantic, 2008)
- "So far, Internet is overrated as campaign tool." (Democratic general and direct-mail consultant for county supervisor in the West, 2008)
- "[It helps with] inviting people to events or low dollar fundraisers. But, and I have to stress this, it never replaces having a volunteer pick up the phone and invite people to something." (Democratic manager for mayor in the West, 2008)
- "The Internet has not replaced old-fashioned organizing, including fundraising and volunteer management. The Internet is a tool that can make these actions simpler, but it has not replaced the human factor involved in this work. Younger consultants might differ on this and I believe they are mistaken." (Democratic campaign manager for superior court judge in the West, 2004)

Internet Optimists

On the other side are the Internet optimists, sometimes called Web evangelists (Watkins 2009) or cyber utopians (Semiatin 2007), who believe that the

Internet has fundamentally changed political campaigns and American democracy and allows managers to do things never before possible. The majority of political analysts, political professionals, and academics would fall into this category, and they often point to the Dean campaign of 2004 as the beginning of a vast transformation. Internet optimists often point to the Web's overall positive impact on politics and society and how the campaign and voters have been the beneficiaries of this change. Many researchers "find that Internet use increases the likelihood of voting and civic engagement; it also promotes higher incomes for African Americans and Latinos in particular" (Mossberger et al. 2008, 2). Philip Howard (2006), after his extensive ethnographic study of Internet technology (IT) professionals in campaigns over election cycles in the early 2000s, found that the Internet was such a transformative tool in political campaigns that the very structure of American democracy was at stake, rightly or wrongly. Others have found that the Internet increases engagement in campaigns from a more diverse audience (Howard 2006; Boyd 2009). Overall, Internet optimists seem to believe that the more the Web is in use in campaigns, the better.

Returning to the survey, as mentioned earlier, the political operatives were asked how they felt the Internet had changed political campaigns. The majority of the respondents were incredibly enthusiastic about how they had already employed the Internet in their campaigns and how they planned to do so in the future. They were particularly effusive about how the Internet helps in fund-raising. For example:

- "Ease of reaching otherwise unreachable donors." (online fund-raiser for Republican candidate for federal Senate in the Midwest, 2004)
- "Neighbor to Neighbor was a HUGE breakthrough especially in rural areas." (GOTV director for Democratic presidential candidate in the Pacific Northwest, 2008)
- "Fundraising! Our opponent ran a totally bull**** ad a week out (she saw the polling and got scared) that was denounced by observers on both sides of the aisle for being wrong, full of lies, and out of place. The day that ad hit the airwaves and made news across the country, our site traffic went up 10 fold as did our contributions from ActBlue. The next day we had a response ad out that slowed our servers to a crawl because it was hit with more traffic from across the country than we could have

ever planned for. . . . [That] was the singular tipping point that drove us
to win." (Internet consultant for Democratic federal Senate challenger
in the Southeast, 2008)

In fact, the general enthusiasm for the Web was so pervasive that many
respondents decried the lack of Internet savvy or intensity on the part of
their campaigns. For example:

- "Allows the distribution of information to happen quickly. My candidate did not want to take advantage of the Internet—even to the objection of the entire campaign staff." (manager of a Democratic open-seat state legislature candidate in the Midwest, 2008)
- "The Republican Party was just starting to get the idea about the power of the Internet, and as I was not the final decision maker, we didn't use the Internet for as much exposure as we should have." (media consultant for a Republican federal Senate challenger in the Northeast, 2008)

With Barack Obama's active use of Facebook, Twitter, MySpace, and various other sites, many Internet optimists pointed to his presidential campaign as the clearest example that the Web has changed everything. His campaign disproves perhaps the biggest criticism of the Internet pessimists, namely, that Internet campaigning cannot be trusted to put feet on the ground and bodies in the voting booth. Arianna Huffington, editor of the *HuffingtonPost.com*, stated definitively after Obama won the presidency that "were it not for the Internet, Barack Obama would not be president. Were it not for the Internet, Barack Obama would not have been the nominee" (Schiffman 2008).

Both Internet optimists and Internet pessimists used and saw the Internet put to use in political campaigns. They fundamentally differed, however, on how influential they saw the Web on campaign strategy and success, which led to the second Internet campaign question. I asked consultants whether they thought the Internet fundamentally changed how campaigns were run in this country, or did the Internet simply allow campaigns to engage in the same activities with better toys? I analyzed the attitudes toward the Internet across how long a consultant had worked in politics, what type of campaign they were running, and political party.

TABLE 5.1 Attitude toward the Internet in campaigns by years as a campaigner

	Years				
	1–4	*5–10*	*11–15*	*16–20*	*More than 20*
	N (%)	*N (%)*	*N (%)*	*N (%)*	*N (%)*
The Internet simply allows campaigns to engage in the same activities they always have, just through a different medium	28 (37.3)	26 (51.0)	9 (39.1)	2 (20.0)	2 (15.4)
The Internet allows campaigns to do new things they were never able to do before	47 (62.7)	25 (49.0)	14 (60.9)	8 (80.0)	11 (84.6)
Total	75 (100)	51 (100)	23 (100)	10 (100)	13 (100)

Note: N = actual number of responses. (%) = percentage of total.

Looking at the results of political operative views based on years in the business provided mixed results (Table 5.1). The relationship between attitudes toward the Internet and years as a campaigner were not statistically significant, so the proscriptive possibilities from these results are limited. We will simply look at them to see what they might mean about the sample. The longer campaigners had been in the field, the more likely they were to say that the Internet allowed campaigns to do things they had never been able to do before. In fact, 84 percent of the consultants that worked in the profession for twenty years or more said that the Internet was transformative. What was more telling, however, were the consultants who had worked on campaigns for five to ten years. In this range they worked on anywhere from two to three federal campaign cycles and possibly more locally, and they were evenly split on whether the Internet was really impacting how campaigns were run. What might explain this response? Campaigners in this range had worked just long enough to see some changes, but perhaps not long enough to make a sustained comparison to the "dark ages." And as we will discuss later, "change" in campaign strategy has a lot to do with where a campaigner started. We now look at how the status of a campaigner's candidate influenced how they felt about the transformative nature of the Internet in campaigns.

The type of campaign that political operatives ran did not seem to have a huge impact on how they felt about the transformative nature of the Internet on campaigns[8] (Table 5.2). The majority of operatives for challengers, incumbents, and open-seat candidates said that the Internet was a transformative

TABLE 5.2 **Attitude toward the Internet in campaigns by candidate status**

| | Type of Race | | |
	Incumbent N (%)	*Challenger* N (%)	*Open seat* N (%)
The Internet simply allows campaigns to engage in the same activities they always have, just through a different medium	22 (43.1)	12 (25.0)	33 (45.2)
The Internet allows campaigns to do new things they were never able to do before	29 (56.9)	36 (75.0)	40 (54.8)
Total	51 (100)	48 (100)	73 (100)

Note: N = actual number of responses. (%) = percentage of total.

TABLE 5.3 **Attitude toward the Internet in campaigns by political party**

	Republican N (%)	*Democrat* N (%)
The Internet simply allows campaigns to engage in the same activities they always have, just through a different medium	16 (30.8)	43 (43.4)
The Internet allows campaigns to do new things they were never able to do before	36 (69.2)	56 (56.6)
Total	52 (100)	99 (100)

Note: N = actual number of responses. (%) = percentage of total.

tool. We do note that the least enthusiastic were the incumbents. This result is congruent with our earlier discussion of the progression of Internet campaign strategy. Incumbent campaigners are much more risk averse, and therefore they are much less likely to see the Internet as a place to make big changes. Finally, we look at how different campaigners viewed the influence of the Internet by party identification.

The results are opposed to what we would expect, given the current literature and political observation. While the majority of both Republican and Democratic campaign operatives felt that the Internet was allowing campaigns to do things they had never done before, Republicans (69.2 percent) were more intense in this belief than Democrats (56.6 percent). What might explain this result? The answer takes us back to our earlier discussion of penetration, speed, and of course comfort.

Democrats as Internet Pessimists

Democrats have used the Internet in vast and extensive ways on the national level, with the help of grassroots activists, for years. Left-wing conventions like *Netroots Nation*, and Web sites like *Democratic Underground*, *ActBlue*, and *Moveon.org* are no longer outside the mainstream in regards to Democratic campaign strategy. In his campaign memoir, *The Audacity to Win*, Obama chief campaign manager David Plouffe epitomizes this attitude among Democrats even in the 2008 campaign. In describing the campaign's online strategy he said, "We had hired an enormous e-mail team within new media that worked under Rospar's direction (I assume in future campaigns this department will be called digital strategy, not new media—it's not new anymore and it's not just media), and also made sure all the states had their own fully staffed new media and email teams" (2009, 329).

The Internet is not allowing campaigns to do things that they were never able to do before in the minds of Democratic campaigners because the Internet is *how* they have been doing things for so long. Internet campaign strategy is so diffuse and normalized in left-wing and Democratic political campaigns in America that Internet innovations are normalized instead of considered transformative. The Republican Party, which has only recently begun using the Internet as consistently and organically as the Democratic Party, is still more likely to see the Web as introducing new concepts to campaigning because these are strategies that they have not employed before. An example can be seen in early 2007 when *Wired* published a story on the new band of campaign innovators in the Republican Party. Focusing on consultant David All, the story discussed how Generation X political consultants were working to get the GOP up to speed: "A former communications director for Republican Congressman Jack Kingston, All is one of a coterie of young conservatives who are trying to both goad and help his party catch up to the Democrats' online organizing and fundraising efforts. Call them the next-generation Karl Roves" (Stirland 2007; see also Rhoads 2009). All and his cohort went so far as to encourage Republican candidates to not skip the CNN-YouTube primary debate of 2008. Many of the campaigners on the GOP side considered this event to be a gimmick but were encouraged to think outside the box on the event as a way to connect with new voters.

The movement to enhance Republican use of the Internet has been a slow and difficult process. In an early 2010 *Washington Post* column titled "How Republicans Won the Internet," Republican Web consultants Mindy Finn and Patrick Ruffini explain why it took so long for the GOP to get serious about going online:

> It's not as though GOP organizers woke up last fall and realized they'd better learn to use this Internet thing. Our party is out of power—and the party out of power has the stronger incentive to innovate. If it doesn't, the base will. It was just that during the years that the netroots really took off—2004 to 2008—Republicans were not angry enough (or desperate enough) to use all the weapons in their arsenal. A single, unifying outrage, like the Democrats' opposition to the Iraq war and to President George W. Bush, was missing. . . . Netroots protests dragged the Democratic Party into the 21st century kicking and screaming in 2006 and 2008. Frustrated with the president and health-care reform, the conservative "tea party" movement has done the same for the Republicans in the past year.

By the fall of 2010, while Democrats were humming along using the Internet with the same comfort and stability that they had been for the past decade, Republicans were breaking down barriers, even within their own party.

In another example of how the GOP was running full speed to catch up with the Democrats, we take a look at James Lankford from Oklahoma. Lankford was a long-shot candidate for the Republican nomination for Oklahoma's Fifth Congressional District, but he turned to the Web to level the playing field: "Greatly outspent by two of his Republican rivals in the race to succeed Rep. Mary Fallin in Congress, Lankford has relied heavily on Facebook, Twitter and YouTube to get his message out. As part of that, the church camp director has employed a unique Facebook application that targets people who are old enough to vote and live in the 5th Congressional District. In just a couple of weeks, the application has used Lankford supporters to contact more than 4,000 people who meet the criteria" (Casteel 2010). Lankford won his race and is now member of the Republican Party's freshman class of 2011.

This discussion of Internet optimism and pessimism and the party differences in need and attitude toward the Internet has identified important trends. Campaign innovation, especially with the Internet, seems to be

TABLE 5.4 **Internet Penetration by U.S. Region**

Some 59% of American adults had Internet access at the end of 2002, up from about 50% in 2000. The use of the Internet by Americans over age 18 varies by region, however, as shown below.

Region	Adults with Internet Access in December 2002 (%)
New England (Connecticut, Maine, Massachusetts, New Hampshire, Vermont, Rhode Island)	66
Mid-Atlantic (Delaware, New Jersey, New York, Pennsylvania)	58
National Capital (Maryland, Virginia, Washington, DC)	64
Southeast (Florida, Georgia, North Carolina, South Carolina)	57
South (Alabama, Arkansas, Kentucky, Louisiana, Mississippi, Tennessee, West Virginia)	48
Industrial Midwest (Illinois, Indiana, Michigan, Ohio)	56
Upper Midwest (Minnesota, North Dakota, South Dakota, Wisconsin)	59
Lower Midwest (Iowa, Kansas, Missouri, Nebraska, Oklahoma)	55
Border States (Arizona, New Mexico, Texas)	60
Mountain States (Colorado, Idaho, Montana, Nevada, Utah, Wyoming)	64
Pacific Northwest (Oregon, Washington)	68
California	65

Source: http://www.pewInternet.org/Reports/2003/Internet-Use-by-Region-in-the-US.aspx?r=1; Spooner 2003

TABLE 5.5 **Consultant Internet Optimism vs. Internet Pessimism by Region of the Country**

	The Internet simply allows campaigns to engage in the same activities they always have, just through a different medium N (%)	*The Internet allows campaigns to do new things that they were never able to do before* N (%)	*Total* N (%)
Northeast	11 (36.7)	19 (63.3)	30 (100)
Mid-Atlantic	11 (40.7)	16 (59.3)	27 (100)
Southeast	16 (50.0)	16 (50.0)	32 (100)
South	2 (20.0)	8 (80.0)	10 (100)
Midwest	13 (31.0)	29 (69.0)	42 (100)
Southwest	4 (33.3)	8 (66.7)	12 (100)
West	5 (45.5)	6 (55.5)	11 (100)
Pacific Northwest	5 (62.5)	3 (37.5)	8 (100)

Note: N = actual number of responses. (%) = percentage of total.

TABLE 5.6 Consultant Internet optimist and pessimist attitudes by campaign
district type

	The Internet simply allows campaigns to engage in the same activities they always have, just through a different medium *N (%)*	*The Internet allows campaigns to do new things that they were never able to do before* *N (%)*	*Total* *N (%)*
Mostly rural	13 (40.6)	19 (59.4)	32 (100)
Somewhat rural	4 (57.1)	3 (42.9)	7 (100)
Mixed rural and suburban	26 (35.1)	48 (64.9)	74 (100)
Suburban	16 (37.2)	27 (62.8)	43 (100)
Urban	8 (50.0)	8 (50.0)	16 (100)

Note: N = actual number of responses. (%) = percentage of total.

driven by long-shot candidates or candidates who do not necessarily have a great deal of cash on hand to start. We also see that there are party differences in attitudes toward Internet campaigning and that there may be a host of other factors, demographic, regional, or structural, that impact how political operatives employ Internet strategy.

Internet Strategy as a Regional Enterprise

Several researchers have found that where one lives in the country can have an impact on whether they access the Internet and to what extent they make use of online resources. The Pew Center on the Internet in American Life produced a study in 2002 demonstrating that there are differences in the country on Internet use stemming from where one lives (Spooner 2003) (Table 5.4). Peslak (2004), using the Pew study as a guide, went further to show that there are in fact regional differences in Internet use that are not simply racially or economically driven. In discussing the Dean campaign of 2004, Chakravarty and Caldwell (2004) also found evidence of a regional effect on online use. Given this existing evidence, it might be fair to assume that campaign strategists are affected by regional differences as well. Might a campaign in a rural area view the value of the Internet as a campaign tool differently than a campaign in a major metropolitan area? We start by taking a look at the Pew Charitable Trusts Institute's results showing how Internet use changes depending on the region of the country.

Now, similar to Peslak, we will examine if the results from the consultants in the survey affirm what Pew showed about campaign use. To compare the results, we examine if there is a significant relationship between whether consultants are Internet optimists or pessimists by the region of the country that they are campaigning in.

Although the relationships were statistically significant in the survey, the results do not exactly agree with the Pew Charitable Trusts Institute's and existing work on regional influences on Internet use and strategy. The three regions in our study with the fewest Internet "optimists" were the Southeast, the West, and the Pacific Northwest. According to the Pew study, the regions of the United States with the lowest levels of Internet penetration in 2002 were the South and the Midwest. Although our study seems to confirm years later that the southern region might be less inclined to inspire campaigners to Internet innovation, the results indicate Internet pessimism in regions of the West and Pacific Northwest, which have some of the highest Internet penetration rates in the nation. Some of these results are likely skewed due to a small sample size of Pacific northwestern and western regions of the survey. However, even if you combine all survey responses from the "West," campaigners were still just barely more optimistic than pessimistic about the value of the Internet as a transformative campaign tool. What might explain why an area that is flush with connected voters would have consultants who are less inclined to say that campaigns are innovating because of the Web?

In the next table we examine attitudes toward the Internet by rural and urban environments for campaigners in our sample.

Again we have a curious result. Campaigners in somewhat rural environments and urban environments were more likely to identify with Internet pessimism than consultants in other campaign districts. The suburbs and mixed regions, where Internet penetration is high, elicited campaigners who saw the transformative power of the Internet, even more so in rural areas where the Internet gave campaigners a chance to connect with voters they might not have been able to see otherwise.

I believe that even with the small sample size available, these results capture a phenomenon similar to what we observed with "Internet optimists" and "Internet pessimists" among Democrats and Republicans. With high Internet penetration rates in California going back much longer and higher than most other parts of the country, Internet campaigning is normalized in California and much of the West and is thus not seen as transformative. The same might be said for at least urban regions in the United States where broadband technology was available and affordable long before it was in the suburbs and rural parts of the country. Is political science late getting into online campaign research? Has the Internet become so ingrained in the minds of some campaigners that e-campaigns are already normalized and the lack of research on consultants has led the discipline to miss some element of this phenomenon?

In the next section we will take a look at where the current political science literature is on Internet campaigning and then turn to see if it reflects the campaigners in the sample.

The State of the Discipline

The current political science research on political campaigns and the Internet is consistent but in many cases is still lacking in the core conceit of this book, namely, that consultant views should play a key role in campaign research. The few works on e-campaigning that have involved political consultant views have resulted in impressive work on the inner workings of modern campaigns. Schneider and Foot noted that when examining campaign Web sites during a presidential primary, consultants put their best foot forward, which improved their ability to analyze the sites: "US presidential primary campaigns also function as a kind of clearing-house for political professionals seeking to burnish their skills and credentials for the political marketplace in the coming general election featuring gubernatorial, Senate and House campaigns. For these reasons, it is reasonable to assume that primary election campaign Web sites, especially as viewed in a common time frame just prior to the New Hampshire primary, should function as a particularly good window through which to view the state of the Web campaigning at a particular point in time" (2005, 1).

Taking a more direct approach on the influence of consultants, Vaccari's research showed that political consultants and campaign managers began to view their target audiences differently with online campaigning. He suggested that campaign professionals viewed their core constituents more with online campaigning than traditional campaigns of the past. After conducting interviews with more than thirty Web consultants from the Bush and Kerry campaigns of 2004, he concluded, "In 2004, e-campaign consultants dedicated most of their activities to bridging the gap between their Internet audiences and the material, off-line reality of the campaign. . . . However, while scholars stress that online organizing tools can only result in empowering those that are already involved . . . campaign professionals strive to convert these energies into viable electoral resources, which can result in increased voter mobilization and participation" (2008, 7).

While researching online versus televised messaging, Druckman et al. (2010b) surveyed political consultants working for House and Senate candidates. They found that there were slightly different strategies influencing online strategy depending on certain contextual campaign factors.

The most extensive existing work on political operatives and Internet campaigning has been done by Philip Howard, who spent five election cycles, ending in 2004, interviewing, observing, and providing an ethnographic analysis of IT political operatives in campaigns. Howard's intimate studies showed that there were two types of political consultants using modern Internet campaigns (what he dubbed *hypermedia*). One group was composed of campaign professionals, and the other group was composed primarily of IT professionals who were less concerned about partisanship and ideology than they were in changing the way that American campaigns were run. "Few members of the e-politics community are tied to the big political parties. They enjoy freelance work, which gives them the option to leave politics altogether and to market other kinds of products with other kinds of consumer campaigns" (2006, 47).

Howard ultimately made a telling point about the difficulty in studying political consultants during the Internet age, if not in general. While he studied IT campaigners from 1996 to 2004, the bulk of his research focused on campaigners in the 2000 and 2004 election cycles. In his conclusion, he stated, "By now, many of the campaigns, lobbyists, candidates and political consultants I studied have come and gone. Other political consultants with expertise in hypermedia have taken their place" (ibid.). Although some of the extensive turnover he noted might have been reflective of the tech bubble bursting in the early 2000s, he also made an even more salient point. There is a difference between IT professionals who work on campaigns and campaign professionals who use Internet technology. The former may be driven by money or a desire to change democracy; the latter are driven by the desire to win a campaign for their client or party.

When looking at the main campaign tenets that also constitute the greater part of this book, researchers have begun to examine specifically how online campaigning influences negative advertising, positioning, and messaging in modern campaigns. Xenos and Foot (2004), studying 2002 campaign Web sites, found that candidates were not making great strides in their position taking on their Web sites, but there were differences based on the type of election. Overall, they found that incumbents spent less time on online issue content than did challengers or those in open-seat races and often attempted to be vaguer about policy stances online than the opposition. Druckman et al. (2009) found similar results, noting that in campaign Web sites from 2002 to 2006 candidates remained selective in what issues they approached online, even though a Web site gives them more freedom to express detailed policy views. In discussing negative advertising online, Druckman et al. noted that Democrats were much more likely to attack their opponents online through Web sites and blogs than were Republicans. He also found that the level of campaign being run, including the House versus the Senate, strongly influenced if Web sites were more negative than radio or television negative advertising. Regarding candidates, Dolan (2005), in examining Web sites for female congressional candidates in 2000 and 2002, found no evidence that issue positioning changed based on gender stereotypes or beliefs.

The driving forces behind campaign strategy by campaigners are surprisingly consistent with much of what we have learned before in this work. Long-shot candidates, challengers, and open-seat candidates are more likely to employ innovative Web strategies than incumbents (Semiatin 2007; Klotz 1997). Democrats are traditionally more likely to use new campaign practices, but that is rapidly changing as Republicans catch up. The competitiveness of a race, where a candidate stands in the polls, and what position they are seeking round out the most consistently discovered factors that influence current Web strategy in political science work (Foot and Xenos 2009; Benoit 2000; Schneider and Foot 2005; Vaccari 2008; Druckman et al. 2010a; Druckman, Kifer, and Parkin 2007). Of particular interest is the influence the demographics or region might play in campaign strategy online. Herrnson and Stokes found that young voters and educated voters were the most active online and thus better targets for online campaigning, noting that the "digital divide" is overstated. Baumgartner and Morris in their study of youth online engagement in 2007 discovered that while young people were online, they were not necessarily any more engaged politically due to social networks (2010, 24). Studying campaign practices in 2000, Dulio and O'Brien found that the Web worked best when rallying whites, Republicans, and young people, beyond which they stated: "For campaign strategists, this means one of two things. For campaigns hoping to mobilize or shore up these groups, using the web can be efficacious. Campaigns that look to mobilize groups not found on this list are well advised to either develop web plans that creatively draw in new groups or direct few resources to the web" (quoted in Thurber and Nelson 2004, 192). Finally, Gaziano and Liesen (2009) and the Pew Charitable Trusts (Lee and Horrigan 2002) performed studies demonstrating that Web use is region specific, meaning that we might want to consider whether e-strategy could be affected by regional norms of Internet use as well.

An important point in all of the above discussion is that the years in which these analyses took place may have a huge impact on how these researchers came to their conclusions. The tendency in political science work on online campaigning is to look at specific years or election cycles and not examine a wide swath of campaigners who may or may not have been working on campaigns at the same time or level. If one were to look at campaigners in a much wider arc, we might get a better idea how consultants actually feel about campaigning online.

Tools of the Trade

If we are going to examine how political operatives used the Internet and what drove that behavior, we have to also look at the tools of the trade. What exactly did campaigners use online to make their campaigns more successful? For this research we will look specifically at how campaign managers and political operatives employed social networking sites (SNS) in campaign strategy. When asked to discuss online innovations, consultants in the sample consistently volunteered Facebook and Twitter as important components to their campaigns. For example:

- "Facebook has become a very useful tool for mobilizing and identifying potential volunteers." (GOTV director for incumbent state legislator in the Southeast in 2008)

- "Sites like Facebook provide a great way to get in touch with voters more efficiently." (Republican manager for incumbent state legislator in the Southeast in 2009)
- "In 2007, Twitter didn't exist, only college students were on Facebook, and many people didn't have "smart phones" that would make fundraising by 'blast email' terribly effective. Now, with Twitter, Facebook, smart phones, etc. you can add immediate 'action items' to communications with activists and donors." (deputy campaign manager and scheduler for Democratic gubernatorial challenger candidate in the Southeast in 2008)
- "Facebook generates turnout, it expands networks, it provides data, and it raises profile." (field organizer for Democratic presidential candidate in the Midwest in 2008)
- "In 2006 the Internet was not used like it is today, Facebook did not exist. If I were running that campaign today Facebook and Twitter would be used. Vote Builder is another advancement that has made organizing voters easier." (GOTV director state legislature challenger in the Southeast in 2006)

Both Web sites have skyrocketed in popularity among important voting populations in the country, and technological advances have made them a regular part of many people's lives. Facebook as of this writing has begun to outstrip massively its onetime rival MySpace to become the most popular Internet site in North America that is not a search engine. Although there is debate about how effective social networking sites really are in engaging and involving voters (Kissane 2010; Baumgartner and Morris 2010), this study will focus more on SNS than blogs. While blogs clearly have a role in modern campaign strategy and have been cited as wonderful outlets for fundraising and political communication, their extensive range and variability make them less valuable for this research. Every campaign can start a blog; there are literally thousands of blogs that exist in this country that are nominally political and wax and wane in influence and popularity depending on the season. A campaigner, looking to be as efficient and creative as possible, is more likely to employ a standing campaign resource like Facebook, My-Space, or Twitter rather than trying to drive traffic to a self-created blog or become the hot topic on an existing blog. We will go through a brief discussion of some of the most popular standing social networking sites and their political impact before going forward.

Facebook

Facebook gained notoriety as a campaign tool due to the easy manner in which people could start political organizing. The two most famous examples are university students Meredith Segal (Bowdoin) and Farouk Olu Aregbe (University of Missouri at Columbia) who each started fan sites dedicated to Barack Obama without any direct contact with his campaign. "Students for Obama" and "One Million Strong for Barack," respectively, are credited with creating a groundswell of support for Obama in locations across the nation where he had not even actively campaigned yet. When Obama came to visit George Mason University for a rally a mere eight months after Segal's site was created, there were more than 62,000 students and more than eighty chapters of "Students for Obama" (Watkins 2009, 195; see also Vargas 2007).

Political scientists Williams and Gulati found that Facebook had incredible value for modern campaigns due to the Web site's own efforts. Facebook actually initiated a candidate feature in 2006 allowing federal politicians to have their own sites with unique features for individual campaigns. This helped make Facebook into one of the premiere social networking sites for political campaigns. "Facebook's efforts with Election Pulse and its streamlining of the process for connecting candidates and supporters seemed to encourage a substantial number of candidates to integrate the site into their online strategies" (2007, 6). Later they found that Facebook fans and memberships on campaign Web sites actually had a correlation to vote share, even if a campaign had Facebook friends that were not actually located in the campaign district. Although Baumgartner and Morris (2010) specifically questioned this conclusion, the fact remains that the power and influence of Facebook and to an increasingly lesser extent MySpace have infiltrated most campaigns in modern politics.

MySpace

Although MySpace has rapidly lost popularity in the years since the 2008 presidential campaign, many people forget that at the time the site was on equal footing with Facebook. Many lower-level candidates used MySpace and

Facebook in the late 2000s, although Facebook was already beginning to pull ahead as far as memberships and usefulness for campaigns. Unlike Facebook, MySpace did not have a set site preference for candidates, which meant that anyone running for public office could potentially see another Web site with their name pop up on the site, and they would have no recourse other than to ask the person nicely to pull the site down (Sabato 2010, 195). One of the unique values of MySpace for the Obama campaign in 2008 and earlier campaigns was that MySpace had a more socioeconomically and racially diverse membership than Facebook (Boyd 2009). MySpace had its roots in the music and arts community in California in the early 2000s compared to Facebook, which was in existence for a full year before anyone other than college students were allowed to join. Because of this gap, MySpace initially offered a more diverse mix of young people and millennials to communicate with online. The Obama campaign made young minority voters a key part of their e-campaign targeting strategy, not only having an active page on MySpace but also running ads and putting up profiles on minority-tailored Web sites such as Blackplanet, MiGente, or AsianAvenue. The Obama campaign's success in gaining hits and visits to its various Web sites was seen as a direct correlation to his ability to get young people and previously disconnected voters to the polls on election day. "Obama had five times the number of visits to his MySpace site as McCain had to his; seven times the number of visits to his Facebook pages; about fifteen times the number of mentions in the blogosphere than either McCain or Palin, as tracked by Technorati; and 89% of citizen visits to websites (to McCain's 12)" (Denton 2005, 235).

Twitter

The 2008 presidential campaigns did not make as much use of Twitter as did campaigns in the following off-year elections and heading into 2010. Part of the reason for this is that Twitter remains a viable piece of Internet campaign technology if properly used, but many people are not active users of the site. A relatively small group of Twitter users account for the bulk of Twitter activity. By most analyses, 5 percent of Twitter users account for 75 percent of all Tweets, so as a campaign resource it is often a challenge for candidates to get citizens on Twitter to begin with, but once they are linked, it is an effective medium to transfer ideas and strategy (Cheng and Evans 2009). Twitter users are on average older than users of other sites, with a median age of thirty-one, even though the young create most of the Tweets, and 35 percent live in urban areas. Lassen and Brown conducted research showing certain factors that predict Twitter use in campaigns: "Members are more likely to adopt Twitter if their party leaders urge them to, if they are young, or if they serve in the Senate. Surprisingly, we find that electoral vulnerability has little or no effect on Twitter adoption or use" (2010). Republicans have recently begun to use Twitter extensively, making it a highlight of their campaigns in 2009 and through the midterms of 2010.

Wyeth Ruthven (2010), an analyst at Qorvis Communications, noted in his research that Twitter feeds fall primarily into three categories: calls to action, conversation with voters, and self-promotion. His work focused on the governors' races in New Jersey and Virginia in 2009 and the special Senate election in Massachusetts to replace Ted Kennedy in early 2010. Ruthven pointed out that Twitter, like most Internet tools, must be used properly to have any significant effect on a campaign's chance of winning. He noted that losing candidates, such as Creigh Deeds in Virginia, tended to dilute their Twitter authenticity by having too many Tweets on various subjects rather than keeping to a focused message. What's more, voters enjoy following Twitter feeds because they feel they are getting the direct thoughts and musings of the candidate they support. Even if everyone knows that Scott Brown's Twitter feeds are coming from a campaign staffer, at least his feed is the only one from the campaign. Deeds had Twitter feeds from not only himself but also other members of his staff, as well as feeds based on specific scandals and events from the campaign. The most effective uses of the site were for targeted messaging and to rally voters heading into important election events. It is also worth noting that in each of these three races, Republicans won in Democratically held seats, employing new media technology that had been anathema to the party just two short cycles earlier.

YouTube

If there is one SNS that represents the "Wild West" era of Internet campaigns, it would be YouTube. The ability to download videos from a cell phone or a camera almost instantly and for free is a wonderful resource for both good and evil during campaigns. In one of the more pointed responses from the survey of campaign operatives, the problems associated with

YouTube were made clear: "This is not specific to the campaign I am using in this survey, but I feel the most detrimental and useful invention on the Internet is YouTube. Opposition trackers videotape candidates at every event, record every speech, and if the candidate makes one misstep—which they always do, it only matters which one makes the more critical error—it can throw the entire election. I find it both amazing and disgusting."

YouTube was not the first time that video images could be rapidly sent during a campaign, but the site certainly made it easier. During the 2004 presidential election the Bush campaign sent out a forty-five-second e-mail video titled *Unprincipled* that brought up many of the issues that would be part of the campaign's criticisms of Kerry in the fall (Denton 2005, 22). This video went out to thousands of Bush supporters and received substantial coverage on television, but the video did not become what we now refer to as "viral" (Wallersten 2010, 163). When YouTube was introduced in the spring of 2005, it revolutionized how video images and information could be spread. For the first time in campaign history there was a free, easily accessible clearinghouse where any political information could be spread by people watching the videos and subsequently sending them to their friends. With the relatively low costs of video production mixed with a forum of potentially millions of viewers every day, YouTube has become a frighteningly level playing field for candidates running for office. The impact of this Web site has trumped just about all others in the world of political consulting. Joe Trippi, former campaign manager for the Dean campaign, put the power of YouTube for the Obama campaign in stark terms: "'The campaign's official stuff they created for YouTube was watched for 14.5 million hours,' Mr. Trippi said. 'To buy 14.5 million hours of broadcast TV is $47 million'" (C. C. Miller 2008).

Political scientists have found mixed results regarding the influence of YouTube on campaign politics. David Karpf noted that despite all the hype surrounding YouTube, candidates' embarrassing moments caught on tape and posted on the site do not really drive fund-raising any more than other political events and drives (2010, 143). Lawrence and Rose found that YouTube can be a ripe environment to foster hostile racial and gender dialogue that is unhampered by moderators or ombudsmen (2010, 198). Gulati and Williams showed that YouTube is most valuable to campaigners running in minority-populated districts, incumbent candidates, and those who have more money at their disposal. This is ironic given that in most cases research shows that it

TABLE 5.7 **Candidate Obama versus Obama Girl: YouTube video hit comparison**

Obama girl videos		*Videos of Barack Obama speeches*	
"I've Got a Crush on Obama"	12.6 million (2007–2008)	Iowa Caucus victory speech	3 million (February 2008)
Iowa Caucus video	2.9 million (2008)	"Yes We Can" in New Hampshire	2.5 million (February 2008)
Telling Hillary to "stop the attacks"	2.2 million (2008)	"Convention Address"	1.5 million (August 2008)
Battle with "McCain Girls"	4.2 million (2008)	"Election-Night Address"	5 million (November 2008)

is "outsider" campaigns that are more driven to innovate online, but they make a compelling case. After conducting interviews with online campaigners, they noted that challengers and open-seat candidates who were not as well known to the district used YouTube less, since they needed to get out and actually meet voters face-to-face rather than conduct introductions online. In comparing the value of YouTube in 2008 compared to other SNS sites, they made the case for the rise of YouTube vis-à-vis other sites: "We find YouTube to be more attractive to candidates than Facebook proved in 2006. This is likely the case because YouTube more closely mirrors the demographic profile of the general voting population. It is also more attractive than campaign websites were in their early days, again probably because more people are online and have broadband connections today, making Internet hosted sites like YouTube widely available to the general population" (2009, 16).

YouTube is the SNS most likely to represent the good and bad of the "bottom-up" strategy initiated by the Dean campaign in 2004 (Denton 2005, 227; Wolf 2004). In theory, using it is a great idea; we have already noted how a couple of college kids created Facebook pages that resulted in thousands of supporters for a presidential candidate. But what is the flip side to this uncontrolled content? As our previous consultant already noted, YouTube allows candidates' every word to be recorded and put online for millions to see almost instantly and can create a barrage of back-and-forth videos—but at least in those cases, it is the actual candidate speaking and possibly making a mistake. What happens when your campaign supporters are out of control? YouTube is the epitome of this conundrum.

There are positive and negative examples of this throughout the campaign season, especially during the presidential election of 2008. We already discussed at the start of this chapter how a YouTube video put an end to a brewing fight between Obama and Hillary supporters, but YouTube also began one of the biggest unpredictable sensations of the campaign as well. In 2007 Amber Lee Ettinger, a model and student at New York's Fashion Institute of Technology, was hired by *BarelyPolitical.com* to star in a video titled *I Have a Crush on Obama*. *BarelyPolitical.com* specialized in creating comedy viral videos with a political slant, and Ettinger, in sexy clothing, danced around in the video pledging her Britney Spears–like love for then candidate Barack Obama. The video became an Internet sensation, going viral in less than a week (meaning it was e-mailed to thousands of individuals who had not seen the content on the original site). Ettinger soon became known as "Obama Girl" and produced a series of videos, each one featuring her in tight-fitting clothing or in one instance a camouflaged bikini, all pledging undying affection for Barack Obama and daring anyone (be it Hillary or the knock-off McCain Girls) to try to stop her "man" from winning the White House. There was both excitement and controversy surrounding Ettinger's videos. Some decried them as sexist titillation and borderline soft porn. Candidate Obama, when asked about the videos, was careful to not throw water on youthful Internet support for his campaign, stating to the *Des Moines Register* in 2007, "It's just one more example of the fertile imagination of the Internet. More stuff like this will be popping up all the time" (Clayworth 2007). But at the same time he suggested such Internet material may not always be appropriate. Obama himself did not like the videos and commented that they made his daughters uncomfortable. But it is hard to avoid being associated with an Internet sensation who is calling herself "Obama Girl." Ettinger's teeny-bopper love for Obama put the campaign in a complicated situation: While her popularity was seen as harmless fun by millions, she also helped bolster the image that Obama was a vapid celebrity, with fawning fans who worshiped him like a pop star rather than someone running for the highest office in the land. It was no coincidence that the McCain campaign's series of ads suggesting that Obama was more teen idol than world leader went on the air during Obama Girl's peak. From the political and academic analysts' standpoint, an even more disturbing trend was noticed due to this YouTube sensation. By the end of the campaign season "Obama Girl's" hits on YouTube rivaled and in some cases beat out YouTube videos by Obama himself (Table 5.7). What did it say about American elec-

TABLE 5.8 **Significant predictors on use of certain Internet tools during a campaign**

	Significant predictor	*More likely to use this Internet tool if:*
Campaign web site	Federal or state race	running for federal office
	Elections after 9/11	election took place after 9/11
Twitter	Executive or legislative position sought	running for executive office
	Region of the country	you are *not* running in the West
	Percentage of minorities in the district	higher percentage of minorities
	Income level in district	district income is high
MySpace	Executive or legislative position	running for executive office
	Federal or state race	running for federal office
YouTube	Executive or legislative position	running for executive office
	Federal or state race	running for federal office
Facebook	Party identification	you are a Republican
	Executive or legislative position	running for executive office
	Federal or state race	running for federal office
Other Internet resources	Minority percentage	higher number of minorities in district

tions that any random individual can put up videos that rival or supersede those of an actual election campaign?

As we see from the table, Obama Girl was as popular as the man she was swooning over. Political analysts often lament the possibility that public discourse could be highjacked by the Internet. But the complications of YouTube run even deeper than starry-eyed fans. Candidates are often placed in the unenviable position of having to justify, defend, or condemn the behavior of their supporters based on what they place on YouTube. It is easy to ignore one screaming fan in a crowd who calls your opponent a name, but when that screaming voter makes a YouTube video of their anger that gets 15,000 hits in three hours, a campaign has to respond or risk being associated or accused of tacitly accepting the content.

Driving Factors and Social Networking Sites

With all the major social networking sites accounted for and existing literature reviewed, I decided to take my findings to the consultants in the sample.
Will the factors driving online campaign behavior identified in political
science hold true when campaign operatives are involved? Will online campaigning be yet another area where campaign context proves more important than an overriding theory? I performed a binary logistic regression on
each of the major SNS sites that I identified in the survey and determined what
independent variables drove how often campaigners used these sites. The potential Web resources were a campaign Web site, Twitter, MySpace, Facebook, YouTube, or "other Internet resources." I used the standard predictor
variables established in this book and the current research, with one excep-
tion for interpretation purposes. In many of the analyses I used the variable
"9/11" to see if dependent variables changed values depending on if a campaign occurred before or after September 11, 2001. In this case MySpace
(2005), YouTube (2005), Facebook (2006), and Twitter (2007) did not exist
before 9/11. However, 2001 would have been the last year before the first Internet campaign of 2004. For that reason we will consider this variable a
proxy for the pre- and post-Internet era of political campaigns. In Table 5.9
the left column features the Web tool that was being investigated as an independent variable. The second column features the variables that were found
to be significant in influencing the use of the Web tool, and the third column shows how the variables interacted.

Two variables stand out the most in regards to driving the use of Internet
tools in campaigns among the consultants. Those running for executive positions (governor, president, mayor) and those running for federal office
(Congress, presidency) were the most likely to employ free resources like
MySpace, Facebook, and Twitter. Remaining true to its demographic of
young, diverse professionals, Twitter was most likely used in campaign areas that were higher in income and with larger minority populations. It is
worthy of note, however, that "other Internet resources" were driven by minority communities being larger in a consultant's campaign district. As
mentioned earlier, there are many Web sites such as Blackplanet, MiGente,
and AsianAvenue that are frequented just as much if not more by Web
surfers as the other major sites like Facebook and MySpace. However, if one

TABLE 5.9 **Analysis of consultant views on value of campaign Web site for certain activities**

	Significant predictor	*More likely to use your campaign Web site for this if:*
Fund-raising	Party identification	you are a Democrat
	Type of election	you are a challenger or in an open-seat race
	Federal or state race	you are running for federal office
	Region of the country	you are *not* in the West
	Regional election after 9/11	your campaign took place after 9/11
Connecting with voters	Federal or state race	you are running for federal office
	Election after 9/11	your campaign took place after 9/11
Organizing events	Executive or legislative race	you are running for executive office
	Federal or state race	you are running for federal office
	Polls midway	you are behind in the polls at the midway point
Voter registration	Executive or legislative race	you are running for executive office
	Federal or state race	you are running for federal office
Other Web site uses	Party identification	you are a Republican
	Type of election	you are a challenger or in an open-seat race
	Federal or state race	you are running for federal office

has a message that they want to specifically target at the growing Asian population in the Virginia suburbs of Washington, D.C., or the African American population in urban Detroit, culture- and race-specific Web sites are the best strategic option.

These results suggest that at least some existing political science work captures the use of political strategists' use of online tools but not very specifically. While existing theory notes differences in House and Senate usage of campaign tools online, or even incumbency or challenger status, more work should be done to include multiple independent variables.

We have looked at the impact of several variables on the use of SNS Web sites, but what about the actual campaign Web sites that many consultants worked with? Federally, there are no incumbent senators or representatives who do not have Web sites for either major party, and campaign sites are becoming standardized at all campaign levels. Moving away from SNS, let us examine what variables drove consultant attitudes on specific uses of campaign Web sites. Table 5.9 is set up like Table 5.8.

The results are a treasure trove of information about how campaigners use their Web sites during campaigns, so we will discuss each use of a campaign Web site specifically.

Fund-Raising

Using one's campaign Web site is more likely when consultants are Democrats, challengers, and consultants working on open-seat campaigns and running for federal office. Democrats' use of campaign Web sites for fund-raising has been a long-established practice, as well as by challengers, who are more likely to need to raise money online than an established incumbent. My use of the 9/11 proxy seems effective thus far, with consultants working on campaigns after 2001 reporting that they were more likely to use their sites for fund-raising. In the first indicator of regional differences in campaign strategy, online consultants who worked on campaigns in the western part of the United States reported that they were less likely to use their sites for fund-raising.

Connecting with Voters

Candidates who ran for federal office were more likely to use their Web sites to connect with voters. This makes sense strategically. Federal candidates have a larger area to cover in their campaigns usually, and thus the Web site becomes a useful tool to connect with voters, state- or regionwide. Compare this to local candidates, who can often travel their smaller districts in person without using the Web site.

Organizing Events

Candidates running for federal and executive offices were more likely to use their campaign Web sites to organize events. This activity is distinct from simply connecting with voters. Connecting with voters could simply be a blog or allowing voters to watch videos or send e-mails. Organizing events is a much more complex and interactive process that might include getting RSVPs and collecting volunteers to host events at their homes or in local communities. All of these are key activities for federal races. It is not entirely clear why consultants working for executive candidates would be more inclined to want to organize events online except that perhaps consultants working for candidates for executive office needed to exert more control over how events in their campaigns were run. Finally, this is the only element of either Web site or social network use that was influenced by where a consultant's candidate was in the polls, but again it makes sense strategically. If a candidate is behind in the polls at the midway point of a campaign, organizing events is going to be one of the top priorities in order to pull the campaign back even with the competition.

Voter Registration

Voter registration efforts are somewhat complicated on the state level, but federal candidates must make registration a critical part of their campaign organization. Again we see that consultants for executive candidates exhibited a greater desire to control or organize their campaigns than candidates for executives, something that we will explore further in this chapter's conclusion.

Other Web Site Uses

Part of living and campaigning in the "Wild West" era is the reality that campaign strategy can change in fundamental ways every election cycle, if not within cycles. That is why I included an "other Internet resource" option for consultants in the survey. Republicans, challengers, open-seat candidates, and those running for federal office were more likely to use their Web sites for campaign activities beyond the four uses above. What were those other activities? Vaccari (2008) noted that some campaign Web sites provided supporters with phone numbers to local media outlets to call in and advocate for their candidates or provided form letters that could be sent to local newspapers across the nation. Other campaign Web site uses included downloading pages where supporters could print flyers or other campaign paraphernalia. Regardless of what those other uses might have been, the fact that Republicans and outsider candidates were more likely to employ them speaks to the larger theme in existing campaign research that it is the outsider candidates or out parties that are more likely to innovate in online strategies.

Conclusion

"No Internet. No Obama. . . . There are other important differences, of course: the caucus strategy, the glamour, the oratory, the speech forthrightly addressing the prejudice. But none of these would have been decisive without the money Obama raised online, the videos Obama posted online, and, above all, the millions of people who connected with the Obama campaign on their own times and terms online. Yes, it did make a difference" (Cornfield 2008). Cornfield's quote exemplifies the complexity of the study of Internet campaigns in political science today. On the one hand, it is clear that campaigns have been changed by the Internet, but just how far that change has gone, and whether it is still dependent on keeping up with classic campaign strategy, is still unclear. One way that this confusion could be cleared up is with more systematic integrations of campaign operatives in analyses of campaign strategy by political science. This chapter suggests that when it comes to what drives some aspects of campaign strategy, political science has done reasonably well with including political activists. It approaches a political truth now that "outsider" candidates either by self-proclamation or actual campaign position are the real innovators of e-campaigning. However, the minutia associated with political campaigning online is still being missed. For all of the existing studies on whether MySpace and Facebook are mobilizing voters, it would stand to reason that those running the campaigns through these sites should be a part of the discussion. The significant results found here suggest that there is work to be done on who uses social networking sites and why during a campaign. Plus, we have also seen that many more factors that drive campaigns in general, like position in the polls and running for federal races or executive races, play a role that has heretofore been missed in campaign studies in political science.

As we head to the conclusion, bear in mind that we have only just begun to scratch the surface of what campaigners contribute to the discipline of political science, and we will review all of those influences as well as what the implications are of this book to the future of campaign studies and political practitioners.

6

Conclusion

The arguments and evidence presented in this book provide a unique and previously unseen look at the world of campaign managers and political operatives in the United States. While many works in political science, journalism, and political commentary have attempted to look at campaign managers, none has attempted an undertaking this large or extensive. Specifically, it is an attempt to examine campaign operatives' behavior across races, places, and spaces in the main areas of political campaigning. In order to do this research, I took both methodological and theoretical risks, some of which may be unconventional or controversial, but the end results speak for themselves. These methods have confirmed the theoretical foundation of much existing political science work by demonstrating that theories actually apply to real practitioner decision making. At the same time, this work has highlighted critical areas in need of improvement and reevaluation in the discipline.

A political scientist studying campaigns can no longer justifiably overlook the role that political consultants and operatives play in basic campaign elements like messaging, candidate presentation, Internet campaigning, policy positioning, and negative advertising. By creating theories on campaigns that do not consider the roles and influences of political operatives, political scientists risk creating theories that may be exciting and understandable but bear no resemblance to the real-life events that they purport to be explaining. Over the past five chapters I have discussed how several basic areas of campaign practices are influenced by political consultants and how these influences are often not captured in political science. My task is now to assess the larger implications of these discoveries and what that might mean for political science, political operatives, outside observers, and American elections in general. This discussion will take place in three parts. First, I will review what we have learned in each of these major campaign areas and what the implications of this research are for political science and American politics in general. Second, I will discuss possible future avenues for research in political science on campaigns and suggestions on how this should be integrated. Finally I will discuss the most important element of all, namely, what have we learned from this work about what it takes to win in political campaigns and how the results of this might give us a preview of elections in the future.

What Have We Learned?

The relationship between a political consultant and their candidate is like an incredibly intense Vegas marriage. It starts with all sorts of passion and excitement because neither side knows if it will last. There is a chance you might wake up in a couple of months and realize this was a huge mistake, or you might find out that you are stuck with each other for years; no one really knows. That is why studying consultant relationships with candidates is so important. While the 1990s brought forth celebrity campaigners who would write books about the candidates and campaigns, years later empirically there was not much in political science about how campaigners looked at candidates strategically.

We learned from this book that campaign operatives do not really look at candidate traits in the same way that voters do. Voters look for leadership and integrity, according to most polls. A campaign manager likes these traits, too, but the most important trait to them is that the candidate is willing to work hard and stick with their issue positions. Only when given the same answer choices as voters do political professionals evaluate candidates on the same criteria as voters. And that is how it should be. If my professional livelihood rests on the back of a candidate who is either a great person or willing to knock on a few extra doors to get out the vote on election day, I am going with the candidate with more mud on their shoes.

When given the same options as voters, campaigners evaluate candidates in a manner similar to voters. They too want leadership and integrity from their clients, something that should soothe the minds of many a cultural critic of campaign operatives. Continuing with this theme, campaign managers recognize the value of the political campaign and the role it will eventually play in the governing candidate. James Barber, a renowned political scientist, known for his classifications of presidential personalities, represented a common attitude toward the relationship between campaigning and governing: "But to suppose that how a candidate performs in contemporary campaigning tells us how he will perform in office is absurd—like supposing that a fellow who wins a hockey game is most likely to win a poker game. The campaign game is not the president game" (1990, 180). Yet this work points to the opposite conclusion. Campaigners do think that how a candidate runs their campaigns matters in how they will govern, and they are disappointed if their clients do not serve well. The results of my analysis address two key areas of political science, namely, the never-ending "Do campaigns really matter?" debate and discussions of representation and governance. If how a campaign is run can give the public insight into how this man or woman will run once serving in office, then perhaps the mechanics of a campaign should be more thoroughly investigated by the press and political scientists, not just when the campaign is over but while it occurs. Did the top-down structure of the Bush campaign, run by a small cabal of leaders, explain how he ran his administration? I think you could argue that the presidency of George W. Bush was defined by a tight-knit group of leaders who believed in their own counsel more than that of outsiders. Has the "bottom-up" nature of the Obama campaign in 2008 told us something about how he has managed the presidency thus far? I think it is fair to say that the Obama campaign staff's comfort in delegating authority to campaigners across the nation could explain why Obama the president was so willing to delegate a great deal of authority to the Democratic Congress in pushing through health-care reform.

Future political science work should take a harder look at what campaign consultants really do in the realm of candidate-trait and -image production. Current literature generally fails to consider the role of consultants, either assuming that decisions are driven primarily by the candidate or overlooking the various levels of relationships between campaign operatives and their clients. The current focus in political science on "elite-level" consultants has value but may not give us a wide enough berth on campaign management in this country. Yes, many Senate-level campaigns feature several rounds of interviews where sought-after campaign managers decide for whom and where they will ply their talents for the election season. But that is not the majority of political managers out there. Most of them are part of a larger party system or are referred by a small community of people. They are not so much choosing clients as they are making the most of what they have. Future political science needs to take this distinction to heart.

When a campaign starts, all too often there is a desire to win and a desire to serve but not necessarily much else. David Perlmutter relates in his book a story about one of the early political consultant's experience with a new candidate: "David Garth, another political pioneer, tells the story of meeting with a candidate and asking him why he was running and what he hoped to accomplish for his state. 'I haven't the slightest idea,' the candidate said. 'That's why I'm here.' To which Garth retorted, 'Get the hell out of my office'" (1999, 24). Having a message, a basic reason you are running for office, is essential in political campaigns, and is noted by political practitioners but is not always as clear in political science as it should be. This book has clarified distinctions between theme, slogan, and messaging for campaigns, opening the door for more specific and practical research down the line. I propose that any successful campaign should differentiate between a good theme, slogan, and message. It may be difficult and time-consuming to come up with a "feeling" that you want people to have in a campaign, but it is important as well. My research has shown that there is a strand of campaign communication work on message consistency that is overlooked by some areas of political science. While current literature takes pains to point out that repetition in campaigns is important to maintain voters' attention and passion, the flip side of that equation, the value of message consistency to campaign professionals, was lacking until now. I showed that message consistency in a campaign is seen as incredibly important for a candidate's success, and campaigners swear by its value. More important, the ability of a candidate to stay on message is unique to demographic and not usually contextual factors. When asked what made a candidate veer off message, political operatives in the sample usually said attacks from the opposition.[1]

- "During personal interaction with voters." (media manager for Republican state legislature challenger candidate in the Southeast in 2002)

- "When he had to defend himself against personal attacks." (media manager for Republican federal open-seat race in the South in 2008)
- "He was fairly well-disciplined. Only time he strayed was if someone tried to attack his family." (deputy campaign manager for Democratic challenger for governor in the South in 2008)

But regression analyses did not bear this out. How the opposition defined you, or even negative attack ads, had no statistically significant relationship to whether a candidate stayed on message. What did seem to throw candidates off message was the never-ending influence of race. My research shows that campaigners felt that their candidates were more likely to go off message when white candidates ran against minority candidates. Further, marketing research, especially the use of message boxes, seems to provide a promising avenue for further studies on messaging and analyses showing the basic marketing ploys used to sell products to consumers (Barber 1990). More work should be done in this area in political science.

While this book demonstrates that there are universal messages used to define the opposition in campaigns, there are surely other methods by which messages could be found or even refined beyond what has been presented here. This work confirms existing research that shows that women candidates face unique challenges in how they are discussed and considered by the popular press as well as in negative advertising and campaign rhetoric. However, the persistence of race playing a role in messaging strategy suggests that more and similar work in this area should be done as well. Much of existing race work in political science deals with the ways in which minority candidates must present themselves or their issues to the public, but this work shows that there is also further work to be done on the rhetoric of campaigns between different races of candidates. I would argue that white candidates being thrown off message when competing against African Americans and consistent definitional attacks of "inexperienced" are a complex new area of rhetorical study worth analyzing further. This goes beyond any perceived "Bradley Effect" to the heart of political communication and race work in general. Is there a "black" and "white" or possibly "Latino" rhetorical campaign strategy? The current occupant in the White House makes further study into this area even more crucial.

Candidate Positioning

*As far as candidate strategies towards the election I have al-
ways been in favor of a "base in position." I'll give you an example. Republicans do this well. Democrats always seem to
try to find the middle and stand there. Rather than starting
with their base. An example of this was the patients' bill of
rights. You can't tell me what's in it (this was a huge issue in
the early 2002s); this polls well with the marginal voter, so
we're for it. But nobody knows what it's about. Not only is it
ideologically unsatisfying. It's electorally difficult because
you're constantly shooting for a moving target. The center
changes, and you're going to miss more often than hit.*

—Wyeth Ruthven, Senior Director,
Qorvis Communications, May 16, 2010

*Generally, the Democratic Party moves from the liberal side
and the Republican Party from the conservative side, and
the party eating most successfully into the middle carries the
election. If either party veers too far away from center it
leaves a vacuum into which the other party naturally flows.
If either party "goes to extremes" the center is more open to
capture by its opposition and we can have a landslide such
as the 1964 LBJ avalanche.*

—Herbert M. Baus and William B. Ross,
Politics Battle Plan (1968)

Even though separated by forty years these quotes still demonstrate that
Democrats and Republicans seem to campaign differently; just how that
looks has not been addressed empirically from a political professional's perspective until now. Although political science is replete with discussions of
position strategy, the two most important position strategies in the discipline, the proximity and directional models, seldom included real-world application, which was both enhanced and improved by the introduction of
political consultants to the research model. This book has shown that there
is a provable difference in campaign position strategy by political operatives

who are Democrats or Republicans, and what's more, those strategies may shift over time. The discussion may no longer need to be about whether the directional or proximity model is a better reflection of campaign position strategy but rather that one strategy is employed more by each party. It was the introduction of campaign operatives to the distinctive models that made this solution possible. Future research should examine if these changes are cyclical, like many other political phenomenon, or driven by something other than the political gestalt of the time.

In the area of issue ownership, this work has again confirmed some research and shown holes in other areas. The work of political scientists like Stephen Medvic, who identified "owned issues" by either party, finds support in my results. It appears that partisanship does have an impact on what issues are "held." But there is more that we found in this analysis. There may be a difference in what issues "campaigners" think they own and what the public believes they own. My results showed that when it came to Democratic consultants, the issue they felt they owned was driven by the voters in their district, whereas Republican consultants' sense of issue ownership was driven as much by their own sense of party discipline as anything in the electoral district itself. Future studies of issue ownership should include more involvement from campaign professionals, not just as creators of messages that focus on specific issues, but why they consider one party to own one issue or another. Prior to this work, there has been no extensive investigation into issue-ownership literature that specifically asked what or how political consultants viewed the issue.

The two major contributions to political science from this book in negative advertising research are in definition and strategy. While some political scientists define negative advertising and others do not, definitions were generally inconsistent across the discipline. The truth is that defining negative advertising without the direct input of the purveyors of negative advertising is akin to studying congressional legislation without looking at the members of Congress who make it. No political scientist would do that, but that is what definitions of negative advertising in political science amounted to prior to this work. With the help of campaign managers and operatives, the distinction between negative and attack advertising has been made, and hopefully if applied consistently will give both the supporters (Geer 2006) and the critics of negative advertising an even deeper level of analysis to approach. Perhaps rather than consistently using college students or even teams of graduate coders to analyze negative advertising, a method similar to that used by Theilmann and Wilhite (1998) could be employed. Campaign managers could be shown a series of ads, and they could provide detail on why one was a negative or an attack ad. This is just one of the many methodological improvements that could be derived from these results on negative advertising.

When it comes to strategy, existing work in political science is confirmed by my research. Many of the factors that are identified in political science as influencing negative ads, such as candidate status and the position being sought, were significant in this research as well. Further, the distinction between negative character attacks and policy attacks established in the literature was also congruous with the results of my analysis. The differences, however, were equally stark. Although many factors influence negative advertising in the minds of campaign managers, ultimately ad strategy is driven by the poll numbers. The candidate's standing in the polls right after the primary and the middle of the campaign are crucial times for ad strategy, according to my research. Political operatives change attacks and the content of ads, whether policy- or character-driven ads, based on polling, a discovery in this work not seen in most political science literature dealing with negative advertising. Since existing research does point to how voters often make policy inferences based on candidate traits and character assessments, the work here has implications for political science work in numerous areas. The simple axiom that Republicans attack more than Democrats was certainly disproved in this work, and the nature of the attacks they place against each other might have as much to do with how they position themselves on policy in the minds of voters as anything else. There is a treasure trove of new directions to explore in campaign negative advertising study if campaigners become an essential part of the research model.

Finally, we look at campaign operatives' use of the Internet, and here we see likely the most synergy between this research and existing political science work. In this current era of political consultant research, mixed with the rapidly changing nature of political campaigning online, many political scientists have been more willing to go to the source to learn about campaign political strategy. It is a bit less efficient and valuable to learn about campaign strategy just by looking at Web sites or viral ads. In this way I believe the pervasive nature of campaigning online will actually force political scientists who work on campaigns to establish even closer relationships with the political operatives in order to understand the campaign world better (Howard 2006; Grossmann 2009; Dittmar 2010).

This work has shown that there are regional and situational differences in the use of e-campaigning technology and that the dedicated researcher should consider more environmental factors in doing analysis of online campaigning. The discussion on the transformative nature of the Internet between "Internet optimists" and "Internet pessimists" is over. The optimists have won. You can get people interested in politics based on online work, and you can raise money and get them to vote as well. You can talk to, engage, and attack an opponent's policies faster and with more efficiency online than at any point in the past. In fact, given how valuable the Internet was to consultants in the sample based on their open-ended responses and regression results, there should never be a question again about whether the electronic world has changed campaigns. What is worth looking into is the impact of regional and various other demographic factors on Internet technology campaigns. This work could be expanded to look at whether campaigns are using different types of "apps" for their Web sites, latching on to the increasing number of Americans who go online through their phones. Future research could also look at the impact of "Internet migrations" from one site to another on campaign strategy. As massive numbers of voters move from Friendster to MySpace to Facebook to Twitter, are campaigns following them as well? What might these migrations do to overall strategy on a national level? These are just some of the exciting questions to be addressed in the coming years.

Winner's Circle

Throughout this book I have made a conscious effort to discuss what motivates different strategic behaviors of consultants and not the impact of those decisions. Namely, we have not talked much about "winning" and "losing," even though that is the ultimate goal of this type of work. Yes, if you are working for a long-shot ideological campaign like Ron Paul or Dennis Kucinich for president, then you probably do not really think you are going to win (not that any campaigner would ever say that out loud). But in most

TABLE 6.1 **Winning or losing your campaign based on contextual and demographic factors**

Dependent variable	Independent variable	Impact on winning or losing
Win or lose	Race of opposing candidate	Better chance of winning going against a white candidate
Win or lose	Running as a challenger	None
Win or lose	Running for an open seat	Less likely to win compared to an incumbent
Win or lose	Position in polls at mid campaign point	Ahead in the polls at midway has better chance of winning
Win or lose	Education level of district	None
Win or lose	District party preference	None
Win or lose	War chest	More money you have, the better chance of winning
Win or lose	Message consistency of candidate	Candidates that are on message have a better chance to win
Win or lose	Internet optimist or pessimist	None
Win or lose	Gender of opposing candidate	None
Win or lose	Party identification Republican or Democrat	None

cases you are learning campaign strategy, running ads, creating messages, and posting photos of your candidate, her family, and her pet golden retriever online because you think that is what it will take to win. We have already learned specifically how political science has been enhanced by this work, but what do these conclusions specifically offer to campaign operatives? Based on the survey, there are a few basic things that drive whether you have a chance of winning or losing. Sixty percent of the respondents in the survey won their campaigns, and 40 percent lost, which is a good breakdown to get some insight into what was driving these two results.

I performed a binary logistic regression on the dependent variable of winning or losing with some of the most important environmental and demographic factors that a consultant can run into in a campaign environment. In Table 6.1, the left column is the dependent variable of whether the consultant won or lost their race. The middle column is the variable, and the column on the right is the influence this variable had on whether a consultant won or lost.

The results speak to some basic truths about campaigning. If you are ahead in the polls at the midpoint, have more money than the opposition, and can keep your candidate on message, you have the best chance of winning your campaign. The good news is that each of these factors is actually within some control of the campaign team. The most influential elements on winning in the regression were poll position at the midpoint of the campaign and staying on message. If you can keep your candidate on message, all things being equal, you greatly enhance your chances to actually win the campaign in the end. Our two more curious results have to do again with race and place. Consultants showed that you had a better chance of winning against a white candidate than a black one. I removed campaigners for Barack Obama just to make sure they were not skewing the regression, but the results were the same. So was Geraldine Ferraro correct, and blacks are just favored and lucky when they run for office? I think many would beg to differ. The explanation for this result is fairly simple: African American candidates are rare, in the majority of the districts in the United States, and in many places are only sacrificial lambs. Increasingly, when African American candidates do make it to a general election, they are in districts where there is an inherent Democratic advantage (the majority of African American candidates are Democrats) or where they have received a tremendous amount of party support. Looking at the 2010 midterm elections, where two African American Republicans were elected to Congress (from Florida and South Carolina), an African American woman was elected lieutenant governor of Florida, and a Latina Republican was elected to the governor's mansion in New Mexico, speaks to the power of party support when minority candidates are elected in districts where there is not a majority or plurality of minority voters. Should such successes continue for minority candidates under the GOP and Democratic banners, another re-evaluation of the role of race in candidate success may be in order, but I am not prepared to go there just yet. I am fairly comfortable in saying that I do not think this result shows that black candidates are simply beating whites in elections no matter what. Another winning factor that you cannot control is being a challenger. You have about as much control over running as an open-seat candidate as you do over your opposition's race or gender. So the focus, based on this work, should be in raising money and keeping your candidate on message.

The results above are based on simply looking at whether a candidate wins or loses, but that is the end result. This book has shown that where you are after the primary or the middle of the election influences your chances of success. So I decided to look a little bit closer at the winners and losers. I

TABLE 6.2 **Regression analyzing consultants who came from behind to win**

Dependent variable	Independent variable	Impact on winning or losing
Win or lose	Race of opposing candidate	None
Win or lose	Running as a challenger	None
Win or lose	Running for an open seat	None
Win or lose	Position in polls at mid campaign point	None
Win or lose	Education level of district	None
Win or lose	District party preference	None
Win or lose	War chest	None
Win or lose	Message consistency of candidate	Candidates that are on message have a better chance of winning[a]
Win or lose	Internet optimist or pessimist	Those who see the Internet as allowing campaigns to do something different are less likely to have come-from-behind victories
Win or lose	Gender of opposing candidate	None
Win or lose	Party identification Republican or Democrat	None

[a] This result is significant at the .055 level.

broke them down into two categories, those who were ahead in the polls after the primary who ended up losing their races and those who were behind in the polls after the primary and ended up winning their races.[2] The come-from-behind victory or the embarrassing flameout is just as important to campaigners as the candidate who runs from announcement to election day as a front-runner. I ran a regression on each of these types of winners and losers using the same independent variables above.

Come-from-behind victories seem to be driven by the same forces as many campaigns in general, according to consultants (Table 6.2). Those candidates who stay on message have a better chance of coming from behind to win a campaign. Along the same lines, those who think that the Internet is a new and fabulous game changer are less likely to be come-from-behind winners. This should not dampen anyone's views of Internet optimism, however. If your campaign is already behind in the polls, it is rare that any amount of Internet wizardry (barring an embarrassing YouTube video of your opponent) is going to turn the race around. But perhaps staying on message, and having a good one, might.

TABLE 6.3 Regression analyzing consultants who were in the lead after the primary and lost their campaigns at the end

Dependent variable	Independent variable	Impact on winning or losing
Win or lose	Race of opposing candidate	None
Win or lose	Running as a challenger	None
Win or lose	Running for an open seat	None
Win or lose	Position in polls at mid campaign point	None
Win or lose	Education level of district	None
Win or lose	District party preference	None
Win or lose	War chest	None
Win or lose	Message consistency of candidate	Candidates that do not stay on message are more likely to be in the lead after the primary and then lose the general election
Win or lose	Internet optimist or pessimist	None
Win or lose	Gender of opposing candidate	None
Win or lose	Party identification Republican or Democrat	None

When we look at campaigns that started in the lead and then lost in the end (Table 6.3), again, the primacy of message consistency comes through. Staying on message is a good thing for campaign success. Straying off message is not so good. These results are not meant to suggest that nothing else in a campaign environment matters when it comes to winning or losing. If anything, this book has shown that issues, world events, and a host of other things buffet the campaign world every season and that those forces drive voters to and from different candidates. A good message will not win you an election if it is not heard by anyone or delivered by a candidate who is not respected (although a good campaigner would know to not have their candidate deliver a message that would conflict with public perception of their character). However, these results do tell us that a campaign lives and presumably dies by messaging, and the consultants in this survey thought that winning started with the words coming out of a candidate's mouth.

2010 and Beyond

This book was completed after the 2010 midterm elections, when in the words of President Barack Obama the Democrats got "shellacked" at the

TABLE 6.4 Internet tools use by campaigners, 2009

	Every day to at least once a week N (%)	A couple of times a month N (%)	A few times during the campaign to never N (%)
Campaign Web site	133 (74.7)	8 (4.5)	27 (20.8)
Facebook	74 (41.6)	10 (5.6)	94 (52.8)
MySpace	29 (16.3)	8 (4.5)	141 (79.2)
Twitter	32 (18.0)	7 (3.9)	139 (78.1)
YouTube	51 (28.7)	20 (11.2)	107 (60.1)
Other	57 (32.0)	16 (9.0)	105 (59.0)

Note: N = actual number of responses. (%) = percentage of total. Total = 178.

TABLE 6.5 Internet tools used by campaigners, 2010

	Every day to at least once a week N (%)	A couple of times a month N (%)	A few times during the campaign to never N (%)
Campaign Web site	40 (87.0)	2 (4.3)	4 (8.7)
Facebook	37 (80.4)	2 (4.3)	7 (15.2)
MySpace	3 (6.5)	1 (2.2)	42 (91.3)
Twitter	23 (50.0)	4 (8.7)	19 (41.3)
YouTube	12 (26.1)	12 (26.1)	22 (47.8)
Other	15 (32.6)	3 (6.5)	28 (60.9)

Note: N = actual number of responses. (%) = percentage of total. Total = 46.

polls. The results were unmistakable. Democrats did lose far and wide across the nation, although the full strategic analysis of why is beyond the scope of this book. However, a new CAMP (Consultant Attitudes on Management and Practices) survey has been distributed to campaigners who participated in the 2010 elections, and as those results trickle in, combined with the results of this book, I can make some preliminary assessments of the future of campaign strategy and directions for political science in 2012 and beyond.

First, the shift in the importance of the Internet and differentiating polls online was even more pronounced (Tables 6.4 and 6.5). Although the numbers were not quite as high for the 2010 election survey, there is a noticeable big difference in the use of the Internet.

Though tentative, it would seem that the trend is moving toward almost universal use of campaign Web sites. Further, while this has been heralded in many a tech magazine over the past year, MySpace, certainly as a political outreach tool, is already dead. Twitter continued to grow in popularity, likely bolstered by its wide adoption throughout the Republican Party. A post-2010 midterm election study by Hewlett-Packard showed that seventy of the top one hundred most influential members of Congress on Twitter are Republicans, and GOP campaigns are getting as much activism out of their Twitter followers as Democrats (Dugan 2010; Drake 2011). The "Other" category, capturing smaller Web sites and social networking sites, remains similar to previous surveys. The only seeming dip thus far was YouTube, which is to be expected. We discussed in Chapter 5 that YouTube is more valuable for large-scale campaigns like presidential elections where a viral video has more impact. In a midterm election, YouTube may not carry as much value.

Beyond the increased use of the Internet heading into the 2012 election, I would anticipate a shifting of campaign strategies by both parties as Republicans experience being the out party for only the third presidential election in the past forty years. However, this may diverge from their trusted strategy in order to win back more seats in the Senate or the White House. Republicans should move beyond their core directional position strategy toward more of a proximity strategy to gain swing voters who will make the biggest difference in the 2012 elections. As of right now, this advice falls on deaf ears. With just under a year before the Iowa caucuses, Republican governors across the Midwest have frustrated independents and galvanized the progressive Left by picking fights with state employee unions. While this may be basic Republican strategy, they have also opened up a can of worms that might hurt congressional candidates and a GOP nominee campaigning in the Midwest in 2012. Researchers should also take note of how or to what extent the Obama campaign and the eventual Republican nominee create their message strategy. With the economy hanging in the balance, it will be interesting to see what issues Democrats can claim they own heading into 2012. If the economy improves between Clinton and Obama, the economy may move from being a "leased" issue to an "owned" one by Democrats. If the economy flatlines or gets worse, Republicans will definitely be able to employ defining messages against Obama questioning his competence and whether he is truly "in touch" with the millions of Americans suffering through the extended recession. Even the few off-year elections of 2011 will likely be affected by these trends, and I believe that a strong research agenda in political science to focus on campaigners in these coming years will put

TABLE 6.6 Which is more important in the minds of voters?

That a candidate have a strong plan and vision for the future N (%)	*That a candidate have a strong past record and experience* N (%)
129 (74.6)	44 (25.4)

Note: N = actual number of responses. (%) = percentage of total. Total = 173.

TABLE 6.7 Which of the following best describes your feelings toward the following statement: "The general election is a referendum on the incumbent"?

Strongly agree N (%)	*Agree* N (%)	*Disagree* N (%)	*Strongly disagree* N (%)
53 (30.6)	92 (53.2)	26 (15.0)	2 (1.2)

the discipline and campaign consultants in a better position to succeed practically and politically in the coming years. Ultimately, the elections of the future will boil down to two key questions: how the public feels about the future and how they feel about the incumbent president (or any other public official). The campaigners in my study give us a quick glimpse as to what is the best option for candidates facing both questions (Tables 6.6 and 6.7).

As we study and participate in future campaigns, the message is clear. Campaigners need to be forward-thinking, encouraging their candidates to look forward, not backward. More important for incumbents, either locally or nationally, the ability to control the agenda since they are the ones being looked at by the public is crucial. For political science, we can know that looking forward, the answers to some of the most compelling questions of the discipline can be tackled with the help of campaigners and consultants who are on the front lines of American democracy. The path to the future is the study of political operatives, and our ability to change and grow as a discipline will be a referendum on our current research agenda.

7

Appendix

The Appendix is meant to explain several elements of the research methods in *Political Consultants and Campaigns*. Given the wide range of regressions and analyses, this Appendix will focus on a few key regressions from each chapter that formed the basis of some of the tables used. Those interested in a more detailed background of any individual table, or access to my data, are encouraged to contact me at johnsonja@hiram.edu.

The Appendix is divided into several sections. Section 1 explains the overall research methods employed for the survey itself, the theoretical justifications, and how the survey was conceived, constructed, and distributed. This will include general information about the target audience themselves. The second section explains the methods employed to develop the five messaging themes from Chapter 2 in the book. The final section explains some of the main variables used in the book, as well as how the regressions were performed. This will be followed by a select number of crosstabs and regressions presented in their unrefined form for perusal by specific chapters and sections. Finally, I include the entire survey.

The Survey

The survey that is the basis of *Political Consultants and Campaigns* is an extension of a survey created as part of my dissertation at the University of North Carolina at Chapel Hill (Johnson 2009). The survey is online, has seventy-five questions, and covers roughly five areas that constitute this research: candidate, message, issue positioning, negative advertising, and

Internet campaigning. The survey construction, wording, and format are influenced by previous extensive surveys of political operatives (Thurber 1999, 2000, 2004; Herrnson 1986; Medvic and Lenart 1997).

The definition of the survey subjects and the distribution of the survey itself diverge from more common and standardized approaches to surveys of political experts. I will address each difference below.

The Definition

The most common definition of *consultant* is established by Johnson (Thurber and Nelson 2000, chap. 3). He establishes that there are three tiers of consultants: strategists, specialists, and vendors. He further strongly cautions against mixing and matching these three types and the pitfalls of research that come from doing so (ibid., 39). In this book I specifically sought to "conflate" consultants in the way criticized by Johnson in his early work. The inspiration for the approach of this book is partially inspired by the many volumes of *The Campaign Manager* written by Catherine Shaw. Shaw's practical, step-by-step books about campaign management speak to the lower tier of political operatives in this country that are often missed in political science studies that adhere strictly to the standard established by Johnson. The 2009 edition of *The Campaign Manager* begins with advice about how a candidate should scout potential campaign managers and their campaign team. She suggests public school teachers, who have free summers and are often good at organizing large groups, are a good place to start. Is a public school teacher as sophisticated in campaign strategy as the political director of a statewide race in that same state? Perhaps not, but of the thousands of men and women who run for office at the local, then city, then county level in America, there are a lot more public school teachers, bankers, and CVS night managers running campaigns than most political science captures. And they are winning those races, too.

One of the driving forces behind this work is that there are many more political experts and operatives running campaigns throughout the United States than most political scientists account for. Therefore, the definition of *political operative* for this book is simply "those who were directly involved in the development of campaign strategy from the beginning of the campaign until the end." The survey itself weeded out those who were not qualified by the positions within the campaign offered, as well as the sophistication of the questions. It is unlikely that a campaign volunteer or occasional participant could answer the survey questions. Because of the method I employed to contact campaigns, it is likely that this work captures many of the campaign professionals that Johnson refers to, but the goal was also to find those who may be hidden from more conventional definitions and survey methods. Ultimately, I believe the power of the results of this book, both confirming and enhancing existing political science work, justifies the non-conventional approach and definition taken.

The Method

The common method in political science for establishing the universe for political consultant surveys is to use membership lists from the American Political Consultants Association, to use listings of active consultants from *Campaigns and Elections*, or to call active campaigns on the federal level and ask to speak with the primary manager or consultant (Grossmann 2010; Dittmar 2010; Thurber 2000; Medvic and Lenart 1997; Howard 2006). The survey for this book employed both a random sample like the ones above in addition to a "snowball" sampling method.

Survey respondents were encouraged to forward the survey to others who met the criteria established in the research e-mail. "Snowball" or "respondent-driven" sampling is often employed by social scientists trying to reach populations like bloggers or endangered political dissidents. The belief is that there are many men and women who are political experts behind the scenes at the state and even federal level who cannot be easily identified by calling a campaign (Weible 2005; Salganik and Heckathorn 2004; Li and Walenjko 2008).

There are concerns about the projections that can be made from such a sample. Given that we used mixed methods, the argument could be made that we are diluting a random sample of campaigns called across the nation and that we cannot make any true predictions or general arguments about political operatives. My response to that is twofold. First, this work is predicated on a wider study of political operatives, and thus a mixed method was the best available to discover both "elite-level" and lower-level campaign professionals. Second, the relationships between consultant responses and the variables if statistically significant can still be valuable in making predictions and assessments of political consultants and political science, even if caution might be warranted in some proscriptions. Ultimately, the results of the work, controversial methods aside, ended up being in line with a great deal of existing work, further justifying the methods employed. Another methodological concern is that this book relies heavily on self-reporting by consultants. There is a possibility, however slight, that respondents could "perceive" that they were attacked first in negative advertising, or that their candidate did not veer off message. This is actually what this book seeks to capture. The perceptions of consultants and how those perceptions might influence political science theory are crucial to the core work of this text. I am fully aware that these perceptions might be biased, but they tell us as much about consultant attitudes as direct interviews. Further, in instances where such biases in self-reporting are exposed (see Chapter 4), it provides the discipline with an interesting insight into campaign operative behavior that we seldom are able to capture on a wide scale.

The survey for this book was distributed during the fall of 2009 through the early winter of 2010. The survey used a mixed approach to identify and survey consultants. Using a team of undergraduate students at Hiram College, I went to the secretary of state Web site for all fifty states and identified every candidate who was running for public office in the November 2009 elections. If no state Web site had this comprehensive information, then I obtained the information from state party Web sites. If state party Web sites did not have the information, I filled in the gaps with the blog www.thegreenpapers.com, which collects information on state campaigns. Once campaigns were identified, an Excel spreadsheet was made of all fifty states identifying every candidate who was running for office. All fifty states were divided between a group of undergraduate students (Steven Voytek, Amy Romanow, Michael Walton, and research leader Wiley Runnestrand; the Excel sheet was prepared by Evan Tachovsky).

Chapter 6 features preliminary survey results from the 2010 election that were used to make assessments of future campaigns. The 2010 midterm campaign information was collected by student researchers from Morehouse College and Spelman College in the fall of 2010 in Atlanta, Georgia.

The students were trained to call campaigns around the country and read from a script asking for the campaign manager or political director. This often required calling the same campaign several times, and in some cases campaign numbers were either disconnected right after election day, or the main manager was never contacted. Upon contact, the main manager or highest political operative available was asked if they would be willing to fill out a short anonymous Internet survey to help in the research project. Their name and e-mail address were then collected, and an e-mail was sent to them that day including a brief description of the project and a link to the site. The text of the e-mail is below:

Dear Campaigner X,

Thank you for agreeing to take this survey. This is part of a research project on Campaign Managers from Hiram College in Northeast Ohio. I'm doing research on political consultants/managers, specifically: I'm comparing what political science theory says you're supposed to do to win a campaign with what political consultants actually do in the field. What I am looking for are people who have been campaign managers or political organizers, or have run their own campaigns. Even if your specific title was not "campaign manager," if you worked on a race from beginning to end, such that you knew about how the whole campaign worked, this applies to you as well. I'm interested in respondents at all levels and experience, so if you've worked on anything from school board to city council to a presidential level campaign I'd appreciate you filling out the survey. Over 300 managers and consultants responded to this survey in 2006 and we're seeking even more responses now that the 2008 elections have come to a close. In addition, if you complete the survey yourself feel free to send this link on to anybody that you know who fits the criteria. It is a simple link, and the entire Internet survey only takes about 30 minutes to complete. It does not have to be completed in one sitting; just leave the window open. My hope is that people will fill out the survey within a week of receiving it so that I can start working on my results as soon as possible. Also, it is completely confidential; the program prevents me from tracing any individual response to any particular respondent. Here is the link. Please click on the link to the survey below. If you have any problems clicking the link simply cut and paste it into your URL. http://www.surveymonkey.com/s.aspx?sm=9PZFE3tvEAob4GBWtK_2bBbw_3d_3d

Thank you so much for any help or people that you can send my way for this research (including yourself!) and if you or anyone else has any questions feel free to contact the director of the project.

Jason Johnson, PhD, Political Science
University of North Carolina at Chapel Hill
Political Science Department, Hiram College

This follow-up e-mail for survey respondents was sent two weeks later:

Dear Campaigner X,

A questionnaire on political consultants was sent to you on August 21st. If you have already filled out this survey thank you very much for your time. If you have not completed the *entire* survey, please do so by November 13th, so that your answers can be included in survey results. The response so far to the survey has been fantastic, but it is critical to this research that as many diverse opinions are included as possible, including yours.

As a quick reminder this survey is for academic research comparing how political science suggests you win political campaigns to how consultants actually behave in the field. The results will be used in a research project and for academic purposes. If you have already filled out the survey, or have not but know of others who you feel are more qualified to answer the survey, please feel free to forward this link to them. Thank you for your time.

The site itself was from Surveymonkey.com and allowed for the immediate collection of any information from the respondents. Calls were made for five days following the election on November 3, 2009, not including the weekend. A total of 421 surveys were sent out, and a total of 89 surveys were completed, for a response rate of 21 percent. Many respondents partially completed their surveys, and while the data collected could still be a part of statistical analyses, for our purposes we considered the completed surveys in determining our completion percentage.

Our second method for capturing political operatives began in the second week of November. Over the next several weeks I contacted directors at the Women's Campaign School at Yale University, the University of Akron, Regent University, and the George Washington School of Political Management. I asked if each of these directors would be willing to review the survey and distribute it among their students online. Each director agreed, and the survey was sent out. Although in some cases it took several months before the survey was distributed, each director confirmed that the survey had been sent to students. The goal of the research was to shut down the survey soon after the first month of the new year (2010), when newly elected officials would be taking office. The survey was closed to new respondents on February 11, 2010. A total of 399 respondents started the survey, and a total of 171 completed the survey, for a completion rate of 42.9 percent.

Defining Messages for Chapter 2

In order to develop the themes for the five major defining messages in campaigns, a content analysis was performed. The themes were identified through a review of case studies from *Campaigns and Elections (C&E)* as well as a content analysis of articles from *C&E*. The primary themes selected for this study were identified through the frequency of appearance in *C&E*. Details of these methods follow. To identify message themes of political operatives, I began the analysis with a review of case studies from *C&E*, the premier trade magazine for political consultants in the United States. *C&E* articles have been and continue to be used by the vast majority of both journalists and academics seeking to study or inform themselves about political consultants. While the American Association of Political Consultants does send out pamphlets and information, the depth, consistency, and reliability of information on consultants collected from *C&E* cannot be matched. The magazine has been in publication for twenty-five years, moving from quarterly to bimonthly in 1986 and then to a monthly publication in 1990.

Analysis of data from *C&E* occurred in two parts. In the first part, I examined the entire special series of case studies produced by the magazine between 1999 and 2003 (a total of twenty-two) to find beliefs about campaigns expressed by consultants and how they expressed those beliefs and messages. Case studies that were focused on noncandidate-centered races and referenda were excluded from this analysis (four in all). Of the remaining eighteen case studies, six focused on challenger-versus-incumbent races, ten focused on open-seat races, and two focused on campaigns where two incumbents faced off because of redistricting.

The second part of this analysis involved determining the frequency or systematic appearance of these themes identified from the case studies in the *C&E* literature. This was accomplished by using the ATLAS ti coding program. Articles from July to November of the election years 1996, 1998, 2000, and 2002 were coded using this program. These years were chosen because they were all election years, both on and "off," and provided a diverse array of presidential and congressional victories. The documents selected for the coding analysis were based on the subject headings in *Campaigns and Elections*. I examined all articles with headings of "Electioneering," "Politics . . . Practical," or "Advertising, Political" from the *EBSCOhost* electronic journal's database at the University of North Carolina at Chapel Hill. I selected these subject headings because the articles they contained focused most consistently on consultants' views on voting and campaigns. While other documents may focus on specific election campaigns or interviews with political movers and shakers, these works do not consistently provide as much direct strategy discussion. Clearly, the use of this method of document selection may have excluded some of the more nuanced documents from analysis, but the gain in parsimony of selection more than compensates for anything that may have been lost in more subtle works.

The following are the seven themes that I coded for the content analysis. After discovering each theme in the case studies, I then used specific terms in order to capture these themes in the content analysis:

- *Message*: Terms relating to the slogans, themes, or communicated ideas about the campaign. Coded as: *slogan, message, tag*.
- *Positioning*: Terms relating to taking a centrist or middle-of-the-road policy stance during a campaign. Coded as: *moderate, center, centrist, mainstream, middle, median*; or terms relating to taking strong or extreme policy positions during a campaign. Coded as: *strong, strength, outside, extreme, stand*.
- *Image over Verbal*: Terms referring to the importance of imagery during a campaign as opposed to verbal communication. Coded as: *image, visual, words, debate, writing*.
- *Racial Issues*: Terms referring to the importance or impact of racial dynamics on a campaign. Coded as: *African American, blacks, Asians, Hispanics, ethnic/ethnicity, racial*.

TABLE 7.1 **Frequency and percentage of appearance for themes across years**

Theme	1996	1998	2000	2002	Total	Percentage
Message	96	109	87	91	383	17.9
Voter knowledge	27	157	30	163	377	17.7
Future or past	37	38	77	183	335	15.7
Positioning	56	45	109	82	292	13.7
Negative advertising	32	89	82	33	236	11.1
Image over words	33	59	40	42	174	8.2
Candidate ability	25	20	56	66	167	7.8
Racial issues	0	64	14	60	138	6.5
Definition	1	7	2	22	32	1.5
Total	307	588	497	742	2,134	100

- *Future or Past*: Terms referring to the temporal orientation of voters. Whether consultants considered voters to have prospective or retrospective judgments during campaigns. Coded as: *future, past, vision, experience, history, plans referendum.*
- *Candidate Ability*: Terms referring to unique or valuable abilities of a candidate that may help them during the campaign. Coded as: *ability, skills, speaker, connect, empathy, communication, constituent.*
- *Voter Knowledge*: Terms referring to what kind of information voters have and how they process information. Coded as: *voter information, knowledge, aware, attention, voter intelligence, informed electorate, notice.*

After running these codes through the selected articles with the ATLAS ti program, I received the frequency results shown in Table 7.1. While I had theoretical and academic reasons for wanting to retain all of these results, my goal was to capture consultant beliefs and determine what message themes came from them. I therefore decided to retain only those themes that were held in the top 75 percent of total frequency appearances throughout the texts. The total number of references throughout the entire collected texts was 2,134. I then calculated the percentage of each from the total number of references. The calculations for each theme are shown in Table 7.1.

Using the most referenced themes my final list was composed of: Message, Voter Knowledge, Future or past, Positioning, and Negative advertising. These themes constituted 76.1 percent of the total appearances from the content analysis—close to my initial goal (75 percent) for this analysis.

Determining the frequency of themes through the coding mechanism served two purposes. First, this system helped strengthen the likelihood that the selected themes were important ones and were less biased by my own review. Second, the frequency coding allowed for a method to objectively create boundaries for not only my determination of message themes but the survey itself. Upon analyzing the basic themes of campaign discussions I discovered the five themes that composed the message SWOT box. These were discovered not just by examining the categories listed but by reviewing each and discovering what was being talked about messagewise in each category.

Four interviews were conducted for this book. The interview subjects were selected in part due to their experiences in political campaigns in diverse geographic locations. Further, they provided context and stories that became a part of case studies in the text. Dates and names of interview subjects are below:

Reese Edwards, government affairs consultant, New Mexico, interviewed on May 4, 2010

Wyeth Ruthven, Democratic political operative who now works for Qorvis Communications, interviewed on May 16, 2010

Jordan Lieberman, former publisher of *Campaigns and Elections*, interviewed on July 22, 2010

Dylan Nonaka, executive director of Charles Djou's congressional campaign, interviewed on June 9, 2010

The next section lists the regression tables and the methods employed for several tables throughout the text. As mentioned earlier, because of the extensive number of tables, a general explanation of many regressions is presented rather than the entire collection.

The regressions performed in this book are primarily binary logistic regressions. This means that the dependent variable was coded as "1" or "0" depending on the degree of feeling or amount of behavior being recoded. For example, a question such as "How often were the following Internet tools employed in the campaign?" initially had five choices, from "Every day" to "Never." Therefore, "Every day or at least once a week" was given a value of "1," and the rest of the response was coded as "0." This is why in many cases the results are described in the book as "more likely" or "less likely," because the variables are dichotomized. Below is a list of common independent variables in the survey:

DemGop: Coded as "1" for Democrats and "0" for Republicans

YouCanSex: Coded as "1" for male and "0" for female

EtypeChallengerDum: A dummy variable to represent challengers as opposed to incumbents

EtypeOpenSeatDum: A dummy variable to represent open-seat candidates as opposed to incumbents

ExecorLegSought: Was the consultant running a campaign for an executive or legislative position?

FedorStateSought: A variable noting if the consultant was running a race for a federal- or state-level candidate

CampaignRegionSouthDumVar: A dummy variable for the southern region of the country

DumVarRegionWest: A dummy variable for the West

DumVarRegionMidwest: A dummy variable for the Midwest

Electionb4911: Coded as "1" for elections after 9/11 and "0" for elections before 9/11

PollsMidway3: Consultant's campaign polls at the midpoint of the campaign. Coded as "3" for ahead, "2" for about even, and "1" for behind

UrbanvsRural: Coded as "1" for urban and "0" for rural

MinorityPercent: Coded as "5" for more than 55%, "4" for between 41% and 55%, "3" for between 26% and 40%, "2" for between 10% and 25%, and "1" for less than 10%

EducationLevel: Coded as "5" for far above average, for "4" for above average, "3" for average, "2" for slightly below average, and "1" for below average

DistrictIncomeAv: Coded as "5" for far above average, "4" for above average, "3" for average, "2" for slightly below average, and "1" for below average

PartyPrefDist: Coded as "5" for very Democratic, "4" for slightly Democratic, "3" for about even between Democratic and Republican, "2" for slightly Republican, and "1" for very Republican

Warchest: Coded as "3" for your candidate, "2" for about even, and "1" for your opponent

YourCanRace: Coded as "1" if your candidate is white and "0" if your candidate is black

YourCanSex: Coded as "1" if your candidate is male and "0" if your candidate is female

OnorOffyear: Coded as "1" if your campaign took place during a presidential election year and "0" if your campaign took place in a non-presidential election year

Respondent Demographics

The following is a very basic outline of the consultants in the sample.

TABLE 7.2 **Consultant demographics**

Campaign year N (%)	
1998	2 (0.7)
2000	8 (2.9)
2002	4 (1.4)
2004	21 (7.6)
2006	35 (12.6)
2008	132 (47.7)
Other (mostly 2009)	75 (27.1)
Campaign job N (%)	
Manager	100 (35.8)
Fund-raiser	21 (7.5)
Media	18 (6.5)
Get Out the Vote (GOTV)	20 (7.2)
Other	120 (43.0)
Experience N (%)	
1–4 years	131 (47.0)
5–10 years	82 (29.4)
11–15 years	34 (12.2)
16–20 years	14 (5.0)
More than 20 years	18 (6.5)
Party identification N (%)	
Republican	92 (33.0)
Democrat	155 (55.6)
Independent	32 (11.5)
Win or lose N (%)	
Won	132 (60.3)
Lost	87 (39.7)

Note: Actual number of responses. (%) = percentage of total.

TABLE 7.3 Consultant demographics

Candidate gender N (%)	
Male	216 (77.4)
Female	63 (22.6)

Candidate race N (%)	
White	241 (86.4)
African American	28 (10.0)
Latino	4 (1.4)
Asian	3 (1.1)
Other	3 (1.1)

Position sought N (%)	
President	44 (15.8)
Governor	22 (7.9)
Federal Senate	26 (9.3)
Federal House	70 (25.1)
State legislator	56 (20.1)
Mayor or city manager	13 (4.7)
School board	8 (2.9)
Other	40 (14.3)

Election type N (%)	
Incumbent	72 (25.8)
Challenger	77 (27.6)
Open-seat race	130 (46.6)

Region of the country N (%)	
Northeast	35 (16.0)
Mid-Atlantic	32 (14.6)
Southeast	37 (16.9)
South	17 (7.8)
Midwest	54 (24.7)
Southwest	17 (7.8)
West	17 (7.8)
Pacific Northwest	10 (4.6)

Note: Actual number of responses. (%) = percentage of total.

Appendix for Chapter 1: "The Candidate"

Explanation for Coding of Democratic "Best Traits" Question

- *Good Communicator*: Any reference to the candidate's speaking, expression of ideas, or ability to connect with voters.
- *Honesty/Integrity*: The specific use of the word *honesty* or *integrity* to describe the candidate.
- *Résumé*: Any reference to the candidate's work or life in the past. This includes references to "being from the area," "being a working mom," and the like. This includes achievements that have nothing to do with previous elected office.
- *Intelligence*: Any use of the words *brains, intelligence, brilliance,* and so forth.
- *Personality*: Any reference to the candidate's general demeanor, friendliness, charisma, or personal traits that made them valuable in the consultant's eyes.
- *Hard Worker/Ambition*: Any references to the candidate's work ethic, on or off the campaign trail. Often terms like *passionate* or *committed* fell into this category.
- *Experience*: Specific use of the word *experience.*

I used the following independent variables: Election pre- or post-9/11; Region; State or federal office sought; Incumbent, challenger, or open seat; Campaign war chest; Win or lose; Executive or legislative position sought; Minority percentage in district; Education level in district; District party preference; Your candidate's race; Your candidate's gender.

TABLE 7.4 **Variables in the equation**

		S.E.	Wald Waldorf-	df	Sig.	Exp(B)
	B	Standard error	Chi-Square		Significance	
Step 1[a]	Electionb4911					
	Election before 9/11	-2.681	1.105	5.892	1	.015	.068
	FedOrStateSought	-.006	.384	.000	1	.987	.994
	Dummy variable for region	1.157	.511	5.129	1	.024	3.179
	DumVarregionMidwest	.529	.512	1.068	1	.301	1.697
	DumVaregionWest	.341	.529	.415	1	.519	1.406
	EtypeChallDum	-1.571	.573	7.516	1	.006	.208
	EtypeOpenSeatDum	-.358	.495	.522	1	.470	.699
	ExecorLegislativeSought	.376	.412	.834	1	.361	1.456
	WinorLose	.345	.425	.660	1	.417	1.412
	MinorityPercent	-.015	.209	.005	1	.943	.985
	EducationLevel	.323	.201	2.579	1	.108	1.381
	PartyPrefDistrict	-.112	.141	.634	1	.426	.894
	YourCanSex	.461	.442	1.087	1	.297	1.585
	YourCandRaceWhiteBlack	-.863	.657	1.727	1	.189	.422
	War Chest	-.180	.256	.496	1	.481	.835
	Constant	3.042	1.780	2.921	1	.087	20.956

[a]Variable(s) entered on Step 1: Electionb4911, FedOrStateSought, CampRegionSouthDumVar, DumVarregionMidwest, DumVaregionWest, EtypeChallDum, EtypeOpenSeatDum, ExecorLegislativeSought, WinorLose, MinorityPercent, EducationLevel, PartyPrefDistrict, YourCanSex, YourCandRaceWhiteBlack, and War Chest.

Tables on Candidate Traits Needed for Running or Governing

Traits were recoded as "1" and "0" variables, as explained above. The regressions were run for each trait against the independent variables.

Appendix for Chapter 2: "The Message"

Table 7.5 presents a brief summary of scholarly works that suggest which variables might have an impact on message delivery during a dynamic campaign.

TABLE 7.5 **Scholarly works on variables influencing message delivery**

	Variable	*Impact*
Zaller 1992 Brady and Johnston 2006, 30	Education	Education should influence how and what types of messages a candidate has to create
Burgoon, Pfau, and Birk 1995 Kaid, McKinney, and Tedesco 2003	Gender	Candidate gender may influence press coverage, how messages are delivered, and how they are received by voters
Masters 1994	Race	The race of the candidate may influence message content and certainly delivery and reception
Parmalee 2003	Position Sought	The higher the position, the more consistent and substantive messages should be
Haynes, Flowers, and Gurian 2002a; Haynes and Rhine 1998	Polls	Candidates are known to alter their message depending on their position in the polls
Flowers, Haynes, and Crespin 2003; Haynes, Flowers, and Gurian 2002a	Location	The range of areas that you are campaigning in will influence the messages you deliver
Flowers, Haynes, and Crespin 2003	Money	More money allows greater opportunities to repeat and hammer home message
Bositis, Baer, and Miller 1985	Partisanship	The parties differ in their message delivery and consistency because they serve different constituents

TABLE 7.6 Regression table for impact of contextual variables on consultant feelings about candidate's staying on message

		B	S.E.	Wald	df	Sig.	Exp(B)
Step 1[a]	EtypeChallDum	.498	.678	.538	1	.463	1.645
	EtypeOpenSeatDum	.716	.593	1.456	1	.228	2.046
	ExecorLegislativeSought	-.849	.469	3.278	1	.070	.428
	EducationLevel	.284	.257	1.219	1	.270	1.328
	WarChest	.404	.333	1.473	1	.225	1.498
	UrbanvsRural2	.340	.534	.406	1	.524	1.405
	PollsMidway3	.129	.334	.148	1	.700	1.137
	Constant	-.247	1.037	.057	1	.812	.781

[a]Variable(s) entered on Step 1: EtypeChallDum, EtypeOpenSeatDum, ExecorLegislativeSought, EducationLevel, WarChest, UrbanvsRural2, PollsMidway3.

TABLE 7.7 Impact of demographic variables on consultant feelings about candidate's staying on message

		B	S.E.	Wald	df	Sig.	Exp(B)
Step 1[a]	EtypeOpenSeatDum	.007	.589	.000	1	.991	1.007
	EtypeChallDum	-.736	.625	1.387	1	.239	.479
	DEMGOP	.380	.509	.555	1	.456	1.462
	YourCanSex	.048	.593	.007	1	.935	1.049
	OppCandSex	-.711	.684	1.079	1	.299	.491
	YourCandRaceWhiteBlack	-.608	.862	.497	1	.481	.544
	OpCanRaceWhiteBlack	1.601	.667	5.768	1	.016	4.957
	Constant	1.384	1.228	1.270	1	.260	3.990

[a]Variable(s) entered on Step 1: EtypeOpenSeatDum, EtypeChallDum, DEMGOP, YourCanSex, OppCandSex, YourCandRaceWhiteBlack, OpCanRaceWhiteBlack.

The tables showing contextual and demographic impacts on message use and perception of received messages used the same independent variables as used in the previous table. The message definitions were recorded "1" to "0" along the standard method explained at the beginning of the section.

Appendix for Chapter 3: "The Issues"

Responses to Survey Question

In general, how much tension do you feel there is in developing a strategy that pleases the base and developing a strategy to win over the swing voter?

TABLE 7.8 Crosstabulation of consultant attitudes on directional versus proximity models in general across party lines

			PartyIDDemGOP		
			Republican	*Democrat*	**Total**
DirVsProxGen5	*No tension; these goals were entirely compatible*	Count	7	10	17
		% within PartyIDDemGOP	10.9	8.3	9.2
	Little tension; trade-offs existed, but by and large the goals were compatible	Count	23	47	70
		% within PartyIDDemGOP	35.9	38.8	37.8
	Modest tension; clear trade-offs existed, but they were not severe	Count	22	50	72
		% within PartyIDDemGOP	34.4	41.3	38.9
	High tension; strong trade-offs existed	Count	11	14	25
		% within PartyIDDemGOP	17.2	11.6	13.5
	Incompatible; any effort to please the base, alienated swing voters	Count	1	0	1
		% within PartyIDDemGOP	1.6	0.0	0.5
Total		Count	64	121	185
		% within Party IDDemGOP	100	100	100

TABLE 7.9 Chi-square tests

	Value	*df*	*Asymp. Sig. (2-sided)*
Pearson chi-square	3.806[a]	4	.433
Likelihood ratio	4.008	4	.405
Linear-by-linear association	.227	1	.634
Number of valid cases	185		

[a]Two cells (20.0%) have expected count less than 5. The minimum expected count is .35.

Responses to Survey Question

Now consider your campaign. How much tension did you feel there was between pleasing the base and winning over the swing voter?

TABLE 7.10 Crosstabulation of consultant attitudes on directional versus proximity model in their own campaigns across party lines

			PartyIDDemGOP		
			Republican	Democrat	Total
DirVsProxYour5	No tension; these goals were entirely compatible	Count	7	19	26
		% within PartyIDDemGOP	11.3	16.2	14.5
	Little tension; trade-offs existed, but by and large the goals were compatible	Count	27	46	73
		% within PartyIDDemGOP	43.5	39.3	40.8
	Modest tension; clear trade-offs existed, but they were not severe	Count	16	35	51
		% within PartyIDDemGOP	25.8	29.9	28.5
	High tension; strong trade-offs existed	Count	10	15	25
		% within PartyIDDemGOP	16.1	12.8	14.0
	Incompatible; any effort to please the base, alienated swing voters	Count	2	2	4
		% within PartyIDDemGOP	3.2	1.7	2.2
Total		Count	62	117	179
		% within PartyIDDemGOP	100	100	100

TABLE 7.11 Chi-square tests

	Value	df	Asymp. Sig. (2-sided)
Pearson chi-square	3.806[a]	4	.433
Pearson chi-square	1.836[a]	4	.766
Likelihood ratio	1.840	4	.765
Linear-by-linear association	.609	1	.435
Number of valid cases	179		

[a]Two cells (20.0%) have expected count less than 5. The minimum expected count is 1.39.

TABLE 7.12 **Consultant attitude on catering to the base or seeking the centrist voter by party identification**

			PartyIDDemGOP		
			Republican	Democrat	Total
BaseorCenter2	*Seek the centrist voter*	Count	21	68	89
		% within PartyIDDemGOP	42.0	70.1	60.5
	Cater to the base	Count	29	29	58
		% within PartyIDDemGOP	58.0	29.9	39.5
Total		Count	50	97	147
		% within PartyIDDemGOP	100	100	100

TABLE 7.13 Chi-square tests

	Value	df	Asymp. Sig. (2-sided)	Exact Sig. (2-sided)	Exact Sig. (1-sided)
Pearson chi-square	10.908[a]	1	.001		
Continuity correction[b]	9.763	1	.002		
Likelihood ratio	10.832	1	.001		
Fisher's exact test				.001	.001
Linear-by-linear association	10.834	1	.001		
Number of valid cases	147				

[a]Zero cells (0.0%) have expected count of less than 5. The minimum expected count is 19.73.
[b]Computed only for a 2x2 table.

TABLE 7.14 Significant predictors by which issue position strategy consultants are most likely to use, cater to base or seek centrist voter

	B	S.E.	Wald	df	Sig.	Exp(B)
Step 1[a] DEMGOP	-1.230	.408	9.091	1	.003	.292
YourCanSex	-.364	.484	.566	1	.452	.695
YourCandRaceWhiteBlack	.428	.684	.392	1	.531	1.535
EtypeChallDum	-.581	.654	.789	1	.374	.559
EtypeOpenSeatDum	-.285	.492	.337	1	.562	.752
ExecorLegislativeSought	-.071	.456	.024	1	.876	.931
FedOrStateSought	.241	.444	.295	1	.587	1.273
WinorLose	.037	.484	.006	1	.940	1.037
OnorOffYearElection	-.311	.444	.492	1	.483	.733
Electionb4911	-.599	.672	.794	1	.373	.549
PollsMidway3	.036	.303	.014	1	.905	1.037
UrbanvsRural2	-.149	.472	.100	1	.752	.861
MinorityPercent	.111	.206	.293	1	.589	1.118
EducationLevel	.190	.333	.326	1	.568	1.209
DistrictIncomeAv	-.259	.342	.574	1	.449	.772
PartyPrefDistrict	.314	.151	4.325	1	.038	1.368
Constant	.123	1.695	.005	1	.942	1.130

[a]Variable(s) entered on Step 1: DEMGOP, YourCanSex, YourCandRaceWhiteBlack, EtypeChallDum, EtypeOpenSeatDum, ExecorLegislativeSought, FedOrStateSought, WinorLose, OnorOffYearElection, Electionb4911, PollsMidway3, UrbanvsRural2, MinorityPercent, EducationLevel, DistrictIncomeAv, PartyPrefDistrict.

TABLE 7.15 Significant predictors by directional or proximity model within your campaign, logistic regression analyses

	B	S.E.	Wald	df	Sig.	Exp(B)
Step 1[a] DEMGOP	-1.230	.408	9.091	1	.003	.292
YourCanSex	-.364	.484	.566	1	.452	.695
YourCandRaceWhiteBlack	.428	.684	.392	1	.531	1.535
EtypeChallDum	-.581	.654	.789	1	.374	.559
EtypeOpenSeatDum	-.285	.492	.337	1	.562	.752
ExecorLegislativeSought	-.071	.456	.024	1	.876	.931
FedOrStateSought	.241	.444	.295	1	.587	1.273
WinorLose	.037	.484	.006	1	.940	1.037
OnorOffYearElection	-.311	.444	.492	1	.483	.733
Electionb4911	-.599	.672	.794	1	.373	.549
PollsMidway3	.036	.303	.014	1	.905	1.037
UrbanvsRural2	-.149	.472	.100	1	.752	.861
MinorityPercent	.111	.206	.293	1	.589	1.118
EducationLevel	.190	.333	.326	1	.568	1.209
DistrictIncomeAv	-.259	.342	.574	1	.449	.772
PartyPrefDistrict	.314	.151	4.325	1	.038	1.368
Constant	.123	1.695	.005	1	.942	1.130

[a]Variable(s) entered on Step 1: DEMGOP, YourCanSex, YourCandRaceWhiteBlack, EtypeChallDum, EtypeOpenSeatDum, ExecorLegislativeSought, FedOrStateSought, WinorLose, OnorOffYearElection, Electionb4911, PollsMidway3, UrbanvsRural2, MinorityPercent, EducationLevel, DistrictIncomeAv, PartyPrefDistrict.

TABLE 7.16 **Significant predictors by directional or proximity model in general logistic regression analysis**

		B	S.E.	Wald	df	Sig.	Exp(B)
Step 1[a]	DEMGOP	-1.230	.408	9.091	1	.003	.292
	YourCanSex	-.364	.484	.566	1	.452	.695
	YourCandRaceWhiteBlack	.428	.684	.392	1	.531	1.535
	EtypeChallDum	-.581	.654	.789	1	.374	.559
	EtypeOpenSeatDum	-.285	.492	.337	1	.562	.752
	ExecorLegislativeSought	-.071	.456	.024	1	.876	.931
	FedOrStateSought	.241	.444	.295	1	.587	1.273
	WinorLose	.037	.484	.006	1	.940	1.037
	OnorOffYearElection	-.311	.444	.492	1	.483	.733
	Electionb4911	-.599	.672	.794	1	.373	.549
	PollsMidway3	.036	.303	.014	1	.905	1.037
	UrbanvsRural2	-.149	.472	.100	1	.752	.861
	MinorityPercent	.111	.206	.293	1	.589	1.118
	EducationLevel	.190	.333	.326	1	.568	1.209
	DistrictIncomeAv	-.259	.342	.574	1	.449	.772
	PartyPrefDistrict	.314	.151	4.325	1	.038	1.368
	Constant	.123	1.695	.005	1	.942	1.130

[a]Variable(s) entered on Step 1: DEMGOP, YourCanSex, YourCandRaceWhiteBlack, EtypeChallDum, EtypeOpenSeatDum, ExecorLegislativeSought, FedOrStateSought, WinorLose, OnorOffYearElection, Electionb4911, PollsMidway3, UrbanvsRural2, MinorityPercent, EducationLevel, DistrictIncomeAv, PartyPrefDistrict.

Feelings on policy positions were recoded "1" to "0," and then regressions were run against the same independent variables that have been used this chapter.

Appendix for Chapter 4: "The Negative Ad"

TABLE 7.17 **Predictors and use of negative advertising**

Author	Dependent variable	Predictor	Effect
West 2005	Candidate won or lost	Polls (challenger, incumbent, open seat)	Challenger more likely to attack attack if behind in polls
Peterson and Djupe 2005	Amount of negativity in campaign ads	Polls (challenger, incumbent, open seat), funds raised, timing	More likely to be negative early if challenger behind in polls; incumbent in the primary increases negativity in opposing party primary and general election; more negative at beginning and end of campaign
Skaperdas and Grofman 1995	Likelihood of using negative ads	Position in the polls	Candidates more likely to attack when behind in the polls
Stevens 2005	Level of information learned from negative ads	Amount of exposure to negative advertising, level of political sophistication, education, race, sex	Negative advertising works better for political sophisticates, more sophisticated, more learned from negative ads; exposure to negative ads lowers political knowledge of women and minorities
Benoit 2004	Likelihood of using character attacks in campaign	Party	Republicans more likely to attack character than Democrats
Johnson-Cartee and Copeland 1997	Whether attack ads appear in the campaign and how many	Population, money, level of interest, candidate status	District's unique makeup influences use of negative ads; negative ads are more likely in low-interest/education races; challengers and open seats use more negative ads
Damore 2002	Use of positive or negative ads	Candidate position in polls, days till election, incumbent, challenger, partisanship, issue ownership, attacked first	Candidates behind in the polls will attack more; candidates who are attacked attack back
Haynes and Rhine 1998	Probability of candidate launching negative attack; attack reported by news	Position in polls; candidate has been attacked	If you are behind in the polls but by a small amount, more likely to attack; candidates are more likely to attack when there are fewer people in the race; more likely to attack when attacked first and more likely to attack early in the campaign

(continues)

TABLE 7.17 (*continued*)

Author	Dependent variable	Predictor	Effect
Sigelman and Shiraev 2002	Amount and strategy of negativity in Russian presidential election	Polls, time in the campaign, incumbent versus challenger, voter awareness/education	Incumbents less likely to attack, Challengers more likely to attack, Attacks come before important milestones in campaign, Sophisticated voters lead to more attacks
Hale, Fox, and Farmer 1996	Presence of negative ads in a campaign	Candidate status, competitiveness of race, district population	Each of these should have a significant effect on when negative ads are used; challengers attack more than incumbents; close races are more negative than non-competitive races
Theilmann and Wilhite 1998	Decision to launch negative ads	Challenger, incumbent, partisanship, money, position in polls	Repubs. more likely to attack than Dems.; more likely to attack with less funds; candidate with most funds more likely to attack; wide difference in polls; no difference between Repubs. and Dems.; closer the campaign gets, the more likely the Repubs. will attack; challenger more likely to attack
Lau and Pomper 2002	Success in election polls	Challenger, incumbent, money, party, position sought	Challengers improve in polls when they attack incumbents; incumbents are better off using positive ads than attack ads, as attack ads may actually lower their votes; candidates with huge money advantage or disadvantage more likely to attack; district partisan preference has impact on tone of negativity and candidate success; senators seeking reelection have differing chances if facing challenger governors or major officeholders
Lau and Pomper 2004	Likelihood of attacking	Polls, challengers, money, Republicans	Candidates behind in the polls more likely to attack; candidates in close races are more likely to attack; challengers more likely to attack than incumbents; candidates with fewer funds will attack more; Republican candidates more likely to attack than Democrats

TABLE 7.18 Predictors of how likely a consultant is to attack their opponent's character

		B	S.E.	Wald	df	Sig.	Exp(B)
Step 1[a]	DEMGOP	1.145	.669	2.931	1	.087	3.144
	EtypeChallDum	-.448	1.065	.177	1	.674	.639
	EtypeOpenSeatDum	.215	.755	.081	1	.776	1.240
	ExecorLegislativeSought	-.318	.669	.226	1	.634	.728
	FedOrStateSought	1.002	.573	3.063	1	.080	2.725
	CampRegionSouthDumVar	.367	.756	.235	1	.628	1.443
	DumVarregionMidwest	-.781	.852	.839	1	.360	.458
	DumVaregionWest	.589	.781	.569	1	.451	1.801
	PollPrimary3	*1.136*	*.577*	*3.878*	*1*	*.049*	*3.115*
	PollsMidway3	-1.005	.562	3.194	1	.074	.366
	EducationLevel	-.274	.291	.887	1	.346	.761
	WarChest	-.479	.405	1.398	1	.237	.619
	PartyPrefDistrict	-.307	.223	1.901	1	.168	.735
	Constant	-.610	1.727	.125	1	.724	.543

[a]Variable(s) entered on Step 1: DEMGOP, EtypeChallDum, EtypeOpenSeatDum, ExecorLegislativeSought, FedOrStateSought, CampRegionSouthDumVar, DumVarregionMidwest, DumVaregionWest, PollPrimary3, PollsMidway3, EducationLevel, WarChest, PartyPrefDistrict, OppAttackChar2.

TABLE 7.19 Predictors of how likely a consultant is to attack character when their character was attacked

		B	S.E.	Wald	df	Sig.	Exp(B)
Step 1[a]	DEMGOP	.821	.701	1.369	1	.242	2.272
	EtypeChallDum	-.291	1.048	.077	1	.781	.748
	EtypeOpenSeatDum	.285	.761	.140	1	.708	1.329
	ExecorLegislativeSought	-.341	.666	.262	1	.609	.711
	FedOrStateSought	.746	.601	1.542	1	.214	2.108
	CampRegionSouthDumVar	.617	.784	.620	1	.431	1.853
	DumVarregionMidwest	-.656	.897	.535	1	.465	.519
	DumVaregionWest	.894	.846	1.117	1	.291	2.446
	PollPrimary3	*1.343*	*.599*	*5.031*	*1*	*.025*	*3.832*
	PollsMidway3	*-1.156*	*.564*	*4.195*	*1*	*.041*	*.315*
	EducationLevel	-.387	.300	1.668	1	.197	.679
	WarChest	-.375	.412	.828	1	.363	.687
	PartyPrefDistrict	-.340	.226	2.272	1	.132	.712
	OppAttackChar2	*1.467*	*.649*	*5.112*	*1*	*.024*	*4.337*
	Constant	-1.292	1.748	.546	1	.460	.275

[a]Variable(s) entered on Step 1: DEMGOP, EtypeChallDum, EtypeOpenSeatDum, ExecorLegislativeSought, FedOrStateSought, CampRegionSouthDumVar, DumVarregionMidwest, DumVaregionWest, PollPrimary3, PollsMidway3, EducationLevel, WarChest, PartyPrefDistrict, OppAttackChar2.

TABLE 7.20 Predictors of how likely a consultant is to attack character when their policies were attacked

		B	S.E.	Wald	df	Sig.	Exp(B)
Step 1ᵃ	DEMGOP	.944	.693	1.857	1	.173	2.571
	EtypeChallDum	-.626	1.083	.333	1	.564	.535
	EtypeOpenSeatDum	.197	.756	.068	1	.795	1.218
	ExecorLegislativeSought	-.283	.665	.181	1	.670	.753
	FedOrStateSought	1.060	.583	3.305	1	.069	2.887
	CampRegionSouthDumVar	.371	.764	.236	1	.627	1.449
	DumVarregionMidwest	-.777	.855	.825	1	.364	.460
	DumVaregionWest	.702	.806	.758	1	.384	2.017
	PollPrimary3	*1.083*	*.574*	*3.562*	*1*	*.059*	*2.954*
	PollsMidway3	*-1.048*	*.564*	*3.454*	*1*	*.063*	*.35*
	EducationLevel	-.266	.297	.800	1	.371	.767
	WarChest	-.404	.413	.955	1	.329	.668
	PartyPrefDistrict	-.300	.220	1.852	1	.174	.741
	OppAttackPolicy2	-.739	.614	1.448	1	.229	.477
	Constant	-.204	1.791	.013	1	.909	.815

ᵃVariable(s) entered on Step 1: DEMGOP, EtypeChallDum, EtypeOpenSeatDum, ExecorLegislativeSought, FedOrStateSought, CampRegionSouthDumVar, DumVarregionMidwest, DumVaregionWest, PollPrimary3, PollsMidway3, EducationLevel, WarChest, PartyPrefDistrict, OppAttackPolicy2.

TABLE 7.21 Predictors of how likely a consultant is to attack their opponent's policy

		B	S.E.	Wald	df	Sig.	Exp(B)
Step 1ᵃ	*DEMGOP*	*-.891*	*.450*	*3.915*	*1*	*.048*	*.410*
	EtypeChallDum	.817	.762	1.150	1	.284	2.263
	EtypeOpenSeatDum	.351	.540	.423	1	.516	1.420
	ExecorLegislativeSought	.220	.482	.208	1	.648	1.246
	FedOrStateSought	*.991*	*.464*	*4.565*	*1*	*.033*	*2.693*
	PollPrimary3	-.603	.391	2.377	1	.123	.547
	PollsMidway3	.112	.389	.083	1	.773	1.119
	EducationLevel	.158	.239	.438	1	.508	1.172
	WarChest	.398	.307	1.673	1	.196	1.488
	PartyPrefDistrict	-.019	.169	.013	1	.910	.981
	OnorOffYearElection	.034	.488	.005	1	.944	1.035
	UrbanvsRural2	.529	.496	1.140	1	.286	1.698
	CampRegionSouthDumVar	-.649	.583	1.239	1	.266	.523
	DumVarregionMidwest	-.275	.576	.228	1	.633	.759
	DumVaregionWest	-.641	.618	1.075	1	.300	.527
	Constant	.055	1.323	.002	1	.967	1.057

ᵃVariable(s) entered on Step 1: DEMGOP, EtypeChallDum, EtypeOpenSeatDum, ExecorLegislativeSought, FedOrStateSought, PollPrimary3, PollsMidway3, EducationLevel, WarChest, PartyPrefDistrict, OnorOffYearElection, UrbanvsRural2, CampRegionSouthDumVar, DumVarregionMidwest, DumVaregionWest.

TABLE 7.22 Predictors of how likely a consultant is to attack their opponent's policy when attacked on character

		B	S.E.	Wald	df	Sig.	Exp(B)
Step 1[a]	DEMGOP	-.833	.460	3.286	1	.070	.435
	EtypeChallDum	.820	.758	1.169	1	.280	2.269
	EtypeOpenSeatDum	.380	.543	.491	1	.484	1.462
	ExecorLegislativeSought	.208	.483	.185	1	.667	1.231
	FedOrStateSought	1.047	.475	4.854	1	.028	2.848
	PollPrimary3	-.629	.394	2.551	1	.110	.533
	PollsMidway3	.138	.391	.125	1	.724	1.148
	EducationLevel	.172	.240	.517	1	.472	1.188
	WarChest	.382	.309	1.529	1	.216	1.466
	PartyPrefDistrict	-.017	.169	.010	1	.919	.983
	OnorOffYearElection	.069	.493	.019	1	.889	1.071
	UrbanvsRural2	.514	.496	1.074	1	.300	1.672
	CampRegionSouthDumVar	-.691	.591	1.369	1	.242	.501
	DumVarregionMidwest	-.350	.591	.351	1	.554	.705
	DumVaregionWest	-.703	.627	1.258	1	.262	.495
	OppAttackChar2	-.264	.425	.387	1	.534	.768
	Constant	.120	1.326	.008	1	.928	1.127

[a]Variable(s) entered on Step 1: DEMGOP, EtypeChallDum, EtypeOpenSeatDum, ExecorLegislativeSought, FedOrStateSought, PollPrimary3, PollsMidway3, EducationLevel, WarChest, PartyPrefDistrict, OnorOffYearElection, UrbanvsRural2, CampRegionSouthDumVar, DumVarregionMidwest, DumVaregionWest, OppAttackChar2.

TABLE 7.23 Predictors of how likely a consultant is to attack their opponent's policy when attacked on policy

		B	S.E.	Wald	df	Sig.	Exp(B)
Step 1[a]	DEMGOP	-.635	.472	1.814	1	.178	.530
	EtypeChallDum	1.188	.804	2.184	1	.139	3.280
	EtypeOpenSeatDum	.515	.565	.829	1	.363	1.673
	ExecorLegislativeSought	.070	.497	.020	1	.888	1.073
	FedOrStateSought	1.003	.482	4.327	1	.038	2.726
	PollPrimary3	-.533	.404	1.736	1	.188	.587
	PollsMidway3	.119	.402	.088	1	.767	1.126
	EducationLevel	.123	.247	.250	1	.617	1.131
	WarChest	.355	.322	1.221	1	.269	1.427
	PartyPrefDistrict	.000	.171	.000	1	.999	1.000
	OnorOffYearElection	.044	.508	.007	1	.931	1.045
	UrbanvsRural2	.575	.507	1.284	1	.257	1.776
	CampRegionSouthDumVar	-.617	.603	1.048	1	.306	.540
	DumVarregionMidwest	-.338	.589	.329	1	.566	.713
	DumVaregionWest	-.788	.637	1.530	1	.216	.455
	OppAttackPolicy2	1.042	.443	5.523	1	.019	2.834
	Constant	-.679	1.395	.237	1	.627	.507

[a]Variable(s) entered on Step 1: DEMGOP, EtypeChallDum, EtypeOpenSeatDum, ExecorLegislativeSought, FedOrStateSought, PollPrimary3, PollsMidway3, EducationLevel, WarChest, PartyPrefDistrict, OnorOffYearElection, UrbanvsRural2, CampRegionSouthDumVar, DumVarregionMidwest, DumVaregionWest, OppAttackPolicy2.

Appendix for Chapter 5: "The Internet Campaign"

TABLE 7.24 How do you think the Internet changes campaigns?

		How many years as a consultant crosstabulation					
		1–4	*5–10*	*11–15*	*16–20*	*More than 20*	**Total**
How do you think the Internet changes campaigns?	.00 Count	28	26	9	2	2	67
	% within Howlongasconsultant	37.3	51.0	39.1	20.0	15.4	39.0
	1.00 Count	47	25	14	8	11	105
	% within Howlongasconsultant	62.7	49.0	60.9	80.0	84.6	61.0
	Total Count	75	51	23	10	13	172
	% within Howlongasconsultant	100	100	100	100	100	100

TABLE 7.25 Chi-square tests

	Value	*df*	*Asymp. Sig. (2-sided)*
Pearson chi-square	7.733[a]	4	.102
Likelihood ratio	8.231	4	.083
Linear-by-linear association	2.257	1	.133
Number of valid cases	172		

[a]One cell (10.0%) has expected count less than 5. The minimum expected count is 3.90.

TABLE 7.26 How do you think the Internet changes campaigns?

		Incumbent	*Challenger*	*Open Seat*	**Total**
How do you think the Internet changes campaigns?	.00 Count	22	12	33	67
	% within IncumbentChallengerOpenSeat	43.1	25.0	45.2	39.0
	1.00 Count	29	36	40	105
	% within IncumbentChallengerOpenSeat	56.9	75.0	54.8	61.0
	Total Count	51	48	73	172
	% within IncumbentChallengerOpenSeat	100	100	100	100

TABLE 7.27 **Chi-square tests**

	Value	*df*	*Asymp. Sig. (2-sided)*
Pearson chi-square	5.505[a]	2	.064
Likelihood ratio	5.729	2	.057
Linear-by-linear association	.204	1	.652
Number of valid cases	172		

[a]Zero cells (0.0%) have expected count less than 5. The minimum expected count is 18.70.

TABLE 7.28 **How do you think the Internet changes campaigns?**

		PartyIDDemGOP		Total
		Republican	*Democrat*	**Total**
How do you think the Internet changes campaigns?	.00 Count	16	43	59
	% within PartyIDDemGOP	30.8	43.4	39.1
	1.00 Count	36	56	92
	% within PartyIDDemGOP	69.2	56.6	60.9
	Total Count	52	99	151
	% within PartyIDDemGOP	100	100	100

TABLE 7.29 **Chi-square tests**

	Value	*df*	*Asymp. Sig. (2-sided)*	*Exact Sig. (2-sided)*	*Exact Sig. (1-sided)*
Pearson chi-square	2.297[a]	1	.130		
Continuity correction[b]	1.796	1	.180		
Likelihood ratio	2.336	1	.126		
Fisher's exact test				.161	.089
Linear-by-linear association	2.282	1	.131		
Number of valid cases	151				

[a]Zero cells (0.0%) have expected count less than 5. The minimum expected count is 20.32.
[b]Computed only for a 2x2 table.

TABLE 7.30 **Chi-square tests**

	Value	*df*	*Asymp. Sig. (2-sided)*
Pearson chi-square	147.587[a]	16	.000
Likelihood ratio	167.387	16	.000
Number of valid cases	266		

[a]Six cells (22.2%) have expected count less than 5. The minimum expected count is 2.52.

TABLE 7.31 **How do you think the Internet changes campaigns?**

	Urban or rural campaign region					
	Mostly rural	*Somewhat rural*	*Mixed rural and suburban*	*Suburban*	*Urban*	**Total**
How do you think the Internet changes campaigns?						
.00 Count	13	4	26	16	8	67
% within urban or rural campaign region	40.6	57.1	35.1	37.2	50.0	39.0
1.00 Count	19	3	48	27	8	105
% within urban or rural campaign region	59.4	42.9	64.9	62.8	50.0	61.0
Total Count	32	7	74	43	16	172
% within urban or rural campaign region	100	100	100	100	100	100

TABLE 7.32 **Chi-square tests**

	Value	*df*	*Asymp. Sig. (2-sided)*
Pearson chi-square	2.34[a]	4	.673
Likelihood ratio	2.296	4	.682
Linear-by-linear association	.003	1	.954
Number of valid cases	172		

[a]Two cells (20.0%) have expected count less than 5. The minimum expected count is 2.73.

The survey questions used to perform the binary logistic regressions are below. The independent variables were derived from the consultant information given near the earlier part of the survey.

TABLE 7.33 **How often were the following Internet resources used during your campaign?**

	Every day	At least once a week	A couple of times a month	A few times during the campaign	Never	Total
Campaign Web site	104 (58.4)	29 (16.3)	8 (4.5)	13 (7.3)	24 (13.5)	178 (100)
Twitter	21 (11.8)	11 (6.2)	7 (3.9)	5 (2.8)	134 (75.3)	178 (100)
MySpace	16 (9.0)	13 (7.3)	8 (4.5)	13 (7.3)	128 (71.9)	178 (100)
YouTube	23 (12.9)	28 (15.7)	20 (11.2)	22 (12.4)	85 (47.8)	178 (100)
Facebook	46 (25.8)	28 (15.7)	10 (5.6)	12 (6.7)	82 (46.1)	178 (100)
Other	38 (21.3)	19 (10.7)	16 (9.0)	18 (10.1)	87 (48.9)	178 (100)

Note: Actual number (percentage of total).

TABLE 7.34 **How effective was your campaign Web site in each of the following activities?**

	Extremely effective	Somewhat effective	Somewhat ineffective	Extremely ineffective	No Web site or site did not have this function	Total
Fund-raising	42 (23.6)	57 (32.0)	17 (9.6)	19 (10.7)	43 (24.2)	178 (100)
Connecting with voters	46 (25.8)	60 (33.7)	25 (14.0)	13 (7.3)	34 (19.1)	178 (100)
Organizing events	31 (17.4)	52 (29.2)	28 (15.7)	20 (11.2)	47 (26.4)	178 (100)
Registering voters	14 (7.9)	30 (16.9)	30 (16.9)	24 (13.5)	80 (44.9)	178 (100)
Other	25 (14.0)	21 (11.8)	16 (9.0)	9 (5.1)	107 (60.1)	178 (100)

Note: Actual number (percentage of total).

Appendix for Chapter 6: "Conclusion"

TABLE 7.35 Winning or losing based on campaign environment and demographics

		B	S.E.	Wald	df	Sig.	Exp(B)
Step 1[a]	DEMGOP	-.716	.603	1.410	1	.235	.489
	OpCanRaceWhiteBlack	2.613	1.086	5.789	1	.016	13.643
	EtypeChallDum	-1.122	.855	1.723	1	.189	.326
	EtypeOpenSeatDum	-1.428	.723	3.897	1	.048	.240
	PollsMidway3	1.479	.376	15.443	1	.000	4.390
	EducationLevel	.307	.280	1.203	1	.273	1.360
	PartyPrefDistrict	-.133	.183	.529	1	.467	.875
	WarChest	.703	.332	4.474	1	.034	2.019
	MessCon2	2.846	.814	12.230	1	.000	17.210
	InternetAttitude2	-1.038	.551	3.546	1	.060	.354
	OppCandSex	-.460	.620	.551	1	.458	.631
	Constant	-6.634	2.068	10.288	1	.001	.001

[a]Variable(s) entered on Step 1: DEMGOP, OpCanRaceWhiteBlack, EtypeChallDum, EtypeOpenSeatDum, PollsMidway3, EducationLevel, PartyPrefDistrict, WarChest, MessCon2, InternetAttitude2, OppCandSex.

TABLE 7.36 Frequency table for campaigners whose candidates went from being in the lead in the polls after the primary to losing

		Frequency	Percentage	Valid percentage	Cumulative percentage
Valid	All Others	201	75.6	95.7	95.7
	Ahead by single to double digits after primary to losing	9	3.4	4.3	100
	Total	210	78.9	100	
Missing	System	56	21.1		
Total		266	100		

TABLE 7.37 Frequency table for campaigners whose candidates went from being behind in the polls after the primary to winning

		Frequency	Percentage	Valid percentage	Cumulative percentage
Valid	All others Behind by single to double digits	182	68.4	86.7	86.7
	to victory	28	10.5	13.3	100
	Total	210	78.9	100	
Missing	System	56	21.1		
Total		266	100		

TABLE 7.38 Variables influencing consultants in campaigns where they went from a lead to losing the election

		B	S.E.	Wald	df	Sig.	Exp(B)
Step 1[a]	DEMGOP	-.400	1.097	.133	1	.715	.670
	OpCanRaceWhiteBlack	1.242	1.579	.618	1	.432	3.461
	EtypeChallDum	-17.551	5797.649	.000	1	.998	.000
	EtypeOpenSeatDum	1.004	1.043	.927	1	.336	2.729
	PollsMidway3	1.579	.959	2.713	1	.100	4.849
	EducationLevel	-.131	.477	.075	1	.784	.877
	PartyPrefDistrict	.490	.365	1.797	1	.180	1.632
	WarChest	-.231	.555	.174	1	.676	.793
	MessCon2	-3.001	1.123	7.134	1	.008	.050
	InternetAttitude2	.085	.952	.008	1	.929	1.088
	OppCandSex	19.020	6031.330	.000	1	.997	1.820
	Constant	-25.578	6031.331	.000	1	.997	.000

[a]Variable(s) entered on Step 1: DEMGOP, OpCanRaceWhiteBlack, EtypeChallDum, EtypeOpenSeatDum, PollsMidway3, EducationLevel, PartyPrefDistrict, WarChest, MessCon2, InternetAttitude2, OppCandSex.

TABLE 7.39 Variables influencing consultants in campaigns where they went from losing to winning the election

		B	S.E.	Wald	df	Sig.	Exp(B)
Step 1[a]	DEMGOP	-1.134	.692	2.684	1	.101	.322
	EtypeChallDum	-.728	.987	.544	1	.461	.483
	EtypeOpenSeatDum	-1.060	.841	1.588	1	.208	.346
	PollsMidway3	-1.154	.447	6.665	1	.010	.315
	EducationLevel	-.356	.293	1.485	1	.223	.700
	PartyPrefDistrict	.200	.209	.910	1	.340	1.221
	WarChest	-.857	.500	2.942	1	.086	.424
	MessCon2	2.180	1.135	3.685	1	.055	8.842
	InternetAttitude2	-2.191	.725	9.128	1	.003	.112
	OppCandSex	1.209	.802	2.274	1	.132	3.349
	OpCanRaceWhiteBlack	20.568	9467.550	.000	1	.998	8.560
	Constant	-18.527	9467.550	.000	1	.998	.000

[a]Variable(s) entered on Step 1: DEMGOP, EtypeChallDum, EtypeOpenSeatDum, PollsMidway3, EducationLevel, PartyPrefDistrict, WarChest, MessCon2, InternetAttitude2, OppCandSex, OpCanRaceWhiteBlack.

Survey

This survey is a critical part of ongoing research on political campaigns. Since 2006 the Consultant Attitudes on Management and Professionalism Survey (C.A.M.P.) has been taken by over 800 consultants, managers, and activists during every election cycle. The purpose of this research is to compare and contrast how political consultants think and operate in the field with what most political science theory says about how elections are won. The results of this research will also help the general public understand better what political consultants do and how their work is not only important but essential to how elections work in the United States today. The survey has 10 sections and should take about 25 minutes; however, you do not have to complete the entire survey in one sitting. Just leave the survey open on your screen until you are finished. We ask that you complete the survey within 1 week of activating the link through your email. Questions marked with an asterisk must be answered in order to continue with the survey, questions without an asterisk are optional. The entire process is voluntary and you have the right to stop at any point. This survey program guarantees your privacy, and there is no way that answers can be traced back to any individual survey respondent. If you have any questions or concerns feel free to contact the research team.

Thank you for your time.

Q1. Do you agree with and understand the terms written above?
   Yes
   No

Q2. Some questions on this survey ask about specific campaigns that you have worked on; others ask about your general views. When answering survey questions about specific campaigns, please answer in terms of one or two important campaigns that you have worked on in your career, even if you are a general consultant. Also, complete the survey based on COMPLETED campaigns, not ones you are currently working on. With that in mind, in what year did you work on the campaign that you will refer to most often in this survey?
   2008
   2006
   2004
   2002
   2000
   1998
   Other (please specify)

Q3. What was your campaign position during the election?
   Manager
   Fundraiser
   Media
   GOTV
   Other (please specify)

Q4. How long have you worked as a consultant or campaign organizer?
   1–4 years
   5–10 years
   11–15 years
   16–20 years
   More than 20 years

Q5. What was your candidate's party identification?
   Republican
   Democrat
   Independent
   Other (please specify)

Q6. What were the genders of the candidates running?
    Male   Female
    My candidate was
    The opposition's candidate was

Q7. Your candidate was:
    White
    Black
    Hispanic
    Asian
    Other (please specify)

Q8. Your opponent was:
    White
    Black
    Hispanic
    Asian
    Other (please specify)

Q9. Your candidate's position at the beginning of the race was:
    Incumbent
    Challenger
    It was an open-seat race

Q10. Which of the following best describes the position sought by your candidate?
    President
    Governor
    Federal Senate
    Federal House
    State legislature
    Mayor or city manager
    School board
    Other (please specify)

Q11. Did your candidate win the general election?
    Yes
    No

Q12. In what region of the country was the campaign you were involved in taking place?

Northeast
Mid-Atlantic
Southeast
South
Midwest
Southwest
West
Pacific Northwest

Q13. Immediately after the primaries took place, your candidate was:

ahead of the opponent in the polls by double digits
ahead of the opponent in the polls by single digits
about even with the opponent
behind the opponent in the polls by single digits
behind the opponent in the polls by double digits

Q14. Midway through the campaign, your candidate was:

ahead of the opponent in the polls by double digits
ahead of the opponent in the polls by single digits
about even with the opponent
behind the opponent by single digits
behind the opponent in the polls by double digits

Q15. At the end of the campaign, your candidate:

won by double digits
won by single digits
had a runoff election
lost by single digits
lost by double digits

Q16. Which of the following best describes the region you campaigned in?

Mostly rural
Somewhat rural
Mixed rural and urban area
Suburban
Urban

Q17. Which of the following best describes the minority demographics of your campaign region?

    Less than 10%

    Between 10% and 25%

    Between 26% and 40%

    Between 41% and 55%

    More than 55%

Q18. What was the largest ethnic or racial minority in your campaign area?

    African American

    Asian American

    Latino American

    Other (please specify)

Q19. On average, about 84% of Americans graduate from high school, 26% have a college degree, and around 15% have graduate or professional degrees. Which of the following do you think best describes the educational level of voters in your campaign area?

    Far above average

    Above average

    Average

    Below average

    Far below average

Q20. The median household income across the United States is about $45,000 a year. Which of the following would you say best describes the average income in the area where you campaigned?

    Far above average

    Above average

    Average

    Below average

    Far below average

Q21. What was the general party preference in your campaign area?

    Overwhelmingly Democratic

    Slightly Democratic

    About evenly split between Republicans and Democrats

    Slightly Republican

    Overwhelmingly Republican

Q22. At the beginning of the general election, which candidate had more money in their campaign war chest?
>Your candidate
>Your opponent
>Both about the same

Q23. What was the turnout of eligible voters in your campaign area in the election?
>Less than 35%
>36–45%
>46–55%
>56–65%
>More than 65%

Q24. In planning a campaign strategy, some consultants feel there is a clear tension between developing a strategy that pleases the base and one that can win over the swing voter. Others feel that these goals are entirely compatible. In general, how much tension do you feel there is in developing a strategy that pleases the base and developing a strategy to win over the swing voter?
>No tension; these goals are entirely compatible
>Little tension; trade-offs exist, but by and large the goals are compatible
>Modest tension; clear trade-offs exist, but they are not severe
>High tension; strong trade-offs exist
>Incompatible; if one pleases the base, one alienates swing voters

Q25. Now consider your campaign. How much tension did you feel there was between pleasing the base and winning over the swing voter?
>No tension; these goals were entirely compatible
>Little tension; trade-offs existed, but by and large the goals were compatible
>Modest tension; clear trade-offs existed, but they were not severe
>High tension; strong trade-offs existed
>Incompatible; any effort to please the base alienated swing voters

Q26. In your opinion, in general, how effective is the use of negative advertising in winning a political campaign?
>Highly effective
>Effective
>Neither effective nor ineffective
>Ineffective
>Highly ineffective

Q27. Under each of the following circumstances, how likely would you be to launch a negative advertising campaign against your opponent?

Very likely	Somewhat likely	Neither likely nor unlikely	Somewhat unlikely	Unlikely

Your candidate is far behind in the election
Your candidate is slightly behind in the election
Your candidate is even with the opponent
Your candidate is slightly ahead in the election
Your candidate is way ahead in the election

Q28. Some argue that negative advertising has an adverse affect on voter turnout. Which of the following best describes your opinion on this issue?
Negative advertising greatly increases turnout
Negative advertising somewhat increases turnout
Negative advertising has a neutral impact on turnout
Negative advertising somewhat decreases turnout
Negative advertising greatly decreases turnout

Q29. What is your definition of negative advertising?

Q30. Were any negative advertisements run during your campaign?
Yes, our opponent attacked us first
Yes, we attacked our opponent first
No, there were no negative ads run

Q31. Did any outside groups run attack ads during the campaign?
Yes, outside groups ran attack ads against my candidate
Yes, outside groups ran attack ads against my opponent
Yes, outside groups ran attack ads against my candidate and the opponent
No, outside groups did not run any attack ads

Q32. What were the major themes of your opponent's attack ads against your candidate?

Q33. What were the major themes of your attack ads against your opponent?

Q34. In YOUR attack ads, which of the following best describes how often you focused on your opponent's CHARACTER?

Always
Mostly
Sometimes
Seldom
Never

Q35. In YOUR attack ads, which of the following best describes how often you focused on your opponent's POLICY POSITIONS?

Always
Mostly
Sometimes
Seldom
Never

Q36. In your OPPONENT'S attack ads, which of the following best describes how often they focused on YOUR candidate's character?

Always
Mostly
Sometimes
Seldom
Never

Q37. In your OPPONENT'S attack ads, which of the following best describes how often they focused on YOUR candidate's policy positions?

Always
Mostly
Sometimes
Seldom
Never

Q38. Were any humorous ads run during the campaign?

Yes, my opponent and I both ran humorous ads
Yes, my opponent ran humorous ads against my candidate
Yes, my candidate ran humorous ads against my opponent
No, they were all serious

Q39. In general, do you think that the ads that were run by your opponent against your candidate were unfair?

    Yes, virtually all were unfair

    Yes, more were unfair than fair

    They were mixed; about half were fair and half were unfair

    No, more were fair than unfair

    No, virtually all were fair

Q40. In general, do you think that any of the ads that you ran during the campaign against your opponent were unfair?

    Yes, virtually all were unfair

    Yes, more were unfair than fair

    They were mixed; about half were fair and half were unfair

    No, more were fair than unfair

    No, virtually all were fair

Q41. Defining your opponent is a very critical part of the campaign process. Which of the following best characterizes how you tried to define your opponent during the campaign?

    Out of touch

    Incompetent

    Inexperienced

    Corrupt

    Too old, too long in office

    Other (please specify)

Q42. Which of the following best characterizes how your opponent tried to define YOUR candidate?

    Out of touch

    Incompetent

    Inexperienced

    Corrupt

    Too old, too long in office

    Other (please specify)

Q43. Would you say that your candidate

    always stayed on message

    mostly stayed on message

    frequently was not on message

    never stayed on message

Q44. When or if your candidate did veer from the campaign's main message, what were the usual reasons?

Q45. How often were the following Internet resources used during the campaign?

	Every day	At least once a week	A couple of times a month	A few times during the campaign	Never
Campaign Web site					
Twitter					
MySpace					
YouTube					
Facebook					
Other					

Q46. How effective was your campaign Web site in each of the following activities?

	Extremely effective	Somewhat effective	Somewhat ineffective	Extremely ineffective	No Web site or site did not have this function
Fund-raising					
Connecting with voters					
Organizing events					
Registering voters					
Other					

Q47. Which of the following statements best reflects how you feel about the Internet in political campaigns?

The Internet allows campaigns to do new things they were never able to do before

The Internet simply allows campaigns to engage in the same activities they always have, just through a different medium

Q48. The use of the Internet in political campaigns changes rapidly in every campaign season. Sometimes these changes are positive and sometimes negative. Briefly describe the most significant impact the Internet has had on your campaign work.

Q49. How would you classify the level of political awareness of voters in your campaign area?

> Very aware
>
> Aware
>
> Somewhat aware
>
> Hardly aware
>
> Not at all aware

Q50. Turnout is a key part of any election campaign. In your experience, is it easier to increase or suppress voter turnout?

> Increase
>
> Suppress

Q51. If there is bad weather on election day, which party will be most affected?

> Poor weather has a greater impact on Democratic turnout
>
> Poor weather has a greater impact on Republican turnout
>
> Poor weather doesn't have a greater impact on the turnout for either party

Q52. If you thought it would help your candidate, would you engage in legal activities that are known to depress turnout?

> Yes
>
> No

Q53. Have you ever engaged in activities designed to lower the turnout of the opposition's supporters during an election?

> Yes
>
> No

Q54. Did your opposition engage in any activities designed to lower turnout in favor of YOUR candidate?

> Yes
>
> No

Q55. Despite a recent uptick during presidential election years, American voter turnout is still fairly low. Why do you think most Americans don't bother to vote?

Q56. Which would you prefer as a consultant?

> A small margin of victory in a race with voter turnout above 55%
>
> A large margin of victory in a race with voter turnout below 30%

Q57. Which of the following do you think has a greater impact on whether citizens come out to vote?

Structural factors (close election, easy registration, major public issues)

Psychological factors (civic responsibility, trust of politicians, interest in politics)

Q58. Which of the following best describes the voter registration process in your campaign area?

Same-day registration

Thirty-day registration in advance

Other (please specify)

Q59. In general, how helpful are the following tactics in turning out the vote?

Extremely effective	Effective	Neither effective nor ineffective	Ineffective	Extremely ineffective

Door to door

Phone calls

E-mails

Mail reminders

Rallies

Q60. Which of the following best describes the employment or office your candidate held prior to running?

President

Governor

Federal Senate

Federal House

State legislature

Mayor or city manager

School board

Other (please specify)

Q61. What would you say was your candidate's best attribute?

Q62. How important are the following traits for a candidate running for office?

Very important	Important	Neither important nor unimportant	Unimportant	Extremely unimportant

Integrity
Leadership
Empathy
Competence
Ambition

Q63. How important are the following traits when actually governing and serving as an elected official

Very important	Somewhat important	Neither important nor unimportant	Somewhat unimportant	Very unimportant

Integrity
Leadership
Empathy
Competence
Ambition

Q64. How do you think the traits that someone has as a candidate relate to how they will actually govern?
    They have a very strong correlation. The way they run and behave in a campaign says a lot about how they will govern.
    They have no correlation. Being a great campaigner says little about how you will actually govern.
    I don't know. I don't keep up with candidates after the race is over.

Q65. What was your candidate's position on the most important policy issue you faced in the campaign?

Q66. Which of the following best describes your candidate's position on most issues?
    Conservative
    Slightly conservative
    Moderate
    Slightly liberal
    Liberal

Q67. Which of the following best describes how your opposition positioned him- or herself on most issues?

Conservative
Slightly conservative
Moderate
Slightly liberal
Liberal

Q68. Now think of the campaign through the eyes of the voters. How did your candidate's positions compare to the opposition's?

Much more conservative
More conservative
About the same
More liberal
Much more liberal

Q69. Occasionally, candidates adjust policy stances during the general election campaign. Which of the following best describes your candidate?

Moved markedly to the left
Moved slightly to the left
Remained in the same position throughout the campaign
Moved slightly to the right
Moved markedly to the right

Q70. What was the main reason your candidate shifted positions on issues?

New information was presented that changed our position
The opposition took a new position, and we changed to counter them
Our stance was unpopular and hurting us in the polls
My candidate did not shift on any issues
Other (please specify)

Q71. What was your candidate's strategic motivation on most issue positions?

To cater to their base
To seek the centrist voter

Q72. If your candidate adjusted policy positions during the campaign, which of these policy areas did they shift positions on?
    Foreign policy
    Jobs
    Taxes
    Education policy
    Social/cultural issues
    No policy position changes
    Other (please specify)

Q73. If a candidate changes positions on issues during a campaign, it can confuse voters or, even worse, make you look inconsistent. In general, on which of the following issues would it be the most problematic for a candidate to change their position?

Extremely problematic	Somewhat problematic	Neither problematic nor unproblematic	Not problematic	Extremely unproblematic
Foreign policy				
Jobs				
Taxes				
Education policy				
Social/cultural issues				

Q74. Which is more important in the minds of voters?
    That a candidate have a strong plan and vision for the future
    That a candidate have a strong past record and experience

Q75. Which of the following best characterizes your feelings toward the following statement, "The general election is a referendum on the incumbent"?
    Strongly agree
    Agree
    Disagree
    Strongly disagree

Acknowledgments

Transforming *Political Consultants and Campaigns: One Day to Sell* from an idea to a dissertation to a book was a long process that involved the help and dedication of many people. My family, friends, and God all deserve credit for making this entire endeavor one of the most enjoyable of my life. Specifically, I would like to thank Dr. Andra Gillespie, Dr. Niambi Carter, and Dr. Carlton Haywood Jr.; their assistance professionally, personally, and technically was priceless.

I would also like to thank my advisers at the University of North Carolina at Chapel Hill, Donald Searing and Marco Steenbergen. A special thanks goes to Daniel Gitterman for all of his outside help and watchful eye and last to Dr. N. J. Scheers, my shadow adviser, who taught me that "*done* is good."

Hiram College has been more than an employer; the school has been a home and a stalwart supporter of me and the research that supports this book, from the administration down to the volunteer student researchers. I would particularly like to thank President Tom Chema, Vice President Cheryl Torsney, Dean Detra West, and the Political Science Department. The real meat of the book, the survey of political consultants, took time, dedication, and tedious data entry, and my research team of students at Hiram came through in every way on this project. My lead researcher, Wiley Runnestrand, grew from a student to a future colleague, and Evan Tachovsky, Amy Romanow, Steve Voytek, and Michael Walton put in long hours on the phone calling campaigns around America.

The final months of putting the book together were challenging, but the process was made smoother by the help of the Political Science Departments at Morehouse College and Spelman College. While I was visiting Morehouse, both departments lent me their offices, resources, and, most important, students. The enthusiasm, sense of humor, and discipline of the student volunteers for this book at both colleges ensured that the final months of this project went off without a hitch. Thanks to Alicia Bello, Lovetta Bradley, Lauren A. Anderson, Brittany N. Carter, Katherine E. Ellis, Braxton Street, Joshua Rodgers, Porscha Phillips, Irrisha Hodnett-Sartin, Ashtin Jones, Shenel Hughes, Jacqeline A. Quander, Darius Smith, Lionell Gaines, Terrence Nero, Kenisha Cromity, Tim Whitt, Brittney Johnson, Brandon Howard, and Winston Roberts.

While writing a book there are dozens of people who step in and answer a quick e-mail question or phone call, share a contact, or just provide that additional insight that makes the book that much better. I thank everyone who has helped me in that regard, but in particular Wyeth Ruthven, Gail Garbrandt, Jerry Austin, Matthew Acie, Chuck Cushman, and my editors at Westview Press, Toby Wahl, Melissa Veronesi, and Annette Wenda, who really worked above and beyond to help during this process.

Finally, a special thanks to the following organizations and universities that contributed to this work: the University of Akron, the Yale Women's Campaign School, Regent University, the Graduate School of Political Management at George Washington University, and the American Association of Political Consultants.

Notes

Introduction

1. For the original report, see "Elections Without Choice" 1968.

2. Larry O'Brian was a former campaign manager for John F. Kennedy who went on to become NBA commissioner. The O'Brian Trophy is the championship trophy in the sport. His book *No Final Victories: A Life in Politics from John F. Kennedy to Watergate* was released in 1974.

3. For an interesting discussion on the role of mass media in American politics, see *Annals of the American Academy of Political and Social Science* 472 (1976): 115, 120.

4. Campaign management programs were started at Kent State University, San Francisco State University, the University of West Florida, George Washington University, Georgia State University, the University of Connecticut, and City University of New York.

5. Bill Clinton to consultants Dick Morris and Doug Shoen during the 1996 campaign.

6. Other examples of the celebrity campaign culture of the 1990s include James Carville appearing on several episodes of the popular sitcom *Mad About You* and a pop rock group the Spin Doctors capturing the popularity of the newfound phrase to describe the consultants and managers who were running campaigns.

7. Political cartoonist Tom Tomorrow, in "How I Became the Story of the Great Debate of 1996" (1996), details how "Spin Alley," the room dedicated to consultants trying to influence reporters about their candidate's performance after the debate, negatively impacts politics.

8. A more detailed description of the methods for this work can be found in the Appendix.

Chapter 1

1. President David Palmer from *24* is consistently voted as one of America's favorite "fictional" presidents. He was voted number 1 all time by a Blockbuster video poll. http://www.imdb.com/news/ni0588731/.

2. Tribute to President Bush Convention 2004 (minute 1:03 to 1:25) http://www.youtube.com/watch?v=0ZiE5F-awFs&feature=related.

3. For further accounts of this campaign event, see campaign blogs around the nation, such as Seelye 2008.

4. In the past forty years there have been a large number of women candidates who have sought the nomination of the two major parties, but only a few were considered "legitimate," meaning they received a substantial number of primary votes and at least some press attention. Shirley Chisholm (D), Patsy Mink (D), Bella Abzug (D), 1972; Libby Dole (R), 2000; Carol Moseley Braun (D), 2004; and Hillary Clinton (D), 2008. Those who have been on a major party ticket were only Geraldine Ferraro (D) in 1984 and Sarah Palin (R) in 2008.

5. We will focus more on "valence" issues in Chapter 3.

6. The number of African American men who have declared their candidacy and run for a major party nomination is smaller than even that of women: Jesse Jackson (D), 1984 and 1988; Virginia governor Doug Wilder (D), 1992; Allan Keyes (R), 1996, 2000; Al Sharpton (D), 2004; and Barack Obama (D), 2008.

7. Prominent examples that resulted in victories by African American candidates though by smaller margins than initially reported include former Virginia governor Doug Wilder in 1992 and New York mayor David Dinkins in 1989. In each case substantial poll leads less than a week before the election (ten points or more) evaporated, leading to one- or two-point wins on election day.

8. Since Nixon's infamous "Southern Strategy" to exploit white southerners' fears of integration and intermarriage with African Americans, many researchers have shown the value of playing on white voters fears to turn out the vote. Large public examples of this would be the "Willie Horton" ad in the 1988 presidential campaign and the entirety of the Jesse Helms–Harvey Gantt Senate election in 1992. For a scholarly analysis of how white candidates may explicitly attempt this strategy, see Mendelberg 1997. See also F. Brown 2004.

9. Democratic Congressional Campaign Committee (DCCC) press release, February 22, 2006, http://dccc.org/newsroom/entry/ports/.

10. Quote from Senator Joe Biden in Democratic presidential primary debate, October 30, 2007, Philadelphia.

11. See "Appendix for Chapter 1: 'The Candidate.'"

12. "Mass Backwards" segment, *The Daily Show*, January 18, 2010, minute 5:13 to 5:45.

13. Many political insiders and some writers from *The Wire* have suggested that Clay Davis's character was based on Senator Larry Young who had been expelled from the Senate in the late 1990s. Further, in one episode of the show former senator Young plays a radio host (his actual job now) who interviews Clay Davis on the allegations, further strengthening their real life–to-character connection (*Salon.com* 2008).

14. See "Appendix for Chapter 1: 'The Candidate'" for more detail.

15. This is not meant to suggest that campaign managers are evolutionary biologists, but various studies have shown that more educated people are more likely to care about others beyond their families. A highly educated district would be more inclined to want an empathetic elected leader than a less educated district. Consultants are likely to pick up on that sentiment. "In the current study, Kanazawa argues that humans are evolutionarily designed to be conservative, caring mostly about their family and friends, and being liberal, caring about an indefinite number of genetically unrelated strangers they never meet or interact with, is evolutionarily novel. So more intelligent children may be more likely to grow up to be liberals" (*Science Daily* 2010).

16. Personal conversation with Wyeth Ruthven of Qorvis, November 2010.

Chapter 2

1. http://www.politicalstrategy.org/archives/001208.php.

2. See Appendix for full regression table and variables.

3. Election type is used as both a contextual and a demographic variable in these regressions. Whether you are running a campaign for a challenger, incumbent, or open-seat race completely changes the context of how you run, what you may target in messaging, and what types of issues may eventually surface in the race. Along the same lines, demographic variables such as race and gender, your candidate status as a challenger, and so forth cannot be changed during the campaign.

4. The Asian, Latino, and other categories were so small in the sample that they were added in. They account for less than 10 percent of the total minority candidates.

5. I would argue that Clinton's "theme" was security and responsibility. She wanted Americans to feel safe with her at the wheel of the nation through troubled economic and foreign policy times. Her slogan was "Ready on Day One," which was to make the public feel safe and suggest that Obama would be learning on the job. And her message was that he was an idealist who would learn on the job and that she was the realist prepared and experienced enough to do the job right. Hope and optimism won out over security and certainty.

6. Bill Clinton was not the only one playing the Southern Strategy and being off message. Clinton's convoluted comments about Martin Luther King's needing President Lyndon B. Johnson to fulfill his dream was seen as a subtle jab that Obama could dream like King but it took a strong (white) person to make the dream a reality. For a detailed discussion of this messaging debacle, see also Kilson 2008.

7. I simply removed those respondents who reported running against an African American for president and reran the regression. There was only one in the sample.

8. http://www.localvictory.com/strategy/how-to-beat-an-incumbent.html.

9. http://uploads.democracyforamerica.com/0005/4001/DFA_Training_Manual_2008 _-_Chapter_6_Messaging.pdf.

10. A more detailed explanation of this process can be seen in the Appendix.

11. More specifically, there is little or no chance that the null hypothesis, that these responses have no relationship, is true.

12. Personal conversation with Lenny McAllister.

Chapter 3

1. From transcript of *Fox News Sunday*, November 7, 2004, host Chris Wallace interviews Karl Rove on his views on the key moments of the campaign. http://www.foxnews.com/story/0,2933,137853,00.html.

WALLACE: When Kerry said, "I voted for the $87 billion before I voted against it"?

ROVE: Disbelief. He had been provoked into this by a television spot that we put up in West Virginia before he visited Huntington, West Virginia. We immediately turned it into a revised version of the ad that featured an ending with those words on it. And it's the gift that kept on giving.

2. For other recent examples of candidates being called flip-floppers, see Sakahara 2010; Taylor 2007; Hertzberg 2008; and Rutenberg 2007.

3. For more statistics, see Newport 2000.

4. Also, Dick Morris, the former Clinton-Gore campaign manager, appeared on several programs chastising Gore for his position or lack thereof on the issue.

5. For an interesting discussion on the direction-versus-proximity debate, see Kenny and Jenner 2008.

6. The Bush campaign's successful depiction of Kerry as a flip-flopper is a good recent example. See also Glazer and Grofman 1988.

7. One of the major challenges for this part of the research was creating questions that properly approximated directional and proximity theories. These questions were developed with the assistance of George Rabinowitz, one of the creators of directional theory, to achieve that approximation.

8. Politicians can often be successful in changing their position stances as they seek higher office, but in Beasley's case he was making the change too early.

9. This older set of data is from a consultant survey conducted in the fall of 2006 as part of the dissertation titled "Theory Versus Practice" (Johnson 2009).

10. Bear in mind that consultants in the survey have run campaigns at all levels, from local city council to presidential, and therefore any trends that may or may not occur must be seen in the context of overall attitudes in the respondents across multiple campaign levels.

11. Previous survey data from Johnson 2009.

12. For more information, see Saad 2010.

Chapter 4

1. Scholars that have studied implementation research include Hale, Fox, and Farmer 1996; Theilmann and Wilhite 1998; Thurber and Nelson 2000; West 2005; Geer 2006; and Grossmann 2009.

2. For more information on the effects of negative advertising, see Biocca et al. 1991; Wayne and Wilcox 1992; Kahn and Geer 1994; Ansolabehere and Iyengar 1994; Wattenberg and Brians 1999; Lemert, Wanta, and Lee 1999; Goldstein and Freedman 2002; Hughes 2003; and Stevens 2005.

3. One hundred seventy consultants answered the question.

4. The woman's name was Cynthia Ore, and it was revealed that police had been called about an incident between her and Sherwood in a hotel in 2004. Sherwood apologized for cheating but denied the abuse. http://www.msnbc.msn.com/id/15132240/. Carney came back with a tough ad featuring the woman's father that basically ended any chance that Sherwood would keep the seat. http://www.youtube.com/watch?v=KA14MqFIncM&feature=related.

5. McCain also announced Sarah Palin as his running mate on August 29, 2008, in Dayton, Ohio.

6. "*New York Times* Presidential Poll Tracker," September 5–13, http://elections.nytimes.com/2008/president/whos-ahead/polling/index.html.

7. My point here is to illustrate specific cases where race was deemed as a motivator behind the content of an ad. Thus, I do not mention the Willie Horton ad, since my goal is to discuss those ads directed at minority candidates.

Chapter 5

1. Link to a chat room discussing the supposed event on *Democratic Underground*: http://www.democraticunderground.com/discuss/duboard.php?az=view_all&address=132x4063521. A small Facebook page was created to encourage Obama to use the song as his campaign theme. http://www.facebook.com/group.php?gid=8733253841#!/group.php?gid=8733253841&v=wall. Other blogs where the story caught fire: http://thedemocraticdaily.com/2008/01/

14/99-problems-but-a-bitch-aint-one/; and Stranger Blog, http://slog.thestranger.com/2008/01/music_for_obama_2.

2. Blogger Geekesque (2008) debunked the story. *Politico.com* blogger Ben Smith (2008) did as well, providing YouTube links.

3. During his closing statement in his first presidential debate with Bill Clinton on October 6, 1996, Bob Dole specifically stated, "I ask for your support. I ask for your help. And if you really want to get involved, just tap into my home page, www.DoleKemp96.org. Thank you. God bless America."

4. http://www.internetworldstats.com/am/us.htm; http://maisonbisson.com/blog/post/11088/us-census-on-internet-access-and-computing/; http://www.websiteoptimization.com/bw/0403/.

5. "As a result of Clinton-Gore era initiatives to have the Internet accessed in all secondary schools and libraries (including the $2.25 billion E-Rate programme that subsidized equipment and training" (Oates, Owen, and Gibson 2006, 3; see also Denton 2005, 230–231).

6. Discussion forum on *Democratic Underground*, August 26, 2003, http://www.democraticunderground.com/discuss/duboard.php?az=show_mesg&forum=105&topic_id=136100&mesg_id=136115.

7. Joe Trippi is quoted as saying the race was so tight heading into Iowa that despite beliefs that Gephardt and Dean were front-runners, anyone could have won. "Polls here have Dean, Gephardt and Sen. John Kerry of Massachusetts in a statistical dead heat, with Sen. John Edwards of North Carolina also flexing some muscle; Dean campaign manager Joe Trippi told ABC News the situation is so fluid he wouldn't be surprised if Gephardt came in first" (Culhane and Tapper 2004). The negative ads between Gephardt and Dean became the subject of many fact-check sites and newspapers. http://www.factcheck.org/article128.html.

8. And similar to the previous table, it was not statistically significant.

Chapter 6

1. Survey question 44: When or if your candidate did veer from the campaign's main message, what were the usual reasons?

2. To see the frequencies of these two types of campaigns, see the Appendix.

Bibliography

Abbe, Owen G., and Paul S. Herrnson. 2003. "Public Financing for Judicial Elections? A Judicious Perspective on the ABA's Proposal for Campaign Finance Reform." *Polity* 35, no. 4: 535–554.

Abrajano, Marissa. 2005. "Who Evaluates a Presidential Candidate by Using Non-Policy Campaign Messages?" *Political Research Quarterly* 58, no. 1: 55–67.

Abramowitz, Alan. 1989. "Viability, Electability, and Candidate Choice in a Presidential Primary Election: A Test of Competing Models." *Journal of Politics* 51, no. 4: 977–992.

Adams, David. 2000. "Elian Swings Cuban Voters Back to GOP." *St. Petersburg Times*, November 5. http://www.latinamericanstudies.org/exile/swings.htm.

Alexander, Amy. 2006. "Evaluating Gendered Contexts: A Look at Political Office-Holding and Candidacy in California Cities." Paper presented at the annual meeting of the Western Political Science Association.

Alexander, Deborah, and Kristi Andersen. 1993. "Gender as a Factor in the Attribution of Leadership Traits." *Political Research Quarterly* 46, no. 3: 527–545.

Alvarez, R. Michael, and Lisa Garcia Bedolla. 2003. "The Foundations of Latino Voter Partisanship: Evidence from the 2000 Election." *Journal of Politics* 65, no. 1.

Alvarez, R. Michael, and Garrett Glasgow. 1998. "Do Voters Learn from Presidential Election Campaigns?" Paper presented at the annual meeting of the Southern Political Science Association.

———. 2000. "Uncertainty and Candidate Personality Traits." *American Politics Quarterly* 28, no. 1: 26–49.

Alvarez, R. Michael, and Thad Hall. 2004. *Point, Click, and Vote: The Future of Internet Voting.* Washington, DC: Brookings Institution Press.

Ambinder, Mark. 2010. "We May Be Incompetent: But They're Crazy!" *Atlantic Monthly*, July 28. http://www.theatlantic.com/politics/archive/2010/07/democratic-message-we-may-be-incompetent-but-theyre-crazy/60575/.

Ansolabehere, Stephen, and Shanto Iyengar. 1994. "Riding the Wave and Claiming Ownership over Issues: The Joint Effects of Advertising and News Coverage in Campaigns." *Public Opinion Quarterly* 58: 335–357.

Ansolabehere, Stephen, and Steven Shanto. 1995. *Going Negative: How Political Advertisements Shrink and Polarize the Electorate.* New York: Free Press.

Ansolabehere, Stephen, James M. Snyder Jr., and Charles Stewart III. 2001. "Candidate Positioning in U.S. House Elections." *American Journal of Political Science* 45, no. 1: 136–159.

Apple, R. W., Jr. 1994. "The 1994 Campaign: Massachusetts; Kennedy and Romney Meet, and the Rancor Flows Freely." *New York Times*, October 26. http://www.nytimes.com/1994/10/26/us/1994-campaign-massachusetts-kennedy-romney-meet-rancor-flows-freely.html.

Arbour, Brian. 2007. "You Are the Message: How Political Consultants Use Candidate Background." Paper presented at the annual meeting of the Southern Political Science Association, New Orleans, January 4–7.

Arnold, Benjamin, and Larycia Hawkins. 2002. "Candidate Quality Properly Understood." Paper presented at the annual meeting of the American Political Science Association, Boston, August 28.

Asch, Beth J., Paul Heaton, and Bogdan Savych. 2009. "Minorities: What Explains Recent Trends in the Army and Navy?" *National Defense Research Institute*.

Associated Press. 1998. "Smith, Medlock Back Beasley." *Item Newspaper*, September 11. http://news.google.com/newspapers?nid=1980&dat=19980911&id=46QoAAAAIBAJ&sjid=OAYGAAAAIBAJ&pg=6087,2337628.

Atkinson, L. R., and R. W. Partin. 2001. "Candidate Advertisements, Media Coverage, and Citizen Attitudes: The Agendas and Roles of Senators and Governors in a Federal System." *Political Research Quarterly* 54: 795–813.

Auer, Matthew R. 2003. "Policy Sciences and the Maverick Career: Commentary on Brunner and Willard's 'Professional Insecurities.'" *Policy Sciences* 36, no. 1: 37–45.

Augusta Chronicle Editorial Staff. 1996. "Beasley's Briar-Patch." *Augusta Chronicle*, November 19. http://chronicle.augusta.com/stories/1996/11/19/edi_200699.shtml.

Austin, Sharon Wright, and Richard T. Middleton IV. 2004. "The Limitations of the Deracialization Concept in the 2001 Los Angeles Mayoral Election." *Political Science Research Quarterly* 57, no. 2: 283–293.

Bacon, Perry, Jr. 2006. "Can Lieberman Survive Iraq?" *Time*, June 25. http://www.time.com/time/magazine/article/0,9171,1207783,00.html.

Bailey, Michael, and Ronald A. Faucheux, eds. 2000. *Campaigns and Elections: Contemporary Case Studies*. Washington, DC: CQ Press.

Baker, Frank. 2009. *Campaigns and Political Advertising: A New Media Literacy Guide*. Denver: Greenwood Press.

Ballew, Charles, and Alexander Todorov. 2007. "Predicting Political Elections from Rapid and Unreflective Face Judgments." *Proceedings of the National Academy of Sciences of the United States of America* 104, no. 46: 17948–17953.

Barber, James David. 1990. "The Promise of Political Psychology." *Political Psychology* 11, no. 1: 173–183.

Barkan, Joel, and James E. Bruno. 1974. "Locating the Voter Mathematical Models and the Analysis of Aggregate Data for Political Campaigns." *Western Political Quarterly* 27, no. 4.

Barnes, James, and Peter Bell. 2005. "Hillary in 2008?" *Atlantic*, July–August. http://www.theatlantic.com/magazine/archive/2005/07/hillary-in-2008/4044/.

Bartels, Larry M. 2002. "Beyond the Running Tally: Partisan Bias in Political Perceptions." *Political Behavior* 24: 117–150.

Baumgartner, Jody, and Peter L. Francia. 2010. *Conventional Wisdom and American Elections: Exploding Myths, Exploring Misconceptions*. 2nd ed. Lanham, MD: Rowman and Littlefield.

Baumgartner, Jody, and Jonathan S. Morris. 2010. "MyFaceTube Politics: Social Networking Websites and Political Engagement of Young Adults." *Social Science Computer Review* 28: 24–44.

Baus, Herbert M., and Peter Ross. 1968. *Politics Battle Plan*. New York: Macmillan.

Beiler, David. 2002. "Mark Warner's Five-Year Plan." *Campaigns and Elections* 22, no. 10: 34–43.

Bendavid, Naftali. 2007. *The Thumpin': How Rahm Emanuel and the Democrats Learned to Be Ruthless and Ended the Republican Revolution*. New York: Doubleday.

Benoit, William. 2000. "A Functional Analysis of Political Advertising Across Media, 1998." *Communications Studies*.

———. 2004. "Political Campaigns: The Messages and Their Analysis." http://presidential-campaign2004.coas.missouri.edu/general/rep_and_character.html.

———. 2007. "Incumbency in Political Campaign Discourse." Paper presented at the annual meeting of the Midwest Political Science Association, Chicago, April 12. http://www.allacademic.com/meta/p199437_index.html.

Berke, Richard L. 1996. "GOP Opens Fierce Attack on Clinton over Character and Handling of the Economy." *New York Times*, August 14.

Berkowitz, Jeff. 2008. "Two Major Reasons Why McCain Lost the Presidency." October 29. http://jeffberkowitz.blogspot.com/2008/10/two-major-reasons-why-mccain-lost.html.

Bevan, Tom. 2006. "Hillary the Hawk." *Real Clear Politics.com*, July 22. http://www.realclearpolitics.com/articles/2006/07/hillary_the_hawk.html.

Biden, Joe. 2007. "Primary Debate." Drexel University, Philadelphia, October 30.

Binford, Michael B. 1985. "The Political Science Education of Campaign Professionals." *PS: Political Science and Politics* 18, no. 1.

Biocca, Frank, John Boiney, and David Paletz, eds. 1991. *Television and Political Advertising*. Vol. 1, *In Search of the Model Model: Political Science Versus Political Advertising Perspectives on Voter Decision Making*. Hillsdale, NJ: L. Erlbaum Associates.

Blumenthal, Sidney. 1980. *The Permanent Campaign: Inside the World of Elite Political Operatives*. Boston: Beacon Press.

Blydenberg, John C. 1976. "An Application of Game Theory to Political Campaign Decision Making." *American Journal of Political Science* 20, no. 1: 51–65.

Bositis, David. 1985. "Design Strategies for Theory Testing: The Efficient Use of Field Experimentation in Local Level Political Research." *Political Behavior* 7, no. 4.

Bositis, David A., Denise L. Baer, and Roy E. Miller. 1985. "Cognitive Information Levels, Voter Preferences, and Local Partisan Political Activity: A Field Experimental Study on the Effects of Timing and Order of Message Presentation. *Political Behavior* 7, no. 3: 266–284.

Boyd, Danah. 2009. "The Not-So-Hidden Politics of Class Online." Personal Democracy Forum, New York, June 29.

Brady, Henry E. and Richard Johnston, eds. 2006. *Capturing Campaign Effects*. Ann Arbor: University of Michigan Press.

Brookings Institution. 2000. "American Voters, 2000: Who's Still Swinging, Who's Decided, and Why Brookings Events." November 14. http://www.brookings.edu/events/2000/0914elections.aspx.

Brown, Frank. 2004. "Nixon's Southern Strategy and the Forces Against Brown." Special issue, "*Brown vs. Board of Education* at 50." *Journal of Negro Education* 73, no. 3: 191–208.

Budge, Ian, and Dennis J. Farlie. 1983. "Party Competition–Selective Emphasis or Direct Confrontation? An Alternative View with Data." In *Western European Party Systems: Continuity and Change*, ed. Hans Daalder and Peter Mair, 267–305. London: SAGE Publications.

Burden, Barry C. 2002. "United States Senators as Presidential Candidates." *Political Science Quarterly* 17, no. 1.

Burgoon, J. K., M. Pfau, and T. Birk. 1995. "An Inoculation Theory Explanation for the Effects of Corporate Issue/Advertising." *Communication Research* 22: 485–505.

Caliendo, Stephen Maynard, and Charlton McIlwain. 2007. "Racialized Media Framing in Federal Elections, 1992–2006." Paper presented at the annual meeting of the Midwest Political Science Association, Chicago, April 12–15. http://www.raceproject.org/pdfs/MPSA2007.pdf.

———. 2008. "Racial Priming and Campaign Ads: The Effect of Context." Paper presented at the annual meeting of the Midwest Political Science Association, Chicago, April 2–6.

———. 2009. "Racial Discourse in Political Advertisements: An Historical View." Paper presented at the annual meeting of the American Political Science Association, Toronto, September 3–6. http://www.raceproject.org/pdfs/APSA09.pdf.

Cannon, Carl M. n.d. "The Contenders, 2008—Rudy Giuliani." *Reader's Digest.* http://www.rd.com/your-america-inspiring-people-and-stories/the-contenders-2008-rudy-giuliani/article49737.html.

Cantor, David M., and Paul S. Herrnson. 1997. "Party Campaign Activity and Party Unity in the House of Representatives." *Legislative Studies Quarterly* 22, no. 3: 393–425.

Carville, James. 1996. *We're Right, They're Wrong: A Handbook for Spirited Progressives.* New York: Random House.

Carville, James, and Mary Matalin. 1995. *All's Fair: Love, War, and Running for President.* New York: Simon and Schuster.

Casteel, Chris. 2010. "Oklahoma Congressional Candidate Uses Social Media Extensively to Build Network of Supporters." July 23. http://www.allbusiness.com/government/elections-politics-campaigns-elections/14842788-1.html.

Cesca, Bob. 2007. "The Most Inappropriate Bush War Smirk of 2007." *Huffington Post*, December 26. http://www.huffingtonpost.com/bob-cesca/the-most-inappropriate-bu_b_78357.html.

Chakravarty, Sujay, and Matthew Caldwell. 2004. "Internet Political Campaigns: Delving into the Demography of the Digital Divide." http://ssrn.com/abstract=623701.

Cheng, Alex, and Mark Evans. 2009. "An In-Depth Look Inside the Twitter World." *Sysomos*, June. http://www.sysomos.com/insidetwitter/.

Claassen, Ryan. 2007. "Ideology and Evaluation in an Experimental Setting: Comparing the Proximity and Directional Models." *Political Research Quarterly* 60, no. 2: 263–273.

Clayton, Dewey M., and Angela M. Stallings. 2000. "Black Women in Congress: Striking the Balance." *Journal of Black Studies* 30.

Clayworth, Jason. 2007. "Obama Responds to Crush." *Des Moines Register*, June 19. http://web.archive.org/web/20080211114524/http://blogs.dmregister.com/?p=6506.

Clift, Eleanor. 2003. "Off Message Again." *Newsweek*, May.

Clymer, Adam. 2000. "The Elian Gonzalez Case: The Politics; While Conservatives and Liberals React, Gore and Bush Hedge on Ruling." *New York Times*, June 2. http://www.nytimes.com/2000/06/02/us/elian-gonzalez-case-politics-while-conservatives-liberals-react-gore-bush-hedge.html.

CNN.com. 2000. "Political Reverberations Felt as Elian Gonzalez Case Drags On." April 13. http://articles.cnn.com/2000-04-13/politics/campaign.elian_1_custody-case-al-gore-juan-miguel-gonzalez?_s=PM:ALLPOLITICS.

Cohen, Susan. 2006. "Toward Making Abortion 'Rare': The Shifting Battleground over the Means to an End." *Guttmacher Policy Review* 9, no. 1: 2–20.

Colleau, Sophie M., et al. 1990. "Symbolic Racism in Candidate Evaluation: An Experiment." *Political Behavior* 12, no. 4.

Collins, Jan. 2009. "Putting the State on Your Plate." http://mooreschool.sc.edu/facultyandresearch/researchcenters/divisionofresearch/businesseconomicreview/bereview552/puttingthestateonyourplate.aspx.

Collins, Michael. 1980. "Race and Political Cleavage: Ten Positions in a Local Election." *Journal of Black Studies* 11, no. 1: 121–136.

———. 2008. "Cutting Down the Wrath Bearing Tree." *Callalo* 31, no. 4: 1033–1037.

Cornfield, Michael. 2004. *Politics Moves Online*. A Century Foundation Report. New York: Century Foundation Press.

———. 2005. *The Internet and Campaign 2004: A Look Back at the Campaigners*. Washington, DC: Pew Center on the Internet and American Life. http://www.pewinternet.org/pdfs/Cornfield_commentary.pdf.

———. 2008. "Yes, It Did Make a Difference." *Talking Note*, June 4. http://takingnote.tcf.org/2008/06/yes-it-did-make.html.

Covington, Cary, Kent Kroeger, Glenn Richardson, and J. David Woodard. 1993. "Shaping Candidate's Image in the Press: Ronald Reagan and the 1980 Presidential Election." *Political Research Quarterly* 46, no. 4: 783–798.

Cox, Phil. 2010. "The McDonnell Model." *Campaigns and Elections* (February).

Craig, Stephen C., ed. 2006. *The Electoral Challenge: Theory Meets Practice*. Washington, DC: CQ Press.

Crotty, William, ed. 2008. *Winning the Presidency*. Boulder: Paradigm.

Crowley, Michael. 2008. "There's Real Danger to Obama in a Cry of 'Snob': The Battle Between Barack and Hillary Has Given the Republicans Time to Polish Their Favourite Dark Art." *Observer*, April 20. http://www.guardian.co.uk/commentisfree/2008/apr/20/barack-obama.hillaryclinton.

Culhane, Max, and Jake Tapper. 2004. "Dean Strikes Back at Gephardt Ads." *ABC News*, January 16. http://abcnews.go.com/Politics/story?id=123536&page=2.

Daley, S. 2010. "Creating a Political Campaign Theme." *Ezinearticles.com*, February 26. http://ezinearticles.com/?Creating-a-Political-Campaign-Theme&id=3829573.

Damore, David F. 2002. "Candidate Strategy and the Decision to Go Negative." *Political Research Quarterly* 55, no. 3: 669–686.

Darcy, R., and Sarah Slavin Schramm. 1977. "When Women Run Against Men." *Public Opinion Quarterly* 41, no. 1.

Davis, Steve. 2005. "Presidential Campaigns Fine-Tune Online Strategies." *Journalism Studies* 6, no. 2: 241–244.

DCCC Press Release. 2006. "Republican Pre-9/11 Mindset Wrong for Port Security." February 26. http://dccc.org/newsroom/entry/ports/.

Denton, Robert. 2005. *The 2004 Presidential Campaign: A Communication Perspective*. Lanham, MD: Rowman and Littlefield.

DeVries, Walter. 1989. "American Campaign Consulting Trends and Concerns." *PS: Political Science and Politics* 22, no. 1: 21–25.

Dickerson, John. 2007. "Lazy Fred: Is Fred Thompson Too Lazy to Get Nominated?" *Slate.com*, May 31. http://www.slate.com/id/2167411/.

———. 2008. "Hope, Inc.: How Obama's Message Found Its Mark." January 3. http://www.slate.com/id/2181272/.

Dinzes, Deborah, Michael D. Cozzens, and George G. Manross. 1994. "The Role of Gender in 'Attack Ads': Revisiting Negative Political Advertising." *Communication Research Reports* 11: 67–75.

Dittmar, Kelly. 2010. "Negotiating Gender: Campaign Practitioners' Reflections on Gender, Strategy, and Campaigns." Paper presented at the annual meeting of the American Political Science Association, Washington, DC, August 31.

Dlouhy, Jennifer. 2010. "Murphy Boasts $1.45 Million Warchest; Gibson Claims Grassroots Support." *Times Union*, September 6. http://blog.timesunion.com/nypotomac/murphy-boasts-1-45-million-warchest-gibson-claims-grassroots-support/3682/.

Doherty, Kathryn, and James G. Gimpel. 1997. "Candidate Character vs. the Economy in the 1992 Election." *Political Behavior* 19, no. 3.

Dolan, Kathleen. 2004a. "The Impact of Candidate Sex on Evaluations of Candidates for the U.S. House of Representatives." *Social Science Quarterly* 85: 206–217.

———. 2004b. "Women Running for Congress: An Overview of the 2002 Elections." *PS: Political Science and Politics* 37, no. 1: 59–60.

———. 2005. "Do Women Candidates Play to Gender Stereotypes? Do Men Candidates Play to Women? Candidate Sex and Issues Priorities on Campaign Websites." *Political Research Quarterly* 58: 31–44.

Downs, Anthony. 1957. *An Economic Theory of Democracy*. New York: Harper.

Drake, Bruce. 2011. "Republicans Catch Up with Democrats in Use of Social Media for Politics." January 27. http://www.politicsdaily.com/2011/01/27/republicans-catch-up-with-democrats-in-use-of-social-media-for-p/.

Druckman, James N., Lawrence R. Jacobs, and Eric Ostermeier. 2004. "Candidate Strategies to Prime Issues and Image." *Journal of Politics* 66: 1180–1202.

Druckman, James N., M. K. Kifer, and M. Parkin. 2007. "The Technological Development of Congressional Candidate Websites: How and Why Candidates Use Web Innovations." *Social Science Computer Review* 25: 425–442.

———. 2009. "Campaign Communications in U.S. Congressional Elections." *American Political Science Review* 103: 343–366.

Druckman, James N., et al. 2010a. "Issue Engagement on Congressional Candidate Websites (2002–2006)." *Social Science Computer Review* 28, no. 1: 3–23.

———. 2010b. "Timeless Strategy Meets New Medium: Going Negative on Congressional Campaign Websites, 2002–2006." *Political Communication* 27: 88–103.

Dugan, Lauren. 2010. "Republicans More Influential on Twitter than Democrats." November 22. http://www.mediabistro.com/alltwitter/republicans-are-more-influential-on-twitter-than-democrats-study_b534.

Dulio, David A., and Candace Nelson. 2004. "Campaigning with the Internet: The View from Below." In *Campaigns and Elections American Style*, ed. James A. Thurber and Candice J. Nelson, 173–194. 2nd ed. Boulder: Westview Press.

Dulio, David A., and Costas Panagopoulos. 2005. "The Role of Women Political Consultants in U.S. Elections." Paper presented at the Southern Political Science Association, New Orleans, January 6.

Edsall, Thomas, and Hanna Rosin. 1999. "Bauer Says He Did Not Have Affair: 2 Ex-Aides Make Public Allegation." *Washington Post*, September 30.

Egan, Patrick. 2006. "Issue Ownership and Representation: A Theory of Legislative Response to Constituency Opinion." Paper presented at the annual meeting of the American Political Science Association, Philadelphia, August 31.

Ekstrand, Laurie E., and William A. Eckert. 1981. "The Impact of Candidate's Sex on Voter Choice." *Western Political Quarterly* 34, no. 1.

Elder, Larry. 2008. "Warming Up to Obama's Message of Hope and Change." June 12. http://townhall.com/columnists/larryelder/2008/06/12/warming_up_to_obamas_message_of_hope_and_change.

"Elections Without Choice." 1968. *Economic and Political Weekly* 3, no. 44.

Everson, David H. 1992. "The Decline of Political Parties." *Proceedings of the Academy of Political Science* 34, no. 4.

Farnsworth, Stephen J., and Diana Owen. 2004. "Internet Use and the 2000 Presidential Election." *Electoral Studies* 23, no. 3: 415–429.

Faucheux, Ronald A. n.d. "Presidential Politics Teach Us to Get the Message Right." http://www.winningcampaigns.org/Winning-Campaigns-Archive-Articles/Presidential-Politics-Teach-Get-The-Message-Right.html.

Faucheux, Ron. 2008. "Get the Message Right." http://www.winningcampaigns.org/Articles/Get-The-Message-Right-Nov.html.

Faucheux, Ronald A., and Paul S. Herrnson, eds. 2002. *Campaign Battle Lines: The Practical Consequences of Crossing the Line Between What's Right and What's Not in Political Campaigning.* Washington, DC: Campaigns and Elections.

———. 2004. *The Good Fight: How Political Candidates Struggle to Win Elections Without Losing Their Souls.* Washington, DC: Campaigns and Elections.

Feldman, Stanley, and John Zaller. 1992. "The Political Culture of Ambivalence: Ideological Responses to the Welfare State." *American Journal of Political Science* 36, no. 1: 268–307.

Filipov, David. 2010. "In Short Race, Coakley Picks Targets Carefully." *Boston.com*, January 13. http://www.boston.com/news/politics/2008/articles/2010/01/13/campaigns_brevity_shapes_coakley_image_on_trail/.

Finn, Mindy, and Patrick Ruffini. 2010. "How the Republicans Won the Internet." *Washington Post*, January 24. http://www.washingtonpost.com/wp-dyn/content/article/2010/01/22/AR2010012202286.html.

Flowers, Julianne F., Audrey A. Haynes, and Michael H. Crespin. 2003. "The Media, the Campaign, and the Message." *American Journal of Political Science* 47, no. 2: 259–273. Bloomington, IN: Midwest Political Science Association. http://www.jstor.org/stable/3186137.

Foot, Kirsten, and Michael Xenos. 2009. "Not Your Father's Internet: The Generation Gap in Online Politics." In *Civic Life Online: Learning How Digital Media Can Engage Youth*, ed. L. Bennett, 51–70. The John D. and Katherine T. MacArthur Series on Digital Media and Learning. Cambridge: MIT Press.

Fox, Richard L. 1997. *Gender Dynamics in Presidential Elections.* Thousand Oaks, CA: SAGE Publications.

Fox, Richard L., and Jennifer Lawless. 2005. "To Run or Not to Run for Office: Explaining Nascent Political Ambition." *American Journal of Political Science* 49, no. 3: 642–659.

Fox, Richard L., and Eric R. A. N. Smith. 1998. "The Role of Candidate Sex in Voter Decision-Making." *Political Psychology* 19, no. 2: 405–419.

Francis, Wayne L., and Lawrence Kenny. 1996. "Position Shifting in Pursuit of Higher Office." *American Journal of Political Science* 40: 768–786.

Funk, Carolyn. 1996. "The Impact of Scandal on Candidate Evaluations: An Experimental Test of the Role of Candidate Traits." *Political Behavior* 18, no. 1: 1–24.

———. 1997. "Implications of Political Expertise in Candidate Trait Evaluations." *Political Research Quarterly* 50, no. 3: 675-697.

———. 1999. "Bringing the Candidate into Models of Candidate Evaluation." *Journal of Politics* 61, no. 3.

Gardner, Amy. 2009. "Takes Deeds Off Message on Charter Schools." *Washington Post*, October 23. http://voices.washingtonpost.com/virginiapolitics/2009/10/potts_takes_deeds_off-message.html.

Garecht, Joe. n.d. "How to Beat an Incumbent." http://www.localvictory.com/strategy/how-to-beat-an-incumbent.html.

Gay, Claudine. 2001. "The Effect of Black Congressional Representation on Political Participation." *American Political Science Review* 95, no. 3: 589–602.

Gaziano, Joe, and Laurette Liesen. 2009. "The Use of Campaign Websites by Low Visibility State and Local Candidates." Paper presented at the annual meeting of the Midwest Political Science Association, Chicago, April.

Geekesque. 2008. "*NY Post* Lies About Obama; Pro-Clinton Bloggers Spread the Lie." *Daily Kos.com*, January 14. http://www.dailykos.com/storyonly/2008/1/14/135113/083.

Geer, John G. 1988. "Assessing the Representativeness of Electorates in Presidential Primaries." *American Journal of Political Science* 32, no. 4: 929–945.

———. 2006. *In Defense of Negativity: Attack Ads in Presidential Campaigns*. Chicago: University of Chicago Press.

Gershtenson, Joseph. 2004. "Ideological Centrism and the Electoral Fortunes of U.S. Senate Candidates." *Social Science Quarterly* 85, no. 2: 497–508.

Gimpel, James, and Kathryn Doherty. 1997. "Candidate Character vs. the Economy in the 1992 Election." *Political Behavior* 19, no. 3: 213–222.

Glaser, James. 1996. "The Challenge of Campaign Watching: Seven Lessons of Participant-Observation Research." *PS: Political Science and Politics* 29, no. 3: 533–537.

Glazer, Amihai, and Bernard Grofman. 1988. "Limitations of the Spatial Model." *Public Choice* 58, no. 2: 161–167.

Goldenberg, Edie, Michael Traugott, and Frank Baumgartner. 1985. "Preemptive and Reactive Spending in U.S. House Races." *Political Behavior* 8, no. 1: 3–20.

Goldstein, Ken, and Paul Freedman. 2002. "Campaign Advertising and Voter Turnout: New Evidence for a Stimulation Effect." *Journal of Politics* 64, no. 3.

Goldthwaite, Dannagal. 2002. "Pinocchio v. Dumbo: Priming Candidate Caricature Attributes in Late-Night Comedy Programs in Election 2000 and the Moderating Role of Political Knowledge." Paper presented at the annual meeting of the American Political Science Association, Boston, August 28.

Goren, Paul. 2002. "Character Weakness, Partisan Bias, and Presidential Evaluation." *American Journal of Political Science* 46: 627–641.

———. 2005. "Party Identification and Core Political Values." *American Journal of Political Science* 49: 881–896.

Graf, Joseph, Grant Reeher, Michael Malbin, and Costas Panagopoulos. 2006. *Small Donors and Online Giving: A Study of Donors to the 2004 Presidential Campaigns*. Washington, DC: Institute for Politics, Democracy, and the Internet, George Washington University.

Grant, Lorie. 2003. "Net Powers Christmas Day Sales." *USA Today*, December 23. http://www.usatoday.com/money/industries/retail/2003-12-24-xmasbuy_x.htm.

Grossmann, Matt. 2009. "What (or Who) Makes Campaigns Negative?" Paper presented at the annual meeting of the Midwest Political Science Association, Chicago, April 2.

Gschwend, Thomas. 2007. "Ticket-Splitting and Strategic Voting Under Mixed Electoral Rules: Evidence from Germany." *European Journal of Political Research* 46, no. 1.

Gulati, Jeff, and Christine B. Williams. 2007. "Social Networks in Political Campaigns: Facebook and the 2006 Midterm Elections." Paper presented at the annual meeting of the American Political Science Association, Chicago.

GurglingCod.com. 2006. "Put Your State on Your Plate." September 7. http://thegurglingcod.typepad.com/thegurglingcod/2006/09/put_your_state_.html.

Hacker, Kenneth L., et al. 2000. "Components of Candidate Images: Statistical Analysis of the Issue-Persona Dichotomy in the Presidential Campaign of 1996." *Communication Monographs* 67, no. 3: 227–238.

Hajnal, Zoltan. 1998. "The Puzzle of Black Incumbent Success: Why White Support Increases Dramatically After Black Candidates Win Office." *American Political Science Association* (September).

Hale, Jon F., Jeffrey C. Fox, and Rick Farmer. 1996. "Negative Advertisements in U.S. Senate Campaigns: The Influence of Campaign Context." *Social Science Quarterly* 77, no. 2.

Hall, Wynton C. 2002. "Reflections of Yesterday: George H. W. Bush's Instrumental Use of Public Opinion Research in Presidential Discourse." *Presidential Studies Quarterly* 32, no. 3: 532–558.

Hansen, Susan B., and Laura Wills Otero. 2007. "A Woman for U.S. President? Gender and Leadership Traits Before and After 9/11." *Journal of Women, Politics, and Policy* 28, no. 1: 35–57.

Hardy, Bruce, and Kathleen Hall Jamieson. 2005. "Can a Poll Affect Perception of Candidate Traits?" *Public Opinion Quarterly* 69, no. 5: 725–743.

Hawaii Free Press. 2009. "RNCC vs. Ed Case: A Career Politician in Search of an Office." March 30. http://www.hawaiifreepress.com/main/ArticlesMain/tabid/56/articleType/ArticleView/articleId/578/categoryId/48/RNCC-vs-Ed-Case-quotA-Career-Politician-in-Search-of-an-Officequot.aspx.

Hayes, David. 2005. "Candidate Qualities Through a Partisan Lens: A Theory of Trait Ownership." *American Journal of Political Science* 49, no. 4: 908–923.

Haynes, Audrey, and Julianne F. Flowers. 2003. "News Norms and the Strategic Timing of Candidate Messages." *Journal of Political Marketing* 1, no. 4: 1–22.

Haynes, Audrey, Julianne F. Flowers, and Paul-Henri Gurian. 2002a. "Getting the Message Out Early: Candidate Messaging Strategy During the Invisible Primary." *Political Research Quarterly* 55, no. 3: 633–652.

———. 2002b. "The Media, Campaign, and the Message." *Political Research Quarterly* 55, no. 3: 633–652.

Haynes, Audrey, and Staci L. Rhine. 1998. "Attack Politics in Presidential Nomination Campaigns: An Examination of the Frequency and Determinants of Intermediated Negative Messages Against Opponents." *Political Research Quarterly* 51, no. 3.

Hedlund, Ronald D., et al. 1979. "The Electability of Women Candidates: The Effects of Sex Role Stereotypes." *Journal of Politics* 41, no. 2.

Herrnson, Paul S. 1986. "Do Parties Make a Difference? The Role of Party Organizations in Congressional Elections." *Journal of Politics* 48, no. 3: 589–615.

———. 1988. *Party Campaigning in the 1980s.* Cambridge: Harvard University Press.

———. 1989. "National Party Decision Making, Strategies, and Resource Distribution in Congressional Elections." *Western Political Quarterly* 42, no. 3: 301–323.

———. 1992. "Campaign Professionalism and Fundraising in Congressional Elections." *Journal of Politics* 54, no. 3: 859–870.

Herrnson, Paul S., and Jennifer C. Lucas. 2006. "The Fairer Sex?" *American Politics Research* 34: 69–94.

Hershey, Randon. 1973. "Incumbency and the Minimum Winning Coalition." *American Journal of Political Science* 7, no. 3: 631–637.

Hertzberg, Hendrick. 2008. "Obama's Flip-Flop Flap." *New Yorker*, July 14. http://www.msnbc.msn.com/id/25673270/.

Hiebert, Ray, et al., eds. 1971. *The Political Image Merchants (the Campaign Workers Handbook): Strategies in the New Politics.* Washington, DC: Acropolis Books.

Hindman, Matthew. 2005. "The Real Lessons of Howard Dean: Reflections on the First Digital Campaign." *Perspectives on Politics* 3: 121–128.

Hines, Nico. 2010. "Veteran Democrat Howard Dean Says Clegg Can 'Do an Obama.'" *Times,* April 22. http://www.timesonline.co.uk/tol/news/politics/article7104964.ece.

Holian, David B. 2004. "He's Stealing My Issues! Clinton's Crime Rhetoric and the Dynamics of Issue Ownership." *Political Behavior* 26: 95–124.

Hollinger, David A. 2008. "Obama, the Instability of Color Lines, and the Promise of a Post Ethnic Future." *Callalo* 31, no. 4: 1033–1037.

Holmes, Steven A. 1996. "Dick Morris' Behavior, and Why It's Tolerated." *New York Times,* September 8.

Homer, Pamela M., and Rajeev Batra. 1994. "Attitudinal Effects of Character-Based Versus Competence-Based Negative Political Communications." *Journal of Consumer Psychology* 3, no. 2.

Horn, Rachel. 2010. "5 Expert Takes on Why So Many Women Are Running for Office in 2010." *Atlantic,* October 31. http://www.theatlantic.com/politics/archive/2010/10/5-expert-takes-on-why-so-many-women-are-running-for-office-in-2010/65456/.

Howard, Philip. 2006. *New Media Campaigns and the Managed Citizen.* Cambridge: Cambridge University Press, 2006.

Howell, Susan. 1980. "Local Election Campaigns: The Effects of Office Level on Campaign Style." *Journal of Politics* 42, no. 4.

Howell, Susan E., and William P. McLean. 2001. "Performance and Race in Evaluating Minority Mayors." *Public Opinion Quarterly* 65, no. 3: 321–343.

Huddy, Leonie, and Nayda Terkildsen. 1993a. "The Consequences of Gender Stereotypes for Women Candidates at Different Levels and Types of Office." *Political Research Quarterly* 46, no. 3: 503–525.

———. 1993b. "Gender Stereotypes and the Perception of Male and Female Candidates." *American Journal of Political Science* 37, no. 1: 119–147.

Hughes, Andrew. 2003. "Defining Negative Political Advertising: Definition Features and Tactics." http://smib.vuw.ac.nz:8081/WWW/ANZMAC2003/papers/ADV21_hughesa.pdf.

Hunt, Kasie. 2010. "House a Stepping Stone for Ben Quayle." *Politico.com,* October 7. http://www.politico.com/news/stories/1010/43244.html.

IMBD. 2008. "Favorite On-Screen President." October 22. http://www.imdb.com/news/ni0588731/.

Institute of Politics at Harvard University, eds. 2006. *Campaign for President: The Managers Look at 2004.* Lanham, MD: Rowman and Littlefield.

Iyengar, Shanto. 2006. "Negative Ads Turn Off Voters, Enthrall News Media." *WashingtonPost.com,* November 15. http://pcl.stanford.edu/press/2006/wp-negative.pdf.

Iyengar, Shanto, and Donald Kinder. 1985. "Psychological Accounts of Media Agenda-Setting." In *Mass Media and Political Thought,* ed. Sidney Kraus and Richard Perloff. Beverly Hills: SAGE Publications.

Jamieson, Kathleen Hall, and Paul Waldman. 2001. *Electing the President 2000: The Insider's View—Election Strategy from Those Who Made It.* Philadelphia: University of Pennsylvania Press.

Jeffries, Judson L. 2002. "Press Coverage of Black Statewide Candidates: The Case of L. Douglas Wilder of Virginia." *Journal of Black Studies* 32 (July): 673–698.

Johnson, Dennis W. 2000. *No Place for Amateurs: How Political Consultants Are Re-Shaping American Democracy.* New York: Routledge.

Johnson, Jason Adam. 2009. "Theory Versus Practice." Ph.D. diss., University of North Carolina.

———. 2010a. Interview with Jordan Lieberman. March 9.

———. 2010b. Interview with Wyeth Ruthven. Summer.

Johnson-Cartee, Karen S., and Gary A. Copeland. 1997. *Inside Political Campaigns.* New York: Praeger.

Jones, Charles O. 2000. "Nonstop!" *Brookings Review* 18, no. 1: 12–16.

Kahn, Kim Fridkin. 1993. "Gender Differences in Campaign Messages: The Political Advertisements of Men and Women Candidates for U.S. Senate." *Political Research Quarterly* 46, no. 3: 481–502.

Kahn, Kim Fridkin, and John G. Geer. 1994. "Creating Impressions: An Experimental Investigation of Political Advertising on Television." *Political Behavior* 16: 93–116.

Kahn, Kim Fridkin, and Patrick J. Kenney. 1997. "A Model of Candidate Evaluations in Senate Elections: The Impact of Campaign Intensity." *Journal of Politics* 59, no. 4: 1173–1205.

———. 1999. *The Spectacle of U.S. Senate Campaigns.* Princeton: Princeton University Press.

———. 2001. "The Importance of Issues in Senate Campaigns: Citizens' Reception of Issue Messages." *Legislative Studies Quarterly* 26, no. 4: 573–596.

———. 2004. *No Holds Barred: Negativity in U.S. Senate Campaigns.* Upper Saddle River, NJ: Pearson, Prentice-Hall.

Kaid, Lynda Lee, and Christina Holtz-Bacha. 2006. *The SAGE Handbook of Political Advertising.* Beverly Hills: SAGE Publications.

Kaid, Lynda Lee, Mitchell S. McKinney, and John C. Tedesco. 2000. *Civic Dialogue in the 1996 Presidential Campaign: Candidate, Media, and Public Voices.* Cresskill, NJ: Hampton Press.

Kam, Cindy D. 2007. "Implicit Attitudes, Explicit Choices: When Subliminal Priming Predicts Candidate Preference." *Political Behavior* 29, no. 3: 343–367.

Kanazawa, Satoshi. 2010. "Why Liberals and Atheists Are More Intelligent." *Social Psychology Quarterly* (March): 1–25.

Karpf, David. 2010. "Macaca Moments Reconsidered: Electoral Panopticon or Netroots Mobilization?" *Journal of Information Technology and Politics* 7, no. 2: 143–162.

Kaufmann, Karen M. 2003. "Black and Latino Voters in Denver: Responses to Each Other's Political Leadership." *Political Science Quarterly* 118, no. 1: 107–125.

———. 2004. "Disaggregating and Reexamining Issue Ownership and Voter Choice." *Polity* 36, no. 2: 283–299.

Keeter, Scott. 1987. "The Illusion of Intimacy Television and the Role of Candidate Personal Qualities in Voter Choice." *Public Opinion Quarterly* 51, no. 3: 344–358.

Kenny, Christopher, and Eric Jenner. 2008. "Direction Versus Proximity in the Social Influence Process." *Political Behavior* 30: 73–96.

Kilson, Martin. 2008. "Obama's Campaign After South Carolina and Super Tuesday." *Black Commentator,* February 7. http://www.blackcommentator.com/263/263_obamas_campaign_after_sc_and_st_kilson.html.

Kilstein, Marc. 2010. "Dems Favor Compromise, GOPers Prefer Holding Firm to Beliefs. *Talking Points Memo,* November 10. http://tpmdc.talkingpointsmemo.com/2010/11/usa-todaygallup-poll-dems-favor-compromise-gopers-prefer-holding-firm-to-beliefs.php?ref=fpc.

Kinder, Donald R., et al. 1980. "Presidential Prototypes." *Political Behavior* 2, no. 4: 315–337.

Kirwan, Michael J., and Jack Redding. 1964. *How to Succeed in Politics*. Washington, DC: Mc-Fadden–Capitol Hill.

Kissane, Dylan. 2010. "A Tale of Two Campaigns: A Comparative Assessment of the Internet in French and U.S. Presidential Elections." Paper presented at the Central European University Conference in the Social Sciences, Budapest, April 16–18.

Klein, Jill, and Rohini Ahluwalia. 2005. "Negativity in Evaluation of Political Candidates." *Journal of Marketing* (January): 131–142.

Klein, Rick. 2010. "Top Line: Steele Off-Message (Again)." January 5. http://blogs.abcnews.com/thenote/2010/01/top-line-steele-offmessage-again.html.

Klotz, Robert J. 1997. "Positive Spin: Senate Campaigning on the Web." *PS: Political Science and Politics* 30, no. 3: 482–486.

Kolodny, Robin, and Angela Logan. 1998. "Political Consultants and the Extension of Party Goals." *PS: Political Science and Politics* 31, no. 2: 155–159.

Kolodny, Robin, James A. Thurber, and David A. Dulio. 2000. "Producing Negative Ads: Consultant Survey—Statistical Data Included." *Campaigns and Elections* (August). http://findarticles.com/p/articles/mi_m2519/is_7_21/ai_64995007.

Kumar, Anita. 2009. "McDonnell Strategy: Stay on Message; Focus Is on Issues, Not Foe's Attacks." *Washington Post*, September 14.

Lake, Celinda. 1989. "Political Consultants: Opening Up a New System of Political Power." *PS: Political Science and Politics* 22, no. 1.

Lakoff, George. 2004. "What's in a Word?" *Alternet.org*, February 18. http://www.alternet.org/story/17876/.

Lassen, David, and Adam Brown. 2010. "Twitter: The Electoral Connection?" Paper presented at the annual meeting of the Midwest Political Science Association, Chicago, April 21–25.

Lau, Richard R., and Gerald Pomper. 2001. "Effects of Negative Campaigning on Turnout in U.S. Senate Elections, 1988–1998." *Journal of Politics* 63: 804–819.

———. 2002. "Effectiveness of Negative Campaigning in U.S. Senate Elections." *American Journal of Political Science* 46, no. 1: 47–66.

———. 2004. *Negative Campaigning: An Analysis of U.S. Senate Elections*. Lanham, MD: Rowman and Littlefield.

Lavine, Howard, and Thomas Gschwend. 2007. "Issues, Party, and Character: The Moderating Role of Ideological Thinking on Candidate Evaluation." *British Journal of Political Science* 37, no. 1: 139–163.

Lawless, Jennifer L. 2004. "Women, War, and Winning Elections: Gender Stereotyping in the Post–September 11th Era." *Political Research Quarterly* 57, no. 3: 479–490.

Lawless, Jennifer L., and Richard L. Fox. 1997. "Why Women's Voices Are Not Heard: Gender and Political Socialization in Kenya." *Current World Leaders* 40, no. 6: 86–105.

Lawrence, Eric, John Sides, and Henry Farrell. 2010. "Self-Segregation or Deliberation? Blog Readership, Participation, and Polarization in American Politics." *Perspectives on Politics* 8, no. 1: 141–157.

Lawrence, Regina, and Melody Rose. 2010. *Hillary Clinton's Race for the White House*. Boulder: Lynne Rienner.

Leal, David. 2004. *Latino Public Opinion*. Austin: Department of Government, University of Texas.

Lee, Rainie, and John Horrigan. 2002. "Getting Serious Online: As Americans Gain Experience, They Pursue More Serious Activities." March 3. http://www.pewinternet.org/

Reports/2002/Getting-Serious-Online-As-Americans-Gain-Experience-They-Pursue-More-Serious-Activities/Summary-of-Findings.aspx.

Lemert, James B., Wayne Wanta, and Tien-Tsung Lee. 1999. "Party Identification and Negative Advertising in a U.S. Senate Election." *Journal of Communication* 49, no. 2.

Lenhart, Amanda, and Susannah Fox. 2009. "Twitter and Status Updating." February 12. http://www.pewinternet.org/Reports/2009/Twitter-and-statusupdating.aspx.

Lewis, Jeffrey B., and Gary King. 1998. "No Evidence on Directional vs. Proximity Voting." *Political Analysis* 8, no. 1: 21–33.

Lewis-Beck, Michael, and Charles Tien. 2009. "Race Blunts the Economic Effect? The 2008 Obama Forecast." *PS: Political Science and Politics* 42, no. 1: 687–690.

Li, Dan, and Gina Walenjko. 2008. "Splogs and Abandoned Blogs: The Perils of Sampling Bloggers and Their Blogs." *Information, Communication, and Society* 11, no. 2: 279–296.

Linaa Jensen, Jakob. 2006. "The Minnesota E-Democracy Project: Mobilising the Mobilised?" In *The Internet and Politics: Citizens, Voters, and Activists*, ed. Sarah Oates, Diana Owen, and Rachel K. Gibson, 39–58. London: Routledge.

Liu, Baodong. 2003. "Deracialization and Urban Racial Context." *Urban Affairs Review* 4, no. 38: 572–591.

Lodge, Milton, Marco R. Steenbergen, and Shawn Brau. 1995. "The Responsive Voter." *American Political Science Review* 89, no. 2: 309–326.

Lublin, David. 1999. "Racial Redistricting and African-American Representation: A Critique of 'Do Majority-Minority Districts Maximize Substantive Black Representation in Congress?'" *American Political Science Review* (March).

Luntz, Frank. 2006. *Words That Work: It's Not What You Say but What They Hear*. New York: Hyperion.

———. 2007. "Words Work." Interview with Terry Gross. *Fresh Air*, January 9. http://www.npr.org/templates/story/story.php?storyId=6761960.

Lyttle, Steve. 2009. "Lassiter, Kinsey, Carter Are Primary Winners." *Charlotte Observer*, September 19. http://www.charlotteobserver.com/2009/09/15/949006/lassiter-kinsey-carter-are-primary.html.

Maddeus, Gene. 2008. "Ferraro Defends Controversial Comments on Barack Obama." *Daily Breeze*, March 11. http://www.dailybreeze.com/ci_8533832.

Magleby, David, and Kelly Patterson. 1998. "Consultants and Direct Democracy." *PS: Political Science and Politics* 32 (June): 160–169.

Magnet, Myron. 1999. "What Is Compassionate Conservativism?" *Wall Street Journal*, February 5.

Marlantes, Liz. 2004. "This Race's Big Issue: Beating Bush; Democrats Consider Electability the Deciding Factor, Above All Others, Prompting Many to Back Kerry on Primary Eve." *Christian Science Monitor*, January 27. http://www.highbeam.com/doc/1G1-112560300.html.

Martin, Jonathan. 2009. "The Virginia Governor's Race Heats Up." *Politico.com*, September 7. http://www.politico.com/news/stories/0909/26849.html.

Masters, Roger D. 1994. "Differences in Responses of Black and Whites to American Leaders." *Politics and the Life Sciences* 13, no. 2: 183–194. http://www.jstor.org/stable/4236039.

Mayer, W. G. 1996. "In Defense of Negative Campaigning." *Political Science Quarterly* 111, no. 3: 437–455.

Mayhew, David R. 1974. *Congress: The Electoral Connection*. New Haven: Yale University Press.

McGann, Anthony J., William Koetzle, and Bernard Grofman. 2002. "How an Ideologically Concentrated Minority Can Trump a Dispersed Majority: Nonmedian Voter Results for Plurality, Run-Off, and Sequential Elimination Elections." *American Journal of Political Science* 46, no. 1: 134–137.

McGirt, Ellen. 2008. "Brand Obama Thrills Broadcasters with Record Ad Spend, but Cheap Video and Democracy Are the Big Winners." October 27. http://www.fastcompany.com/blog/ellen-mcgirt/strike-indicator/brand-obama-thrills-broadcasters-record-ad-spend-cheap-video-and-.

McIlwain, Charlton, and Stephen Maynard Caliendo. 2011. *Race Appeal: How Candidates Invoke Race in U.S. Political Campaigns.* Philadelphia: Temple University Press.

McShea, Kathy. 2008a. "The Campaign Message Box the Zone to Stay on Message." February. http://www.emeraldstrategies.net/buzz/articles/2008/200802-campaign-message-box-how-to.htm.

———. 2008b. "Message Development: The Secrets of Creating a Sticky Message." Slideshare presentation, Emerald Strategies.

Medvic, Stephen K. 1998. "The Effectiveness of the Political Consultant as a Campaign Resource." *PS: Political Science and Politics* 31, no. 2: 153–154.

———. 2001. *Political Consultants in U.S. Congressional Elections.* Columbus: Ohio University Press.

Medvic, Stephen K., and Silvo Lenart. 1997. "The Influence of Political Consultants in the 1992 Congressional Elections." *Legislative Studies Quarterly* 22, no. 1.

Medvic, Stephen K., Candice J. Nelson, and David A. Dulio. 2002. "Political Consultants: Campaign Advocacy and the Common Good." In *Shades of Gray: Perspectives on Campaign Ethics,* ed. Candice J. Nelson, David A. Dulio, and Stephen K. Medvic. Washington, DC: Brookings Institution Press.

Mendelberg, Tali. 1997. "Executing Hortons: Racial Crime in the 1988 Presidential Campaign." *Public Opinion Quarterly* 61, no. 1: 134–157.

Meyers, Jessica. 2010. "Texas Agriculture Chief Post Has Proven to Be a Political Stepping Stone." October 11. http://www.dallasnews.com/sharedcontent/dws/dn/latestnews/stories/101110dnmetagsteppingstone.281fb78.html.

Mezey, Michael L. 1970. "Ambition Theory and the Office of Congressmen." *Journal of Politics* 32, no. 3: 563–579.

Milbank, Dana, and Richard Moran. 2004. "Fewer Say Bush Is Serving the Middle Class: Poll Shows Americans Split over Whether President Has Governed Compassionately." *Washington Post,* April 4.

Miller, Arthur, and Warren Miller. 1975. "Issues, Candidates, and Partisan Divisions in the 1972 American Presidential Election." *British Journal of Political Science* 5, no. 4: 393–434.

Miller, Christian. 2000. "For Bush Race Becomes a Question of Heart." *Los Angeles Times,* August 25. http://articles.latimes.com/2000/aug/25/news/mn-10342.

Miller, Claire Cain. 2008. "How Obama's Internet Campaign Changed Politics." *New York Times* "Bits" Blog, November 7. http://bits.blogs.nytimes.com/2008/11/07/how-obamas-internet-campaign-changed-politics/.

Mitchell, Alison. 2000. "Bush Draws Campaign Theme from More than the Heart." *New York Times,* June 11.

Moon, Woojin. 2004. "Party Activists, Campaign Resources, and Candidate Position Taking: Theory, Tests, and Applications." *British Journal of Political Science* 34: 611–633.

Moore, James, and Wayne Slater. 2003. *Bush's Brain: How Karl Rove Made George W. Bush Presidential.* Hoboken, NJ: J. Wiley.

Morley, Jefferson. 2002. "Fetal Mistake: The Abortion Rights Crowd Squanders a Victory." *Slate.com*, February 14. http://www.slate.com/id/2062056/.

Morrill, Jim. 2009. "Fox Wins Race for Charlotte Mayor." *Charlotte Observer*, November 3.

Morris, Dick. 1997. *Behind the Oval Office: Winning the Presidency in the Nineties*. New York: Random House.

———. 1998. *Behind the Oval Office: Getting Reelected Against All Odds*. Los Angeles: Renaissance Books.

Mossberger, Karen, Caroline Tolbert, and Ramona McNeal. 2008. *Digital Citizenship*. Cambridge: MIT Press.

Mossberger, Karen, Caroline Tolbert, and Mary Stansbury. 2003. *Virtual Inequality: Beyond the Digital Divide*. Washington, DC: Georgetown University Press.

Murphy, John M. 2003. "'Our Mission and Our Moment': George W. Bush and September 11th." *Rhetoric and Public Affairs* 6: 607–632.

Nadeau, Richard, Richard G. Niemi, and Timothy Amato. 1995. "Emotions, Issue Importance, and Political Learning." *American Journal of Political Science* 39, no. 3: 558-574. Bloomington, IN: Midwest Political Science Association.

National Journal. 2006. "Webb Blasts Allen for Cutting and Running; Wadhams/Jarding Spar." June 27. http://hotlineoncall.nationaljournal.com/archives/2006/06/webb-blasts-all.php.

Nelson, Candice J. 1998. "Inside the Beltway: Profiles of Two Political Consultants Inside the Beltway: Profiles of Two Political Consultants." *PS: Political Science and Politics* 31, no. 2: 162–166.

Nelson, Candice J., David A. Dulio, and Stephen K. Medvic, eds. 2002. *Shades of Gray: Perspectives on Campaign Ethics*. Washington, DC: Brookings Institution Press.

Nelson, Candice J., Stephen K. Medvic, and David A. Dulio. 2002. "Hired Guns or Gatekeepers of Democracy?" In *Shades of Gray: Perspectives on Campaign Ethics*, ed. Candice J. Nelson, David A. Dulio, and Stephen K. Medvic, 75–97. Washington: Brookings Institution Press.

Nelson, Michael. 2005. *The Elections of 2004*. Washington, DC: CQ Press.

Neumayr, George. 2006. "Safe, Legal, and Remorseless: Why Are Democrats Calling Abortion Bad? Real 'Pro-choicers' Want to Know." *National Review Online*, March 2. http://old.nationalreview.com/comment/neumayr200603020818.asp.

Newport, Frank. 2000. "Americans Continue to Favor the Return of Elian Gonzalez to Cuba." *Gallup*, April 4. http://www.gallup.com/poll/3034/Americans-Continue-Favor-Return-Elian-Gonzalez-Cuba.aspx.

Nichols, John. 2004. "Avoiding Dean's Mistakes." *Nation*, March 19. http://www.thenation.com/blog/avoiding-deans-mistakes.

Niemi, Richard G., Harold W. Stanley, and Ronald J. Vogel. 1995. "State Economies and State Taxes: Do Voters Hold Governors Accountable?" *American Journal of Political Science* 39, no. 4.

Nimmo, Dan. 1970. *The Political Persuaders: The Techniques of Modern Election Campaigns*. Englewood Cliffs, NJ: Prentice-Hall.

Niquette, Mark, and Joe Hallat. 2010. "Strickland Campaign Comes Out Firing." *Columbus Dispatch*, May 13. http://www.dispatchpolitics.com/live/content/local_news/stories/2010/05/13/copy/strickland-campaign-comes-out-firing.html?sid=101.

Niven, David. 2006. "A Field Experiment on the Effects of Negative Campaign Mail on Voter Turnout in a Municipal Election, 2006." *Political Research Quarterly* 59, no. 2: 203–210.

Norpoth, Helmut, and Andrew H. Sidman. 2007. "Mission Accomplished: The Wartime Election of 2004." *Political Behavior* 29: 175–196.

Norrander, Barbara. 1989. "Ideological Representativeness of Presidential Primary Voters." *American Journal of Political Science* 33, no. 3: 570–587.

Norton, Michael I. and George R. Goethals. 2004. "Spin (and Pitch) Doctors: Campaign Strategies in Televised Political Debates." *Political Behavior* 26, no. 3: 227–248.

Oates, S., and R. K. Gibson. 2006. "The Internet, Civil Society, and Democracy: A Comparative Perspective." In *The Internet and Politics: Citizens, Voters, and Activists*, ed. S. Oates, D. Owen, and R. K. Gibson, 20–38. London: Routledge.

Oates, S., D. Owen, and R. K. Gibson. 2006. *The Internet and Politics: Citizens, Voters, and Activists*. London: Routledge.

"On the Record: South Carolina Gov. Jim Hodges." 2000. *Stateline.org*, March 16. http://www.stateline.org/live/ViewPage.action?siteNodeId=136&languageId=1&contentId=13959.

Orey, Byron D., and Boris E. Ricks. 2007. "A Systematic Analysis of the De-Racialization Concept." *University of Nebraska at Lincoln*: 325–334. http://digitalcommons.unl.edu/cgi/viewcontent.cgi?article=1024&context=poliscifacpub.

O'Shaughnessy, N. J. 1990. "High Priesthood, Low Priestcraft: The Role of Political Consultants." *European Journal of Marketing* 24, no. 2: 7–23.

Panagopoulos, Costas. 2006. "Political Consultants, Campaign Professionalization, and Media Attention." *PS: Political Science and Politics* 39, no. 4: 867–869.

Parkinson, Hank. 1970. *Winning Your Campaign: A Nuts-and-Bolts Guide to Political Victory*. Englewood Cliffs, NJ: Prentice-Hall.

Parmalee, John H. 2003. *Meet the Candidate Videos: Analyzing Presidential Primary Campaign Videocassettes*. Westport, CT: Praeger.

Patterson, Kelly, and David Magleby. 1998. "Consultants and Direct Democracy." *PS: Political Science and Politics* 31: 160–169.

Perlmutter, David D. 1999. *The Manship School Guide to Political Communication*. Baton Rouge: Louisiana State University Press.

Perry, James. 1968. *The New Politics: The Expanding Technology of Political Manipulation*. London: Weidenfeld and Nicolson.

Peslak, Alan. 2004. "Regional and Demographic Differences in United States Internet Usage." *First Monday* 9, no. 3. http://firstmonday.org/issues/issue9_3/peslak/index.html.

Peterson, David A. 2005. "Heterogeneity and Certainty in Candidate Evaluations." *Political Behavior* 27, no. 1: 1–24.

Peterson, David A., and Paul Djupe. 2005. "When Primary Campaigns Go Negative: The Determinants of Campaign Negativity." *Political Research Quarterly* 58, no. 1.

Petracca, Mark P. 1989. "Political Consultants and Democratic Governance." *PS: Political Science and Politics* 22, no. 1: 11–14.

Petrocik, John R. 1996. "Issue Ownership in Presidential Elections with a 1980 Case Study." *American Journal of Political Science* 40: 825–850.

Pew Research Center for the People and the Press. 2005. "An In Depth Look at Dean Activists: Their Profile and Prospects." April 6. http://www.pewtrusts.org/uploadedFiles/wwwpewtrustsorg/Reports/Public_opinion_and_polls/PRC_Dean_0405.pdf.

Pierce, Patrick A. 1993. "Political Sophistication and the Use of Candidate Traits in Candidate Evaluation." *Political Psychology* 14, no. 1: 21–35.

Plane, Dennis L., and Joseph Gershtenson. 2004. "Candidates' Ideological Locations, Abstention, and Turnout in U.S. Midterm Senate Elections." *Political Behavior* 26, no. 1: 69–93.

Plotz, David. 1998. "The Gambling Gamble: South Carolina Democrats Bet the Farm." *Slate.com*, October 23. http://www.slate.com/id/5155/pagenum/all/.

Plouffe, David. 2009. *The Audacity to Win: The Inside Story and Lessons of Barack Obama's Historic Victory*. New York: Viking.

Price, D., and M. Lupfer. 1973. "Volunteers for Gore: The Impact of a Precinct-Level Campaign in Three Tennessee Cities." *Journal of Politics* 35, no. 2: 410–438.

Pritchell, R. 1958. "The Influence of Professional Campaign Management Firms in Partisan Elections in California." *Western Political Quarterly* 11: 278–300.

Rabinowitz, George, and Stuart MacDonald. 1998. "A Directional Theory of Issue Voting." *American Political Science Review* 83: 93–121.

Rabinowitz, George, et al. 2003. *Directional Politics and the 1996 Presidential Election*. Ann Arbor: University of Michigan Press.

———. 2004. "Bush v. Gore: Policy Issues in the 2000 U.S. Presidential Election." *Tidsskrift for Samfunnsforskning* 45: 185–213. Reprinted in H. M. Narud and A. Krogstad, eds., *Voters, Parties, and Political Representation*. Oslo: Universitetsforlaget.

Rahn, M. Wendy, John Aldrich, and Eugene Borgida. 1994. "Individual and Contextual Variations in Political Candidate Appraisal." *American Political Science Review* 88 (March): 193–199.

Rampton, Sheldon, and John Stauber. 2004. *Banana Republicans: How the Right Wing Is Turning America into a One-Party State*. New York: Tarcher/Penguin.

Randon Hershey, Marjorie. 1984. *Running for Office: The Political Education of Campaigners*. London: Chatham House.

Rapoport, Ronald B., Kelly L. Metcalf, and Jon A. Hartman. 1989. "Candidate Traits and Voter Inferences: An Experimental Study." *Journal of Politics* 51, no. 4: 917–932.

Rhoads, Christopher. 2009. "Playing Catchup: The GOP Is All Atwitter About the Internet." *Wall Street Journal*, January 30. http://online.wsj.com/article/SB123309277668321299.html.

Riley, Naomi Schaefer. 2006. "Mr. Compassionate Conservatism." *Wall Street Journal*, October 21.

Roe, Jeff. 2010. "Targeting the Right Voters, with the Right Message, at the Right Time." *Politics* (February).

Rosenberg, Shawn W., and Patrick McCafferty. 1987. "The Image and the Vote Manipulating Voter's Preferences." *Public Opinion Quarterly* 51, no. 1.

Rosenbloom, David Lee. 1973. *The Election Men: Professional Campaign Managers and American Democracy*. New York: Quadrangle Books.

Rosenwasser, Shirley M., et al. 1987. "Attitudes Toward Women and Men in Politics: Perceived Male and Female Candidate Competencies and Participant Personality Characteristics." *Political Psychology* 8, no. 2: 191–200.

Rothberg, Stuart. 2009. April 27. "April Madness: Can the GOP Win Back the House in 2010?" April 27. http://rothenbergpoliticalreport.com/news/article/april-madness-can-gop-win-back-the-house-in-2010.

Rowland, Christopher. 2010. "Opponents See Lessons in Brown Win." *Boston.com*, February 25. http://www.boston.com/news/nation/washington/articles/2010/02/25/opponents_see_lessons_in_brown_win/.

Russell, Tom. 1996. "The Power of a Simple Message: How a 27-Year-Old with a Famous Name Won a Democratic Congressional Primary in California—Former White House Aide Michela Alioto." *Campaigns and Elections* (August).

Rutenberg, Jim. 2007. "Ex-Aide Says He's Lost Faith in Bush." *New York Times*, April 1. http://www.nytimes.com/2007/04/01/washington/01adviser.html?_r=2&hp=&adxnnl=1&adxnnlx=1175368218-cyyjPeRPtD7iIVo8lP6hOw&oref=slogin.

Ruthven, Wyeth. 2010. "Twitter Trends in Off Year Elections: Virginia, New Jersey, Massachusetts." http://www.qorvis.com/sites/qorvis.com/files/Ruthven_Twitter_Study.pdf.

Saad, Lydia. 2010. "Tea Partiers Are Fairly Mainstream in Their Demographics." April 5. http://www.gallup.com/poll/127181/tea-partiers-fairly-mainstream-demographics.aspx.

Sabato, Larry J. 1983. *The Rise of Political Consultants: New Ways of Winning Elections.* New York: Basic Books.

———. 1984. *Power: Inside the World of Political Action Committees.* New York: W. W. Norton.

———. 1989a. *Campaigns and Elections: A Reader in Modern American Politics.* Glenview, IL: Scott Foresman.

———. 1989b. *Paying for Elections: The Campaign Finance Thicket.* New York: Priority Press Publications.

———. 1989c. "Political Influence, the News Media, and Campaign Consultants." *Political Science and Politics* 22, no. 1.

———. 2006. *Divided States of America: The Slash and Burn Politics of the 2004 Presidential Election.* Glenview, IL: Pearson Education.

———. 2010. *The Year of Obama: How Barack Obama Won the White House.* New York: Longman.

Sabato, Larry J., and Bruce Larson. 1987. *The Party's Just Begun: Shaping Political Parties for America's Future.* Boston: Little, Brown, College Division.

Sakahara, Tim. 2010. "Early Voting Begins; Abercrombie Answers Flip Flop Issue." *Hawaii News Now,* October 19. http://www.hawaiinewsnow.com/Global/story.asp?S=13353703.

Saleton, William. 2004. "Kerried Away: The Myth and Math of Kerry's Electability." *Slate.com,* February 11. http://www.slate.com/id/2095311.

Salganik, Matthew J., and Douglas D. Heckathorn. 2004. "Sampling and Estimation in Hidden Populations Using Respondent-Driven Sampling." *Sociological Methodology* 34: 193–239.

Salmore, Barbara, and Stephen A. Salmore. 1989. *Candidates, Parties, and Campaigns: Electoral Politics in America.* 2nd ed. Washington, DC: CQ Press, 1989.

Salon.com. 2008. "'Hot Off the Wire': *Salon* Staff Discusses Episode 7 of *The Wire.*" February 18. http://www.salon.com/entertainment/tv/feature/2008/02/18/wire_wrap_6/print.html.

Sanbonmatsu, Kira. 2002. "Gender Stereotypes and Vote Choice." *American Journal of Political Science* 46, no. 1.

Schaefer, Naomi. 2006. "Mr. Compassionate Conservatism." *Wall Street Journal,* October 21. http://www.freedomworks.org/news/mr-compassionate-conservatism.

Schaller, Thomas. 2004. "Dean's Dizzying Descent: How and Why Did the Vermont Juggernaut Implode So Quickly?" *Salon.com,* February 3. http://www.salon.com/news/feature/2004/02/03/trippi_neel.

Schiffman, Betsy. 2008. "The Reason for the Obama Victory: It's the Internet, Stupid." *Wired,* November 7. http://www.wired.com/epicenter/2008/11/the-obama-victo/.

Schlesinger, Joseph A. 1996. *Ambition and Politics: Political Careers in the United States.* Chicago: Rand McNally.

Schneider, Steven M., and Kevin Foot. 2005. "Web Campaigning by U.S. Presidential Primary Candidates in 2000 and 2004." In *The Internet Election: Perspectives on the Web's Role in Campaign 2004,* ed. A. Williams and J. Tedesco. Lanham, MD: Rowman and Littlefield.

Schouten, Fredreka. 2006. "Internet Critical Tool for Political Cash." *USA Today,* December 18. http://www.usatoday.com/news/washington/2006-12-17-internet-cash_x.htm.

Schrader, Esther. 2000. "Gore Goes to Fla., Leaves Elian Issue Behind." *Los Angeles Times,* April 8. http://articles.latimes.com/2000/apr/08/news/mn-17388.

Schultz, C., and S. M. Pancer. 1997. "Character Attacks and Their Effects on Perceptions of Political Candidates." *Political Psychology* 18: 93–102.

Science Daily. 2010. "Liberals and Atheists Smarter? Intelligent People Have Values Novel in Human Evolutionary History, Study Finds." February 24. http://www.sciencedaily.com/releases/2010/02/100224132655.htm.

Scott, Hugh, Jr. 1968. *How to Run for Public Office and Win!* Washington, DC: National Press.

Sears, David, and Michael Tesler. 2010. *Obama's Race: The 2008 Election and the Dream of a Post-Racial America.* Chicago: University of Chicago Press.

Seelye, Katharine Q. 2008. "Clinton Misspoke About Bosnia Event Campaign Says." http://thecaucus.blogs.nytimes.com/2008/03/24/clinton-misspoke-about-bosnia-trip-campaign -says/.

Sellers, Patrick. 1998. "Strategy and Background in Congressional Campaigns." *American Political Science Review* 92, no. 1: 159–171.

Semiatin, Richard. 2007. *Campaigns on the Cutting Edge.* Washington, DC: CQ Press.

Shadegg, Stephen C. 1964. *How to Win an Election: The Art of Political Victory.* New York: Taplinger.

———. 1972. *The New How to Win an Election.* New York: Taplinger.

Shaw, Catherine. 2009. *The Campaign Manager: Running and Winning Local Elections.* Boulder: Westview Press.

Shipman, Tim. 2008. "Sarah Palin: Barack Obama 'Palling Around with Terrorists.'" *Telegraph,* October 4. http://www.telegraph.co.uk/news/worldnews/sarah-palin/3137197/Sarah -Palin-accuses-Barack-Obama-of-terrorist-links.html.

Shrum, Robert. 2007. *No Excuses: Concessions of a Serial Campaigner.* New York: Simon and Schuster.

Sigelman, Carol K., Lee Sigelman, Barbara J. Walkosz, and Michal Nitz. 1995. "Black Candidates, White Voters: Understanding Racial Bias in Political Perceptions." *American Journal of Political Science* 39, no. 1: 243–265.

Sigelman, Lee, and Eric Shiraev. 2002. "The Rational Attacker in Russia? Negative Campaigning in Russian Presidential Elections." *Journal of Politics* 64, no. 1: 45–62.

Skaperdas, Stergios, and Bernard Grofman. 1995. "Modeling Negative Campaigning." *American Political Science Review* 89, no. 1.

Smith, Ben. 2008. "Obama's Soundtrack." *Politico.com,* January 14. http://www.politico.com/blogs/bensmith/0108/Obamas_soundtrack.html.

Speakes, Larry. 1988. *Speaking Out: The Reagan Presidency from Inside the White House.* New York: Scribner.

Spooner, Tom. 2003. "Internet Use by Region in the U.S." Pew Center on the Internet in American Life, August 27. http://www.pewinternet.org/Reports/2003/Internet-Use-by-Region -in-the-US/Summary-of-Findings.aspx.

Stanley, Alessandra. 1992. "The 1992 Election: New York State—D'Amato; Senator Proclaims Comeback, and Victory." *New York Times,* November 4.

Steele, Shelby. 2008. "Obama's Post Racial Promise." *Los Angeles Times,* November 5. http://articles.latimes.com/2008/nov/05/opinion/oe-steele5.

Stein, Sam. 2008. "Obama Ad Goes After McCain for Being Old, Incompetent." *Huffington Post,* September 12. http://www.huffingtonpost.com/2008/09/12/obama-ad-goes-after-mccai_n _125896.html.

Stevens, Daniel. 2005. "Separate and Unequal Effects: Information, Political Sophistication, and Negative Advertising in American Elections." *Political Research Quarterly* 58, no. 3.

Stewart, Jon, Rory Albanese, and Josh Lieb. 2010. "Mass Backwards." *Comedy Central*, January 18. http://www.thedailyshow.com/watch/mon-january-18-2010/mass-backwards.

Stirland, Sarah Lai. 2007. "New Wave of Strategists Tap Web to Transform GOP." *Wired*, August 23. http://www.wired.com/politics/law/news/2007/08/rove#ixzz16ifQBTGr.

Stoker, Laura. 1993. "Judging Presidential Character: The Demise of Gary Hart." *Political Behavior* 15, no. 2: 193–223.

Stokes, Donald E. 1963. "Spatial Models of Party Competition." *American Political Science Review* 57: 368–377.

Strickland, Ruth Ann, and Marcia Lynn Whicker. 1992. "Comparing the Wilder and Gantt Campaigns: A Model for Black Candidate Success in Statewide Elections." *PS: Political Science and Politics* 25, no. 2: 204–212.

Strother, Raymond. 2003. *Falling Up: How a Redneck Helped Invent Political Consulting*. Baton Rouge: Louisiana State University Press.

Sullivan, Amy. 2003. "General Election: Insiders Say It's Too Late for Wesley Clark to Win the Primaries. They're Wrong." *Washington Monthly*. http://www.washingtonmonthly.com/features/2003/0309.sullivan.html.

Swift, Mike. 2009. "Facebook Becomes More Diverse as Blacks, Latinos Join at Rapid Pace." December 16. http://meapa.com/app/download/1829986304/Facebook+becomes+more+diverse+121709.pdf.

Tapper, Jack. 2008. "Bubba: Obama Is Just Like Jesse Jackson." January 26. http://blogs.abcnews.com/politicalpunch/2008/01/bubba-obama-is.html.

Taranto, James. 2009. "Obama's Post Racial America: Why Stupid Squabbles over Race Are a Sign of Progress." *Wall Street Journal*, September 15. http://online.wsj.com/article/SB10001424052970203917304574414923099147990.html.

Tate, Katherine. 1991. "Black Political Participation in the 1984 and 1988 Presidential Elections." *American Political Science Review* 85, no. 4: 1159–1176.

Taylor, Luke. 2007. "Flip-Flop Fever." December 6. http://minnesota.publicradio.org/radio/podcasts/grammar_grater/archive/2007/12/06/.

Tenpas, Kathryn Dunn. 1998. "The Clinton Reelection Machine: Placing the Party Organization in Peril." *Presidential Studies Quarterly* 28, no. 4: 761–767.

Terrelonge-Stone, Pauline. 1980. "Ambition Theory and the Black Politician." *Western Political Quarterly* 33, no. 1: 94–107.

Tesler, Michael, and David O. Sears. 2010. *Obama's Race: The 2008 Election and the Dream of a Post-Racial America*. Chicago: University of Chicago Press.

Theilmann, John, and Allen Wilhite. 1998. "Campaign Tactics and the Decision to Attack." *Journal of Politics* 60, no. 4.

Thomas, Evan. 2005. *Election 2004: How Bush Won and What You Can Expect*. New York: Public Affairs.

Thompkins, Al. 2004. "How Important Are Campaign Slogans?" *Poynter*, July 29. http://www.poynter.org/content/content_view.asp?id=69125.

Thurber, James A. 1998a. "Political Consultants Survey: Are Campaign Pros Destroying Democracy?" *Campaigns and Elections* (August): 54–61.

———. 1998b. "The Study of Campaign Consultants: A Subfield in Search of a Theory." *PS: Political Science and Politics* 31, no. 2: 145–149.

———, ed. 1999. *Improving Campaign Conduct* packet, Center for Congressional and Presidential Studies, American University, Pew Charitable Trusts.

———, ed. 2001. *The Battle for Congress: Consultants, Candidates, and Voters*. Washington, DC: Brookings Institution Press.

Thurber, James A., and Candace J. Nelson. 2000. *Campaign Warriors: Political Consultants in Elections*. Washington, DC: Brookings Institution Press.

———. 2004. *Campaigns and Elections American Style: Transforming American Politics*. Boulder: Westview Press.

Thurber, James A., Candace J. Nelson, and David Dulio. 2000. *Crowded Airwaves: Campaign Advertising in Elections*. Washington, DC: Brookings Institution Press.

Tomorrow, Tom. 1996. "How I Became the Story of the Great Debate of 1996." *Salon.com*, October 7. http://www.salon.com/media/media961007.html.

Traugott, Michael. 2000. "Polling in the Public's Interest." *Public Opinion Quarterly* 64: 374–384.

Trent, Judith S., and Robert V. Friedenberg. 2000. *Political Campaign Communication: Principles and Practices*. New York: Praeger.

———. 2008. *Political Campaign Communication: Principles and Practices*. 4th ed. Lanham, MD: Rowman and Littlefield.

Trippi, Joe. 2008. *The Revolution Will Not Be Televised*. Rev. ed., *Democracy, the Internet, and the Overthrow of Everything*. New York: Harper Collins.

Trumbore, Peter, and David Dulio. 2009. "Running on Iraq, Running from Iraq: Deliberate Priming in Mid-Term Elections." Paper presented at the annual meeting of the Midwest Political Science Association, Chicago.

United Press International. 2006. "Murphy: GOP 'Out-of-Touch, Out-of-Sync.'" November 4. http://www.upi.com/Top_News/2006/11/04/Murphy-GOP-out-of-touch-out-of-sync/UPI-32481162656600/.

Vaccari, Cristian. 2008. "From the Air to the Ground: The Internet in the 2004 U.S. Presidential Campaign." *New Media Society* 10, no. 4: 647–665.

VandeHei, Jim, and Chris Cillizza. 2006. "In a Pivotal Year, GOP Plans to Get Personal." *Washington Post*, September 10. http://www.washingtonpost.com/wp-dyn/content/article/2006/09/09/AR2006090901079.html.

Vargas, Jose Antonio. 2007. "Young Voters Find Voice on Facebook: Site's Candidate Groups Are Grass-Roots Politics for the Web Generation." *Washington Post*, February 17. http://www.washingtonpost.com/wpdyn/content/article/2007/02/16/AR2007021602084.html.

Waldron, Thomas W., and JoAnna Daemmrich. 1998. "Young Answers Ethics Panel; Md. Senator Responds to Allegations Against Him in Closed Session." *Baltimore Sun*, January 7. http://articles.baltimoresun.com/1998-01-07/news/1998007015_1_ethics-committee-ethics-laws-answers.

Walker, David, and Alan Seacrest. 2002. "Nassau County Revolt." *Campaigns and Elections* 23, no. 3: 34–42.

Wallersten, Kevin. 2010. "Yes We Can: How Online Viewership, Blog Discussion, Campaign Statements, and Mainstream Media Coverage Produced a Viral Video Phenomenon." *Journal of Information Technology and Politics* 7, no. 2: 163–181.

Walsh, Edward. 1992. "Clinton Directs 'Trust' Issue Back at Bush; President Accused of Abusing Powers and Sending Millions on 'Ads He Knew Were False.'" *Washington Post*, October 29.

"Walsh Stayed in Office Too Long." 2006. September 25. http://enterprise.southofboston.com/articles/2006/09/25/news/opinion/opinion01.txt.

Watkins, S. Craig. 2009. *The Young and the Digital: What the Migration to Social-Network Sites, Games, and Anytime, Anywhere Media Means for Our Future*. Boston: Beacon Press.

Watson, Robert P., and Colton C. Campbell. 2003. *Campaigns and Elections: Issues, Concepts, Cases*. Boulder: Lynne Rienner.

Wattenberg, Martin P., and Leonard Brians. 1999. "Negative Campaign Advertising: Demobilizer or Mobilizer?" *American Political Science Review* 93, no. 4.

Wattier, Mark. 2003. "'Vote for Me, I Can Win': Electability in 2000 Republican Presidential Primaries." *Party Politics*: 1–23.

Wayne, Stephen, and Clyde Wilcox. 1992. *The Quest for Office: National Electoral Politics*. New York: St. Martin's Press.

Weible, Christopher M. 2005. "Beliefs and Perceived Influence in a Natural Resource Conflict: An Advocacy Coalition Approach to Policy Networks." *Political Research Quarterly* 58, no. 3: 461–475.

West, Darrell M. 2005. *Air Wars: Television Advertising in Election Campaigns, 1952–2004*. Washington, DC: CQ Press.

Westholm, Anders. 1997. "Distance Versus Direction: The Illusory Defeat of the Proximity Theory of Electoral Choice." *American Political Science Review* 91, no. 4: 865–883.

———. 2001. "On the Return of Epicycles: Some Crossroads in Spatial Modeling Revisited." *Journal of Politics* 63, no. 2: 436–481.

Whitney, Carol. 2002. "Wolves or Watchdogs?" In *Shades of Gray: Perspectives on Campaign Ethics*, ed. Candice Nelson, David A. Dulio, and Stephen K. Medvic. Washington, DC: Brookings Institution Press.

Wielhouwer, Peter W. 2004. "Teaching Campaign Ethics Using Web-Based Scenarios." *Political Science and Politics* 37, no. 4: 865–869.

Williams, Christine, and Girish Gulati. 2007. "Social Networks in Political Campaigns: Facebook and the 2006 Midterm Elections." Paper presented at the annual meeting of the American Political Science Association, Chicago.

———. 2008. "What Is a Social Network Worth? Facebook and Vote Share in the 2008 Presidential Primaries." Paper presented at the annual meeting of the American Political Science Association, Boston, August 28–31.

———. 2009. "Congressional Candidates' Use of YouTube in 2008: Its Frequency and Rationale." January 21. http://blogsandwikis.bentley.edu/politechmedia/wp-content/uploads/2009/01/youtubejan21_final-2.pdf.

Williams, Joseph, and Kevin Baron. 2007. "Military Sees Big Decline in Black Enlistees." October 7. http://www.boston.com/news/nation/washington/articles/2007/10/07/military_sees_big_decline_in_black_enlistees/.

Wilson, James Q. 1966. *The Amateur Democrat: Club Politics in Three Cities*. Chicago: University of Chicago Press.

Wolf, Gary. 2004. "How the Internet Invented Howard Dean." January 1. http://www.wired.com/wired/archive/12.01/dean.html.

Wright, Sharon D. 1995. "Electoral and Biracial Coalition: Possible Election Strategy for African American Candidates in Louisville, Kentucky." *Journal of Black Studies* 25, no. 6: 749–758.

Wuffle, A., et al. 1989. "Finagle's Law and the Finagle Point: A New Solution Concept for Two-Candidate Competition in Spatial Voting Games Without a Core." *American Journal of Political Science* 33, no. 2.

Xenos, M., and K. A. Foot. 2004. "Politics as Usual, or Politics Unusual? Position-Taking and Dialogue on Campaign Websites in the 2002 U.S. Elections." *Journal of Communication* 55: 169–185.

Yang, Carter M. 2000. *Bush Stays on Message*. ABC News, November 4.

Index